EASY KEY TO GERMAN VOCABULARY

Easy Key to
GERMAN
Vocabulary

A Mnemonic List with English Cognates

Harry Murutes

Easy Key to German Vocabulary
Copyright 1995 by Harry Murutes

Library of Congress Number: 95-95192

ISBN: 0-9648579-0-1

Printed in Canton, Ohio

Third Printing, 1996
With Corrections

Harry Murutes
P.O. Box 8184
Canton, Ohio 44711

Table of Contents

Preface

This handbook grew out of my own need to acquire a reading knowledge of German. The book employs an innovative system designed to help the student undertake the daunting task of learning German vocabulary, and is based on the principle that English cognates can be associated with most German words.

Although introductory textbooks of German customarily point out that much of the vocabulary is related to English, the number of examples of cognates given in them is disappointingly small. Regrettably for the beginner faced with learning a broad foreign vocabulary, authors of instructional books of German have ignored the didactic potential of identifying each German word with the English cognates that exist.

Because of that neglect, I was motivated to uncover as many German-English cognates as I could find. My search drew from a variety of authoritative sources, including, not only German and English dictionaries, but Dutch, French, and Italian ones, as well. There I found valuable etymological information explaining sense development in many German words. I integrated my research in an innovative way, arranging the information into an easy to read table which lists each German entry with an etymologically related English word to serve as a mnemonic, an aid to the memory.

Thanks to this method, a broad range of German vocabulary that at an earlier period would have escaped me has stayed firmly fixed in my memory. I no longer experience the difficulty I once had in remembering vocabulary, the problem that previously caused me to avoid reading German. Now I approach such reading with confidence, comprehension and pleasure.

With its unique purpose and method, *Easy Key to German Vocabulary* can be helpful to individuals enrolled in college courses for reading knowledge of German. This book could be useful, as well, to professional scholars, particularly of the humanities, who must consult material in German for purposes of research but feel themselves inadequate in vocabulary. And to those who have already attained fluency in German, the book will offer surprising and fascinating information not only about German words, but English ones, too.

adj.	adjective	MDu.	Middle Dutch
adv.	adverb	ME.	Middle English
anat.	anatomy	MHG.	Middle High German
Arab.	Arabic	ML.	Medieval Latin
arch.	archaic	n.	neuter
archt.	architecture	neg.	negative
AS.	Anglo-Saxon	obs.	obsolete
bs.	basic sense	OFr.	Old French
cf.	compare	OHG.	Old High German
cogn.	cognate	ON.	Old Norse
compar.	comparative	ONeth.	Old Netherlandish
dial.	dialect	orig.	originally
dim.	diminutive	OSax.	Old Saxon
Du.	Dutch	past p.	past participle
Eng.	English	past t.	past tense
esp.	especially	perh.	perhaps
etym.	etymology	pl.	plural
f.	feminine	possib.	possible, possibly
Fr.	French	pref.	prefix
Frk.	Frankish	prep.	preposition
freqtv.	frequentative	prob.	probably
G.	German	refl.	reflexive verb
Gaul.	Gaulish	Scot.	Scottish
gen.	genitive	s.o.	someone
Gk.	Greek	Sp.	Spanish
Gmc.	Germanic	s.t.	something
Goth.	Gothic	Turk.	Turkish
Heb.	Hebrew	ult.	ultimately
IE.	Indo-European	uncert.	uncertain
intens.	intensive, intensive	var.	variation, variant
Ital.	Italian	vi.	verb intransitive
L.	Latin	VL.	vulgar Latin
lit.	literally	vt.	verb transitive
LL.	Late Latin, Low Latin	<	derives from
m.	masculine	>	leads to
MDa.	Middle Danish	*	unattested

Introduction

German Vocabulary Can Be Easy to Learn

Easy Key to German Vocabulary is a reference work designed to assist mature students to learn and remember the German vocabulary they encounter in the classroom, under a tutor, or in readings. Major root words and a wide range of entries naming qualities or things in nature are gathered into a unique system that can dramatically shorten the task of memorizing vocabulary. The manual is intended only as a *supplement* to the principal grammar book and dictionary so essential to a study of German. As this is not meant to replace a conventional dictionary, not all possible meanings of words are listed. Nor are its entries to be taken as representing preferred, contemporary German usage.

Easy Key to German Vocabulary applies an idea that has been largely ignored in instructional books on German. Here, each principal German word is accompanied by an English cognate—a word born of the same root as another—serving as a mnemonic, an aid to the memory. This manual is thus not a gimmicky invention of spurious word associations but a utilization of affiliations between words as recognized by authorities of etymology.

English cognates are employed to facilitate the recall of German terms to which they are related. For instance, the German word *Haut* (skin) is directly related to English *hide* (an animal's skin). And *sieden* (to boil) has its cognate in English *seethe*. However, a word in one language can sometimes develop a meaning different from its cognate in another. For example, *klein* (small) has come to mean something different from its English cognate, *clean*. And German *tasten* (to touch or grope) means something other than its English cognate, *taste*. Widely diverging meanings between cognates are not so frequent, but when encountered should be kept in mind by users of this system.

Most of the English cognates listed in the table are common words. Those that are rare, dialect or obsolete are always defined for the user. Although defunct English words such as *lich* or *fother* are not used elsewhere in print or speech, their inclusion in this table is justifiable because they help to fix in the memory particular German words that might otherwise escape it.

This manual will likely be controversial. Certain instructors will be unsympathetic to a "cognate system," in the belief that it will confuse learning and fail to benefit students. Perhaps true for some users, that should not be assumed true for all; it underestimates the ability of students, particularly the motivated, intelligent, mature ones. To withhold the option of utilizing cognates for absorbing foreign vocabulary would unreasonably restrict the ways individuals can learn.

Easy Key to German Vocabulary offers historical information about German and English words, and traces out many etymologies. When consulted during routine vocabulary study, these pages will help users discover that thousands of German words are only disguised cousins, so to speak, of words existing in English. With this mnemonic system, students will find that German vocabulary can, indeed, be easy to learn!

Features of the Mnemonic System

Prior to using *Easy Key to German Vocabulary* the student should become acquainted with its features. Described in the following list, they reflect the complex nature of the content and purpose of this manual. Most of these features are deliberate and address instructional concerns. But a few were imposed from without, determined either by the material itself or by the restrictions imposed by the cellular format of the table within which the information is presented.

(1) *Nearly all German root words that have an English cognate* have been included in this list. These are arranged in alphabetical order, in a table of rows divided into three cells. The *left* cell has a principal German entry (often accompanied by derivatives), the *middle* cell gives the English meaning, and the *right* one furnishes an English cognate as a mnemonic key.

(2) The small number of German words *lacking* any cognate in English could not, of course, be included in a list dealing only with identifiable cognates. Also not included are obvious words from Latin and Greek, such as *delikat* (delicate) and *Sphäre* (sphere). Many words from Latin or Greek that are inconspicuous or tricky, however, are included.

(3) The table is designed to facilitate *self-testing* in allowing the user to cover any one column and test recall of covered information by referring to the words in the adjoining column cells.

(4) If the principal German entry is followed by *derivatives*, the latter are sometimes listed *according to sense or root* development, not necessarily by alphabetical order. The list does not claim to be comprehensive.

(5) *Explanatory early forms* of words (Anglo-Saxon, Old High German, Middle High German) are often presented, but with *diacritical marks intentionally omitted,* since they are not essential to the present study and might even burden the student.

(6) A few *rare or obsolete* German entries are included because they have legitimate cognates in English, and might be encountered in older literature.

(7) Certain English cognates that are of *rare or dialectical usage, or are obsolete,* are included in this list because they are the sole cognate forms to the German, and fulfill a mnemonic purpose, also.

(8) As in *Steuer[1], Steuer[2],* a *superscript numeral* on the end of a word indicates that two or more entries share identical forms but have different meanings.

(9) Helpful explanation about the *history of English as well as German words* is included in many entries.

(10) Information about German and English vocabulary traced in the word list is drawn from *authoritative German, English and Dutch etymological dictionaries.*

(11) Some entries have *uncertain or disputed etymologies.* In rare cases, the theory of the present author is proposed.

(12) In instances when a *close* English cognate is lacking, a *distantly related word* deriving from a shared Indo-European root is given to allow inclusion of a German entry that would otherwise not be in the list.

(13) Certain related entries with strong changes (e.g., *stehen, Stelle*) are listed separately to avoid long, unwieldy cells that can cause spacing problems in pages. Due to the system of *closed cells in this table,* gaps at the bottom of some pages are *unavoidable.*

The Two Historical Sound Shifts

The letter *t* in certain German words is equivalent to a *d* in English ones. A German *b* corresponds to a *v* in certain English cognates. These are but a few examples of what are called "sound shifts," that is, sounds in German and English that, although different from each other, are actually related, having developed from a common source. Two important historical shifts involving *groups of consonants* have been identified by scholars. For the student of German, a familiarity with these sound shifts is indispensable. Once the correspondences of certain pairs of letters are understood, the alien look to hundreds of German words will vanish and their meanings will come clear.

The First or "Germanic Sound Shift"

The German language, like English, Dutch, Swedish, Norwegian, Danish, and Icelandic, had evolved from an ancestral language which scholars once called "Teutonic," but now designate "Germanic." In the centuries just before the Christian era, this parent Germanic language had undergone changes in certain consonants that were to affect the languages that subsequently developed out of it. Called *the first or "Germanic sound shift,"* the phenomenon was to systematically distinguish certain Germanic words from their kindred forms in Latin and Greek. For example, what was initial *p, t,* and *k* in the Indo-European language shifted respectively to *f, th,* and *h* in Germanic. And what was *b, d,* and *g* in Indo-European shifted, in turn, to *p, t,* and *k* in Germanic. The following examples demonstrate how the first sound shift affected English:

Latin			*Germanic (English)*	
p	(pater)	equals	*f*	(father)
t	(tre)	equals	*th*	(three)
k	(cornu)	equals	*h*	(horn)
b	(lubricare)	equals	*p*	(slip)
d	(duo)	equals	*t*	(two)
g	(iugum)	equals	*k*	(yoke)

The Second or "High German Sound Shift"

A *second sound shift* of consonants took place within the West Germanic language branch, beginning possibly as early as the fifth century and certainly evidenced in the documents of the eighth. This second sound shift had only a limited influence, since it affected German but not Anglo-Saxon or Dutch, the two other major West Germanic languages. Because it originated in the higher, mountainous region of central and southern Germany, the phenomenon has been named the "High German Sound Shift," and the language of Germany "High German." As a distinct entity, High German has a history that has been divided into three chronological phases, the earliest being Old High German, followed by Middle High German and New High German. The three periods are generally assigned the following dates: (1) OHG., 700 to 1100 (the early Middle Ages); (2) MHG., 1100 to 1350 (the high and late Middle Ages); (3) NHG., 1350 to present (Renaissance to modern times).

The High German Sound Shift caused many German words to be differentiated from their counterparts in the other West Germanic languages. The principal changes of the second sound shift consisted, on the one hand, of conversion of the Germanic sounds *p, t,* and *k* respectively into *f/pf, s/z,* and *ch,* and, on the other hand, *b* and *d* respectively into *p* and *t.* The following examples represent principal changes differentiating High German consonants from those of English, another West Germanic language (NOTE: in some cases, *differences in meaning* have developed between two cognates):

West Germanic (English)			*High German*	
p	(help)	shifted to	*f*	(helfen)
p	(slip)	shifted to	*pf*	(schlüpfen)
t	(two)	shifted to	*z*	(Zwei)
t	(water)	shifted to	*s(s)*	(Wasser)
k	(yoke)	shifted to	*ch*	(Joch)
b	(sibling)	shifted to	*p*	(Sippe, *kinship*)
d	(daughter)	shifted to	*t*	(Tochter)

Historians of German have studied the transformations in consonants and grouped them into classifications. That system is both too complex to outline here and lies beyond the scope of this book. What will suffice is the following list showing more pairs of affiliated consonants linking English and German words. Again, the user should note that in some cases, *differences in meaning* have developed between cognates.

English			*High German*	
f	(wife)	can equal	*b*	(Weib, *woman, female*)
ght	(night)	can equal	*cht*	(Nacht)
sc	(scold)	can equal	*sch*	(schelten)
sh	(shoe)	can equal	*sch*	(Schuh)

sk	(**sk**id)	can equal	*sch*	(**Sch**eit)
sl	(**sl**eep)	can equal	*schl*	(**schl**afen)
th	(**th**orn)	can equal	*d*	(**D**orn)
v	(star**v**e)	can equal	*b*	(ster**b**en, *to die*)
v	(**v**at)	can equal	*f*	(**F**aß)
wr	(**wr**ite)	can equal	*r*	(**r**eißen, *to tear, split*)
y	(**w**ay)	can equal	*g*	(**W**eg)

Students should note that German vocabulary includes a number of words that do not conform to the consonant shifts described above. Such terms are often borrowings from Low German or Dutch, languages that were unaffected by the High German sound shift. These words preserve the very consonants that High German had shifted in earlier times. That explains why German has two forms of the same Teutonic word: *Waffe*, "weapon," and *Wappen*, "(coat of) arms," the second example, via Dutch, revealing the unshifted *p*.

In addition to shifts in *consonants*, changes in *vowel* sounds occurred in the evolution of High German to further distinguish German words from their English counterparts. Fortunately, changes in *vowels* are not as important for the student to learn to recognize as shifts in *consonants*. The latter will sufficiently establish that two words are cognates, as is seen in the "skeletal" patterns of *d-gh-t-r* (*daughter*) and *t-ch-t-r* (*Tochter*).

Assimilation and Dissimilation

An understanding of two additional sound changes can facilitate the learning of a limited number of German words that are deceptive in appearance. Recognized in linguistics, these sound changes are called *assimilation* and *dissimilation*.

Assimilation is the process in phonetics which causes one of two neighboring but different consonants to be changed and made *similar* to the other. Assimilation occurs in many languages, including English. It is seen in many compounds formed with Latin prepositions (e.g., Latin *ad*, to; and *con*, with) whose final letter becomes assimilated to the first consonant of certain words to which it is joined, as in *ad + levis*, light > *alleviate*; *con*, together + *robur*, strength > *corroborate*. Thus, the final *d* of *ad*, and final *n* of *con*, are assimilated in the above examples.

Dissimilation is the reverse phonetic process. Involving two neighboring consonants that are already alike, dissimilation causes one of the adjacent consonants to be differentiated from, or made *dissimilar* to, its twin. This process is seen in English in the word *pilgrim*, whose original Latin source, *peregrinus* (one who goes abroad), shows two *r* sounds closely positioned to each other. In time, the *r* sounds became dissimilated, the first *r* becoming an *l*, and, after passing through Old French, arriving into English as the form *pilgrim*. In this example, the original *r* of the first syllable is dissimilated.

The number of German words transformed by assimilation or dissimilation is small. Even so, an understanding of their now disguised roots can make it easier for the student to remember these words. A few examples, *which are explained fully as entries in the table*, are listed here just to demonstrate how these altered words hide other roots within them.

ch - f	(in *Hochfahrt*)	assimilated to	*f - f*	(in *Hoffart*)
m - b	(in *Zimber*)	assimilated to	*m - m*	(in *Zimmer*)
l - l	(in *klovolouh*)	dissimilated to	*n - l*	(in *Knoblauch*)
t - t	(in *Tartoffel*)	dissimilated to	*k - t*	(in *Kartoffel*)

German Word List A to Z

GERMAN WORD	MEANING	ENGLISH COGNATE
A		
Aal (m) • **aalen** (vi) • **aalen** (refl)	= eel = to fish for eel = to laze, lounge like eel, bask	*eel*
Aas (see **essen**)		
Abend (m) • **abendländisch** (adj) [bs: like evening sun, at west]	= evening = western, occidental	*eve, evening*
Achse (f) [cogn. L. *axis*, axis]	= axis, axle	*axis, axle*
Achsel (f) [bs: lateral part < IE. *axla*, suffixed form of *aks-*, cogn. L. *ala*, wing] • **achseln** (vt)	= shoulder = to shoulder	distantly: *aisle* [lateral section of a church, passageway < OFr. *aile, ele*, with intrusive *s* < L. *ala*, wing < IE. *axla*, suffixed form of *aks-*]
Acker (m) • **ackern** (vt & vi) • **Ackerbau** (m)	= field, arable land = to till; (fig.:) work hard = agriculture	*acre*
Adel (see **edel**)		
Adler (m), **Aar** (m) (poet.) ['noble eagle' < MHG. *adelar* < *ad-al*, noble + *are, arn*, eagle (cf. AS. *earn*)] • (see also **edel**)	= eagle	*Adel-, Edel-, Ethel-*, in names *Adelaide, Ethel* [noble] + *1. ern(e)* [a kind of eagle that lives near the sea < AS. *earn*]; *2. Ar(n)-* in names: *Arnold* [mighty like an eagle < *arn* + *-old* < *walt-*, power]
Affe (m) • **äffen** (vt)	= ape = to tease, mock, dupe	*ape*
agieren (vi) [< L. *ago, agere, egi, actum*, to act, perform]	= to act, operate	words < L. *ago, agere, egi, actum*, to act, perform: *1. agent; 2. agile; 3. action*
Ahle (f)	= awl, pricker, reamer	*awl*

GERMAN WORD	MEANING	ENGLISH COGNATE
Ahn, Ahnherr (m), **Ahnfrau** (f) [< IE. *an-*, old woman; ancestor (nursery word), whence L. *anilis*, infirm < *anus*, old woman] • **Ahnenkult** (m)	= ancestor = ancestor worship	distantly: *anile* [infirm, like an old woman < L. *anilis* < *anus*, old woman < IE. *an-*, old woman; ancestor (nursery word)]
ahnden (vt) [bs: hostile intensification of 'onto' < OHG. *anton* < *anto*, suffixed form < *an*, on, upon]	= to avenge, punish	*on, onto*
ahnen (vt) [bs: to be 'onto' s.t. < MHG. *anen* < *an(a)*, on, at, upon, near] • **Ahnung** (f)	= to have a presentiment (of or about s.t.), suspect, divine (cf. Eng. to be 'onto something') = presentiment, hunch	*on, onto*
ähnlich (see **Leiche**)		
Akt (m) [< L. *ago, agere, egi, actum*, to act, perform] • **Akte** (f) • **Aktie** (f) [< Fr. *action*, stock, share]	= act (theat.); deed, action; a nude, posed (en*acted*) figure (ptg., photog., etc.) = document, file = (finan.:) stock, share, certificate	words < L. *ago, agere, egi, actum*, to act, perform: *1.* agent; *2.* agile; *3.* action and transaction
albern (see **wahr**)		
allmählich (see **machen**)		
Alp (m) [< OHG. *alb* (cf. AS. *aelf*)] • **Alpdruck** (m), **Alpdrücken** (n)	= nightmare = nightmare	*elf* [a small sprite exercising magic powers < AS. *aelf*]
alt (adj) • **Alter** (n) • **Altertum** (n) • **altertümlich** (adj) • **älter** (adj) • **altern** (vi) _____ • **Eltern** (pl.) • **elterlich** (adj) • **Elternschaft** (f)	= old = age, old age, seniority = antiquity = ancient, archaic = older; older brother = to age, grow old _____ = parents = parental = parentage, the parents	*1.* old; *2.* elder
Altan (m) [bs: something up high < Ital. *altana*, balcony < L. *altus*, high]	= balcony, gallery, platform	words < L. *altus*, high: *1.* altitude; *2.* altar; *3.* alto [range of the highest male voice]
Amboß (m) [< OHG. *anaboz* < *bozan*, to beat (cf. AS. *beatan*)]	= anvil	*1.* beat [< AS. *beatan*]; *2.* to butt
Ameise (f) [< OHG. *ameiza* (cf. AS. *aemette*)]	= ant	*ant* [orig.: *amt* < ME. *amete* < AS. *aemette*]

GERMAN WORD	MEANING	ENGLISH COGNATE
Amme (f) [believed < echoic utterance of a child]	= wet-nurse	cf. *ma-ma* [< echoic utterance of a child]
Ampel (f) [bs: bottle-shape < L. *ampulla*, a round-bottomed flask]	= hanging lamp, traffic light	*ampule* [a sealed vial containing one dose of medicine < L. *ampulla*, a round-bottomed flask]
Amsel (f) [< OHG. *amsala* (cf. AS. *osle*)]	= blackbird	*ouzel* [a European blackbird < AS. *osle*]
Amt (m) • **amtlich** (adj) • **amtieren** (vi) • **Beamte** (m)	= office, duty, charge = official = to officiate, be in charge = officer, official	*amb-* in *ambassador*
ander (adj) • **(ver)ändern** (vt & refl) • **veränderlich** (adj)	= other, different, next = to alter, change = changeable, variable	*other*
Angst (see **eng**)		
Antlitz (see **Blick**)		
Antwort (f) [< *ant-*, opposing + *Wort*, word] • **antworten** (vi) • **beantworten** (vt)	= answer, reply = to give answer = to answer	*an-* in *answer* [< *and-*, opposing + *swer-*, to declare, swear] + *word*
Arbeit (f) [cogn. Czech *robota*, Russ. *rabota*, to work] • **arbeiten** (vt & vi) • **mitarbeiten** (vi)	= work, labor, toil = to work, fashion; labor = to collaborate, cooperate	distantly: *robot* [< Czech *robota*, work (cf. Russ. *rabota*, to work); root *r-b-t* evident in *Arbeit*]
arg (adj) [orig.: unsteady, then disagreeable activity < OHG. *arag* (cf. AS. *earg*, bad) < Gmc. *arga-*, cowardly < IE. **ergh-*, to move quickly, shake] • **Arg** (n) • **verargen** (vt) • **Argwohn** (m) ['a bad supposition' < *arg* + *wohn* < *wahn*, delusion (cf. Eng. *to ween*, to suppose, imagine)] • **argwöhnen** (vt) • **argwöhnisch** (adj) • **Ärger** (m) • **verärgern** (vt) • **ärglich** (adj)	= bad, wicked, malicious = malice, harm = to blame a person = suspicion = to be suspicious of = distrustful, suspicious = annoyance, vexation = to annoy, vex, anger = annoyed, vexed, angry	*1. eerie* [inspiring fear < ME. *eri*, timid, var. of *erg*, cowardly < AS. *earg*, bad < IE. **ergh-*, to move quickly, shake]; *2.* distantly: *orch-* in *orchestra* [< Gk. *orchesthai*, to dance < IE. **ergh-*, to move quickly, shake]
Arm[1] (m) • **Ärmel** (m) • **umarmen** (vt)	= arm = sleeve = to embrace, hug	*arm*

GERMAN WORD	MEANING	ENGLISH COGNATE
arm² (adj) [cogn. Gk. *erem-* in *eremites*, hermit] • **Armut** (f)	= poor = poverty	distantly: *eremite, hermit* [< Gk. *eremites*, one in desolation]
Armbrust (f) [< ML. *arcuballista* < L. *arcus*, bow + Gk. *ballein*, to throw, shoot]	= crossbow	*arc + ballistics*
Art (f) [cogn. L. *ars, artis*, art, skill] • **entarten** (vi) [*ent-*, opposing, separation + *Art*] • **artig** (adj) [bs: in a proper manner] • **Artigkeit** (f)	= kind, sort, way, manner, nature = to degenerate [< L. *de*, away + *genus*, kind, species] = well-behaved, civil, polite = good behavior, civility, politeness	distantly: *art* [< L. *ars, artis*]
Arzt (m) [lit.: 'chief doctor' < OHG. *arzat* < ML. *archiater* < Gk. *archiatros* < *arch-*, first + *iatros*, physician] • **Ärztin** (f) • **ärztlich** (adj) • **Arznei** (f) • **Hausarzt** (m) • **Tierarzt** (m)	= physician, doctor = female doctor = medical, of medicament = medicine = family doctor = animal doctor, veterinarian	*arch-* in *arch(duke)* [principal, chief < Gk. *archein*, to be first, rule] + *-iat-* < *iatrist* in *psychiatrist, podiatrist* [doctor < Gk. *iatros*, physician, healer (+ *psyche*, soul; *podo-*, foot)]
Asche (f) • **einäschern** (vt)	= ash = to incinerate, cremate	*ash*
Attentat (n) ['an attack' < L. *attentare*, to try]	= assassination	*attempt* [< L. *attentare*, to try]
Attrappe (see **traben**)		
Aue (f) (esp. poetic)	= water-meadow, pasture, green	*-au* in *Nassau* [an old duchy in Germany ('wet meadow' < *naß* +*Aue*)]
Auge (f) [cf. AS. *eage*; LG. *oog*] • **äugeln** (vi) • **ereignen** (vi) ['to come before one's eyes' < *er*, thoroughly + *äugnen* < *Auge*, eye] • **Ereignis** (n)	= eye = to look fondly at s.t. = to occur, happen = occurrence, event	*1. eye* [< AS. *eage*]; *2. to ogle* [< LG. *oog*, eye]; *3. -ow* in *window* [lit.: 'wind-eye,' a hole to let in air, wind < ME. *windoge* < ON. *windauga*]
Auster (f) [< L. *ostreum* < Gk. *ostreion*]	= oyster	*oyster* [< L. *ostreum* < Gk. *ostreion*]
äußern (vt) [bs: to 'give out' a statement < *aus*, out] • **Äußerung** (f)	= to utter, express, advance = utterance, remark	*1. out; 2. utter* [to give out words < *ut*, out]

GERMAN WORD	MEANING	ENGLISH COGNATE
B		
Bach (m)	= brook	*beck* [a brook with a stony bed]
backen (vt & vi) [*backte, gebacken*] • **Gebäck** (n) • **Bäcker** (n)	= to bake = pastry = baker	*bake*
Bad (n) • **baden** (vt & vi) • **Badort** (m) • **Badwanne** (f)	= bath = to give bath to; to go bathing, bathe = watering place; spa, seaside resort = bathtub	*bath*
Bahn (f) [bs: path or track beaten down < IE. *gwhen-*, to strike, beat down, kill (cf. AS. *bana*, slayer)] • **bahnen** (vi) • **Bahnhof** (m) • **Bahnsteig** (m) • **Bühne** (f) [bs: raised 'path' built of boards]	= path, track = to clear or open a way = railway station = railway platform = stage, platform	distantly: *bane* [that which brings harm, orig.: what strikes down < AS. *bana*, slayer < IE. *gwhen-*, to strike, beat, kill]
Bahre (f) ['what holds up a corpse or body' < obs. OHG. *beran* < IE. *bher-*, to carry (up), lift, raise] • **gebaren** (refl) [bs: to carry oneself a cert. way] • **Gebaren** (n) [how one carries oneself] • **Gebärde** (f) • **gebären** (vt) [*gebar, geboren*] • **Geburt** (f) • **angeboren** (adj) • **Eingeborene** (m) • **entbehren** (vt) [bs: bearing nothing < *ent*, without] • **entbehrlich** (adj) [bs: that can be lacking] • **Bürde** (f) • **Gebühr** (f) [bs: a cost to be born] • **gebühren** (vt) • **gebührlich** (adj) • (see also **empor**)	= bier, stretcher, litter = to behave, act = behavior, demeanor = gesture, gesticulation = to bear, give birth to = birth = innate = native = to lack, be wanting in = dispensable, needless = burden = dues, fee, charge = to be due (to one), be proper to = duly, seemly, suitable	words < IE. *bher-*, to carry (up), lift, raise: *1. to bear; 2. born; 3. bier; 4. bar-* in *wheelbarrow;* *5. burden* [anything carried]

GERMAN WORD	MEANING	ENGLISH COGNATE
Balg (m) [< MHG. *balc* < Gmc. *belg*]	= sloughed skin, bag, husk, shell; bellows	*1. bellows* [hollow implement used to blow a fire]; *2. belly*
Balken (m) • **Gebälk** (n) • **Balkon** (m)	= rafter, beam = framework, timberwork = balcony	*1. balcony; 2. to balk* [bs: to be obstructive, 'throw a beam in the way']; *3. bulk-* in *bulkhead* [the upright partitions of a ship, then any wall to hold back water, etc.]
Banause (m) [< Gk. *banausikos,* of the forge, hence, vulgar < *baunos,* forge]	= Philistine (smugly conventional person)	*banausic* [characteristic of a mechanic or the forge; low, vulgar < Gk. *banausikos* < *baunos,* forge]
bang(e) (see **eng**)		
Bank (f)	= bench	*bench*
Bann (m) • **bannen** (vt)	= ban, excommunication = to banish, exorcise; avert (danger)	*ban*
bar (adj) • **Bargeld** (n), **Barschaft** (f) [bs: exposed or ready money, 'bared gold']	= bare, nude, devoid of = ready cash	*bare*
Bär (m)	= bear	*bear*
barsch (see **Borste**)		
Bart (m)	= beard	*beard*
Base (f) [< OHG. *basa,* sister of the father, aunt, cousin]	= female cousin	theorized: *boss¹* [< Du. *baas* < MDu. *baes,* orig.: friend, father, uncle, then governor, master]
basteln (vt & vi) [< Gmc. *bastjan,* to make with bast or thatch, to build, hence OFr. *bastir* > Fr. *bâtir,* to frame, build] • **Bastei** (f) • **Bastler** (m)	= to rig up, build, do handicrafts = bastion = amateur craftsman	*1. to baste* [to sew together loosely]; *2. bast* [fiber used in making mats]; *3. bastion* [a built up fortification]
Bauch (m)	= abdomen, paunch, belly	*1. buck-* in *bucket* [< ME. *boket,* dim. of *buc,* pitcher, belly]; *2. bouk* [Scot. and dial.: belly, trunk, body]
bauen (vt & vi) [< OHG. *bu-,* to dwell] • **Bau** (m) • **baulich** (adj) • **Gebäude** (n) • **Bauer¹** (n) • **Bauer²** (m) • **bäuerlich** (adj)	= to build, construct; till, cultivate, raise = building, construction, structure = structural, architectural = building, edifice = (bird)cage = peasant, farmer, builder = rural, rustic	*1. Bow-* in *Bowery* [district in Manhattan, orig.: 'farmland']; *2. bower* [bs: dwelling, shelter created by branches]; *3. boor* [awkward person]; *4. -bor* in *neighbor* [lit.: 'nearby farmer' < AS. *neah,* nigh, + *boer,* farmer]

GERMAN WORD	MEANING	ENGLISH COGNATE
Baum (m) • **bäumen** (refl) [bs: to go straight up like a tree] • **Purzelbaum** (m)	= tree = to rear up (of a horse), prance = somersault	*1. beam; 2. boom* [a long pole extending from a mast or derrick]
Bausch (m) • **bauschen** (vi & refl) • **bauschig** (adj) ──────── • **pauschal** (adv) [bs: in a lump or pad] • **Pauschale** (f)	= pad, bolster, wad, puff = to swell or bulge out = puffy, swelled, baggy ──────── = all at once = lump sum	distantly: *bush* and *to bush out*
beben (vi) • **Erdbeben** (n)	= to quake, tremble, shiver = earthquake	*to bever* [now dial.: to tremble, shake]
Becher (m)	= cup, beaker, mug	*beaker*
Becken (n) [< LL. *baccinum*, basin]	= basin; pelvis	*basin* [< OFr. *bacin* < LL. *baccinum*, basin]
bedingen (see **Ding**)		
beeinträchtigen (see **tragen**)		
Beere (f)	= berry	*berry*
befehlen (see **Fell**)		
begleiten (see **leiten**)		
behelligen (vt) [original sense: to make tired < MHG. *hel, hellic*, weak, flat < IE. **(s)kel-*, dried out, whence Gk. *skeletos*, skeleton] • **unbehelligt** (adj)	= to importune, bother, molest = unmolested	distantly: *skel-* in *skeleton* [< Gk. *skeletos*, skeleton < IE. **(s)kel-*, dried out]
Behörde (see **hören**)		
behr- (see **Bahre**)		
Behuf (m) • **behufs** (prep) + *gen.*	= purpose, end = for the purpose of	*to behoove* [to be fitting, suit the purpose of] and *behoof* [sake]
Beichte (f) [< OHG. *bigiht, bijiht* < *bi-* + *jiht*, declaration < *jehan*, to declare < IE. **yek-*, to speak, whence L. *joco, jocare*, to say in jest] • **beichten** (vt & vi)	= confession, solemn declaration = to confess	*be-* + distantly: *to joke* [< L. *joco, jocare*, to say in jest < IE. **yek-*, to speak]
Beifall (see **fallen**)		
Beil (n) [cf. AS. *bile*]	= ax, hatchet, cleaver	*bill* [point of an anchor; beak of a bird < AS. *bile*]

GERMAN WORD	MEANING	ENGLISH COGNATE
Bein (n) • **Gebein** (n)	= leg, bone = bones, skeleton	*bone*
beißen (vt & vi) • **Biß** (m) • **Bissen** (m) • **bißchen** (adj, adv) • **bissig** (adj)	= to bite = bite = morsel = a little bit = sarcastic, biting	*bite*
bejahen (vt) [*be + jah*] • **Bejahung** (f)	= to answer in the affirmative, con- cede = affirmation, acceptance	*yeah, yes*
Belang (m) • **belangen** (vt)	= importance, matter, issue = to concern	*to belong* [to be connected to a mat- ter]
bellen (vi) [echoic; ult. < IE. **bhel*, to sound]	= to bark	cf. echoic Eng. *bellow,* to roar [< IE. **bhel-,* to sound]
bequem (adj)	= comfortable, convenient	*becoming*
bereit (adj) • **bereiten** (vt) • **bereits** (adv)	= prepared = to prepare = already	*1. ready; 2. to redd up* [make ready]; *3. array* [< L. *ad,* to + AS. *raedan,* to put in order]
Berg (m) • **Gebirge** (n) • **Bergmann** (m) • **Bergwerk** (n)	= mountain = mountain range = miner = mine	*-berg* in *iceberg*
bergen (vt) [*barg, geborgen* (cf. AS. *byrgan*)] • **Bergung** (f) • **geborgen** (adj) • **Geborgenheit** (f) • **verbergen** (vt) • **verborgen** (adj)	= to save, salvage, shelter; conceal, hide = salvage, recovery = sheltered = safety, security = to conceal, hide = hidden, concealed	*1. bury* [< AS. *byrgan, beorgan*]; *2. burrow* [shelter]; *3. -bor* in *har- bor* [lit.: 'army shelter,' then refuge, esp. for ships < AS. *here,* army + *beorg,* shelter]
Bernstein (m) [< LG. *bernen* (= *brennen*), to burn + *Stein,* stone]	= amber (a brownish-yellow fossil resin)	*burn + stone*
bersten (vi) [*barst, geborsten*]	= to burst, break, explode	*burst*
beschäftigen (see **schaffen**)		
bestätigen (see **stetig**)		
Besteck (see **stecken**)		
beten (vi) • **anbeten** (vt) • **Gebet** (n)	= to pray = to worship, adore = prayer	*bead* [knob on a string used in prayer]

GERMAN WORD	MEANING	ENGLISH COGNATE
Beton (m) [< Fr. *béton*, concrete < L. *bitumen*, pitch used in masonry]	= concrete	*bitumen* [mineral pitch, natural asphalt]
Bett (n)	= bed	*bed*
betteln (see **bitten**)		
Beule (f) • **Beulenpest** (f)	= bump, swelling, boil; dent (on metal) = bubonic plague	*boil* (medic.)
Beute (f) • **erbeuten** (vt) • **ausbeuten** (vt) • **Ausbeute** (f)	= booty, loot; prey, victim = to capture, take as booty = to exploit = gain, profit	*booty* [< ME. *botye, buty*]
Beutel (m) [bs: thing swollen, bulging < OHG. *budila*, prob. ult. < IE. **beu-, *bheu-*, to swell] • **beuteln** (vt) [bs: to use a cloth bag as a sieve] • **beuteln** (refl) • **beutelig** (adj) • **Beutelschneider** (m)	= bag, pouch, purse; cyst = to shake, sift = to bulge, be baggy = baggy = cutpurse, pickpocket	words < IE. **beu-, *bheu-*, to swell: *1. bud; 2. pout* [disagreeable attitude shown by swollen cheeks or jutting lips]; *3. pod; 4. boudoir* [pouting chamber < Fr. *bouder*, to pout]
Bezirk (m) [bs: an area in a defined zone < L. *circus*, circle]	= district, precinct	*circle*
Biber (m)	= beaver	*beaver*
biegen (vt) [*bog, gebogen* (cf. AS. *bugan*)] • **biegsam** (adj) ['bendable'] • **Bogen** (m) • **beugen** (vt & refl) • **vorbeugen** (vt & vi) [bs: to bend forward as to deflect] • **bücken** (refl)	= to bend, curve = pliant, compliant = bend, arch = to bend; bow = to ward off, prevent [cf. *deflect*, to turn to the side < L. *de*, away + *flectere*, to bend] = to bend, stoop to, submit to	*1. to bow* [< AS. *bugan*, to bend]; *2. buxom* [healthy, plump (esp. of a woman), orig.: bendable, compliant, obedient (e.g., 'buxom bride') < ME. *buhsum*]
Biene (f)	= bee	*bee*

GERMAN WORD	MEANING	ENGLISH COGNATE
bieten (vt & refl) [*bot, geboten*]	= to offer, bid	*1. bid; 2. forbid;*
• **darbieten** (vt)	= to present, perform	
• **gebieten** (vt & vi)	= to order, command; to rule, give command	
• **Gebiet** (n) [bs: that governed, area of rule]	= area under one's command, territory, area of jurisdiction	
• **verbieten** (vt)	= to forbid, prohibit	
• **Bote** (m)	= messenger, envoy	*3. to bode (ill or well)*
• **Botschaft** (f)	= message, communication, embassy	
• **Botschafter** (m)	= ambassador	
• **Gebot** (n)	= commandment	
Bild (n) [< OHG. *bilidi*; suggested by some to be distantly cogn. G. *billig*, fair, reasonable, what is right]	= picture, image, illustration	close cogn. lacking; ? *bilewit* [obs. adj: mild, clement, fair, lit.: 'fairminded' < Gmc. *bili-*, reasonable + *wit*, mind]
• **bilden** (vt)	= to form, shape; (fig.:) to educate, train	
• **bildlich** (adj)	= pictorial, figurative	
• **Bildnis** (n)	= portrait	
• **Bildhauer** (m) ['image hewer' < *Bild* + *hauen*, to hew, chop]	= sculptor	
• **Abbild** (n)	= likeness, image	
• **abbilden** (vt)	= to illustrate, represent	
billig (adj) [< OHG. *billih*, reasonable, appropriate]	= orig.: reasonable, fair, then of reasonable price, hence cheap, inexpensive	*bilewit* [obs. adj: mild, clement, fair, lit.: 'fairminded' < Gmc. *bili-*, reasonable + *wit*, mind]
• **Billigkeit** (f)	= justness, fairness, reasonableness	
• **billigen** (vt)	= to approve of, find reasonable	
• **Billigung** (f)	= approval	
• **unbillig** (adj)	= unfair	
bimsen (vt) [< MHG. *bumez* < L. *pumex*, pumice]	= to rub or polish; (fig.:) to drill (as in military)	*pumice* [material used in polishing < L. *pumex*, pumice]
binden (vt & vi) [*band, gebunden*]	= to bind, unite	*1. bind; 2. band; 3. bundle*
• **Band** (m)	= volume, book	
• **Band** (n)	= ribbon	
• **bändigen** (vt) [bs: to put in binds as animals]	= to tame, subdue	
• **Bund** (m)	= alliance, union, federation	
• **Bund** (n)	= bundle, truss	
• **bündig** (adj) [bs: well-bound, tight]	= concise, terse; binding, conclusive	
• **Bündigkeit** (f)	= conciseness, conclusiveness	
Birke (f)	= birch	*birch*
Birne (f) [< L. *pirum*, pear]	= pear; (electric) bulb	*pear* [< L. *pirum*, pear]
• **Glühbirne** (f)	= electric light bulb	

GERMAN WORD	MEANING	ENGLISH COGNATE
birschen (see **Pirsch**)		
bitten (vt) [*bat, gebeten* (cf. AS. *biddan*)] • **Bitte** (f) • **abbitten** (vt) ——————————— • **betteln** (vi) [intensive of *bitten*, to ask for] • **Bettler** (m) • (see also **beten**)	= to ask or beg for = entreaty, request = to beg forgiveness, apologize ——————————— = to beg = beggar	words < AS. *biddan*, to ask, command: **1.** *to bid* (to one); **2.** *bidden* [asked]
blähen (vt) [cf. AS. *blawan*]	= to inflate, make swell out	*blow* [< AS. *blawan*]
blaken (vi)	= to give off fumes, smoke	*black* [orig.: sooted, smoke-black]
blasen (vt & vi) • **Blase** (f)	= to blow, sound or play (a musical instr.) = bubble, blister, bladder	*blast*
blaß (adj) [bs: very light < IE. *bhles-*, to shine, be light] • **Blässe** (f) • **erblassen, verblassen** (vi)	= pale, pallid = paleness = to grow pale	*blaze* [< AS. *blaese, blase*, torch or flame < IE. *bhles-*, to shine, be light]
Blatt (n) • **blättern** (vi) • **Blattgold** (n) • **Blätterteig** (m) and **Blatterkuchen** (m)	= leaf; sheet, page of book = to leaf through a book = gold leaf = puff (leafy) pastry	*blade* [grass; flat bone, metal slab]
blau (adj)	= blue	*blue*
Blei (n) [bs: a white-greyish metal < IE. *bhlei-/*bhel-*, to shine, flash] • **Bleistift** (m) • **bleiern** (adj)	= lead (miner.) = pencil (marker using lead) = leaden, of lead	distantly: *blea-* in *bleak* [bs: pale, light < IE. *bhlei-/*bhel-*, to shine, flash]
bleiben, verbleiben (vi) • **bleibend** (adj) • **Verbleib** (m)	= to remain, stay, be left = lasting, permanent = whereabouts	**1.** *leave* [orig.: to leave a heritage]; **2.** *-lay* in *delay* [to leave until later < OFr. *deslaier < laier <* Gmc.]
bleich (adj) • **bleichen** (vt & vi)	= pale = to make pale, bleach; to lose color, fade	**1.** distantly: *blea-* in *bleak* [bs: pale, light < IE. *bhlei-/*bhel-*, to shine, flash]; **2.** *bleach*

GERMAN WORD	MEANING	ENGLISH COGNATE
Blick (m) [orig.: brilliance, then restricted to a flashing look, glance; cogn. to *bleich* (cf. Goth. *wlits*) < IE. **bhlei-/*bhel-*, to shine, flash]	= glance, look, view	distantly: *1. bleak* [bs: pale, light < IE. **bhlei-/*bhel-*, to shine, flash]; *2. bleach*;
• **blicken** (vi) • **erblicken** (vt)	= to glance, look = to catch sight of, perceive	
• **Blitz** (m) • **blitzen** (vi)	= lightening = to flash, give lightening	*3. blizzard; 4. blitz*
• **Antlitz** (n) [orig.: what shines out and away, aspect < *ent-*, opposing + *-litz*]	= face, countenance	
blind (adj) • **Blindheit** (f) • **blindings** (adv) • **Blinde** (m & f)	= blind; opaque, cloudy = blindness = at·random = a blind person	*blind*
Blitz (see **Blick**)		
bloß (adj) • **Blöße** (f) • **bloßlegen** (vt)	= bare, naked, mere = bareness, nakedness; clearing, glade = to lay bare, expose	*blot* [in backgammon, an exposed man; hence, an exposed point, a failing]
blühen (vi) • **Blüte** (f)	= to blossom, flower = blossom, bloom	*blow*
Blume (f) [ult. < *blühen*, to blossom]	= flower	*1. bloom; 2. blow*
Blut (n) • **bluten** (vi)	= blood = to bleed	*blood*
Bock (m) • **bocken** (vi) • **bockig** (adj)	= buck (male of the deer, goat, ram) = to buck, be obstinate = stubborn, obstinate	*buck*
Bogen (see **biegen**)		
Bohle (f) • **bohlen** (vt)	= plank, board = to lay planks, boards	*1. bole* [stem, trunk of tree]; *2. bul-, boul-* in *bulwark* [timber rampart, 'bole-work'] and *boulevard* [street put on land once of rampart ruins]
bohnern (vt) [bs: to make shiny; < iterative of root *bohn-* < IE. **bha(n)-*, to shine, whence Gk. *phantom*] • **Bohner** (m)	= to polish, wax = polisher	distantly: words < Gk. *phaino*, to make clear or manifest < IE. **bha(n)-*, to shine: *1. phantom; 2. phenomenon*
bohren (vt & vi)	= to bore, drill	*bore*
Boltzen (m)	= dart, bolt, dowel, pin	*bolt* [metal rod or pin; roll of cloth; flash of lightening]

GERMAN WORD	MEANING	ENGLISH COGNATE
Boot (n)	= boat	*boat*
borgen (vt) [cf. AS. *borgian*]	= to borrow; lend	*borrow* [< AS. *borgian*]
• **auf Borg**	= on credit	
• **Bürge** (m)	= security, surety, bond, bailsman	
• **(ver)bürgen** (vt)	= to guarantee, warrant	
Borke (f)	= rind, crust, bark, scab	*bark*
Born (m)	= fountain, well, spring	*bourne* [a well]
Borste (f)	= bristle	*bristle*
• **borstig** (adj)	= bristly	
• **barsch** (adj) ['like bristles']	= rough, gruff	
• **Barschheit** (f)	= gruffness, bluntness	
böse, bösartig, bösewillig (adj) [bs: neg. force added to IE. *beu-, *bheu-, to swell]	= bad, evil, wicked, ill-tempered	distantly: words < IE. *beu-, *bheu-, to swell, expand: *1. boast; 2. bosom; 3. pouch; 4. poach* [to cook in a pouch]
• **Bösewicht** (m) [*Wicht*, wight, creature]	= villain, scoundrel	
• **boshaft** (adj)	= malicious, wicked	
• **Bosheit** (f)	= maliciousness, spite, wickedness	
• **erbosen** (vt)	= to irritate, infuriate, provoke	
• **erbosen** (refl)	= to grow angry	
Bottich (m) [cf. AS. *bodig*]	= barrel, tub, vat	*body* [< AS. *bodig*]
• **Böttcher** (m)	= cooper	
Bracke (m) [Ital. *bracco;* Fr. *brague*]	= hunting dog, pointer	*brack* [orig.: a dog that hunts by scent, now a female hound]
braten (vt)	= to grill, fry, roast	distantly: *1. broth; 2. bread* [< IE. *bhreu-,* to bubble, boil];
• **Bratpfanne** (f)	= frying pan	
• **Braten**[1] (n)	= roasting	
• **Braten**[2] (m) [< OHG. *brato* < Gmc. *braton*]	= roast (meat), joint	*3. brawn* [< OFr. *braon, braion,* piece of flesh < Gmc. *braton*]
• **Wildbret** (n)	= venison, game	
Brauch (m) [cf. AS. *brucan*]	= usage, use, custom, habit	*to brook* [orig.: to enjoy use, then limited to bearing something unpleasant ('I cannot *brook* his insolence') < AS. *brucan,* to use]
• **brauchen** (vt)	= to want, require, use	
• **brauchbar** (adj)	= useful, serviceable	
• **Gebrauch** (n)	= use, employment	
• **gebrauchen** (vt)	= to use, employ	
• **gebräuchlich** (adj)	= in use, current, common	
• **mißbrauchen** (vt)	= to misuse, abuse	
• **mißbräuchlich** (adj)	= abusive, improper	
• **verbrauchen** (vt)	= to use up, consume	
• **Verbraucher** (m)	= consumer	

GERMAN WORD	MEANING	ENGLISH COGNATE
Braue (f)	= eyebrow	*brow*
Braut (f) • **Brautigam** (m)	= bride, fiancee = bridegroom	*bride*
brechen (vt & vi) [*brach, gebrochen*] • **Bröcken** (m) • **bröckeln** (vi) • **bröckelig** (adj) • **brüchig** (adj) • **Verbrechen** (n) • **Verbrecher** (m) • **ehebrechen** (vi) ['to break *Ehe,* matrimony'] • **Ehebrecher** (m) • **Ehebruch** (m)	= to break; break down = piece, fragment = to crumble = crumbly, friable = brittle = crime = criminal = to commit adultery = adulterer = adultery	*break*
Brei (m) [< IE. **bhreu-,* to bubble] • **breiig** (adj)	= pulp, pap, puree, porridge, mush = pulpy, pasty	distantly: *1. barm* [froth on malt liquor fermenting < IE. **bhreu-,* to bubble]; *2. brew, broth*
breit (adj) • **Breite** (f) • **verbreitern** (vt & refl) • **ausbreiten, verbreiten** (vt) • **unterbreiten** (vt) ['to spread s.t. under one's gaze']	= broad, wide = breadth, width = to widen, broaden = to spread, diffuse = to put before one, submit (a plan, etc.)	*broad*
bremsen (vt) [uncert.; theorized bs: to squeeze < L. *premo, premere, pressus,* to press, squeeze (whence Span. *prensa,* press)] • **Bremse** (f)	= to brake, check, retard (from the squeezing system used to brake wheels?) = brake	*1. press; 2. prim-* in *imprimatur* [an approval, orig. an approval to print issued by the Church: 'let there be printed' < passive subjunctive of L. *in,* in + *premo, premere, pressus,* to press, squeeze]
brennen (vt & vi) • **brennbar** (adj) • **Brand** (m) ——————— • **Brunst** (f) [< *brennen,* to burn] • **brünstig** (adj) • **Brunft** (f)	= to burn = combustible = burning, fire, blaze ——————— = (of animals:) heat, rut; (humans:) lust, sexual desire = lustful, in heat = rut	*1. to brand; 2. brandy* [earlier: *brandywine,* lit.: 'burnt wine,' so-called from being distilled]; *3. burn*
Bresche (f)	= breach, gap	*breach*
Brett (n)	= plank, board, shelf, tray	*board*
Brief (m) [< L. *breve (scriptum),* a concise writing]	= letter, missive	*brief* and *brevity*

GERMAN WORD	MEANING	ENGLISH COGNATE
Brille (f) [< MHG. *berille* < L. *beryllus,* a sea-green gem used as a crystal in reliquaries to allow viewing of the contents within] • **Schutzbrille** (f) [< *schutzen,* to safeguard, shelter]	= spectacles, eye glasses = safety glasses, goggles	*1. beryl* [a transparent, green precious stone]; *2. brilliant*
brodeln (vi)	= to simmer, bubble	*broth*
Brodem (m)	= steam, vapor	*breath*
Bruder (m)	= brother	*brother*
Brunnen (m)	= well, spring, fountain	*bourne* [a brook or stream]
Brunst, Brunft (see **brennen**)		
Brust (f) • **Brüstung** (f), **Brustwehr** (f) ['wall breast-high' and 'breast protection' < *wehren,* to defend (loan transl. of Ital. *parapetto,* parapet, 'protecting the breast')]	= breast = balustrade, sill, parapet [wall 'protecting at the breast' < Ital. *parapetto* < *parare,* to guard + *petto,* breast]	*breast*
Brut (f) • **brüten** (vt & vi)	= hatching, incubation, brood, spawn = to incubate, hatch; (fig.:) to scheme	*brood*
Bube (m)	= boy, lad	*booby* [silly fellow]
Buch (n) • **Buchstabe** (m) • **buchstabieren** (vt)	= book = letter (alphab.), type = to spell with letters	*book*
Büchse (f) [(cf. Du. *bus*) < LL. *buxa* (whence LL. dim. *buxula* > Ital. *bussola,* case with magnetic needle) < Gk. *pyxis,* an ancient cylindrical container with a lid] • **Bussole** (f)	= box, case, cylindrical tin or can; also rifle, gun, bec. of its cylindrical barrel [cf. *-bus* in *blunderbus,* an early gun, and *arquebus,* an early gun propped on a *haak,* 'hook' or forked rest < Fr. *arquebuse* < Du. *haakbuse*] = magnetic compass	*1. box* [< LL. *buxa* < Gk. *pyxis,* an ancient container, round box]; *2. bushing* [the cylindrical metal lining of a hole < Du. *bus,* can, box]; *3. to bush* [to fit with bushings]; *4. -bus* in *blunderbus* and *arquebus* [early types of guns]
Bucht (f)	= bay, inlet, creek, bight	*bight* [a bending, bend of river, bay]
Buckel (m) [< OFr. *bocle* < LL. *buccula,* shield with a center hump] • **buck(e)lig** (adj)	= hump, bump, bulge, humpback = humped, humpbacked	*1. buckler* [a small round shield, orig. with a hump in the center < OFr. *bocle* < LL. *buccula,* shield with a center hump]; *2. buckle*
Bude (f)	= stall, hut, booth	*booth*
Büffel (m) • **büffeln** (vi)	= buffalo; oaf = to work like a buffalo, cram for exams	*buffalo*

GERMAN WORD	MEANING	ENGLISH COGNATE
Bug (m)	= joint of the leg, hock, shoulder; bow (of ship)	*bough* ['leg,' or 'joint' of a tree]
Bügel (m) [bs: something with a bent loop < *biegen*, to bend, bow] • **bügeln** (vt) ['to use a loop,' i.e., a loop-handled iron] • **Bügeleisen** (n) ['loop-handled iron'] • **Steigbügel** (n) [lit.: 'mounting loop']	= bow-shaped piece of metal or wood; hoop, loop, handle (of a bucket, etc.) = to press (clothing), use an iron = iron (for pressing cloth) = stirrup	*bow*
Buhle (m) [cf. Du. *boel*, lover] • **Buhlerin** (f) • **buhlen** (+ **um**) (vt) • **buhlerisch** (adj)	= lover, paramour = courtesan, paramour = to make love to; woo, court = amorous, wanton	*bully* [orig.: sweetheart, then a person who hurts or threatens < Du. *boel*, lover]
Bühne (see **Bahn**)		
bühr- (see **Bahre**)		
Bulle (m)	= bull	*bull*
Bummler (m) • **bummeln** (vi) • **bummelig** (adj) • **Bummelei** (f)	= stroller, idler, loafer = to stroll, saunter, loaf = slack, careless, sluggish = carelessness, loafing	*bum*
Bund (see **binden**)		
bunt (adj) [< L. *punctum*, pricked, variegated by points or stitches in textile work] • **Buntheit** (f) • **Buntdruck** (m) • **buntfleckig** (adj) • (see also **kunterbunt**)	= variegated, flecked, multi-colored = gay coloring, variety = color print, chromolithograph = spotted, speckled	*puncture* [< L. *pungo, pungere, punctum*, to prick, puncture]
Burg (f) [a medieval fortification near which houses were built] • **Bürger** (m) • **Bürgerkrieg** (m) • **bürgerlich** (adj)	= castle, citadel = citizen, townsman = civil war = civic, bourgeois, middle-class	*1. bourg* [a medieval town near a castle]; *2. borough* [orig.: fortified place, later a self-governing settlement]; *3. burgher* [citizen of a town]; *4. bourgeoisie* [the middle class < Fr. < OHG. *burg*]
Bürge (see **borgen**)		
Bursch (m) [orig.: a student on a stipend, then any young person < ML. *bursa*, purse, financial aid]	= youngster, lad, fellow, guy	*1. bursar* [treasurer at a university < ML. *bursa*, purse]; *2. purse* [< ML. *bursa*]
Bürzel (see **empor**)		

GERMAN WORD	MEANING	ENGLISH COGNATE
Busen (m)	= bosom, breast	*bosom*
Buße (f) [< OHG. *buoza* (cf. AS. *bot*) < Gmc. **boto*, a making good; also cogn. OHG. *bezziro* (G. *besser*) better]	= atonement, penance	***1.*** *boot, to boot* [orig.: advantage, a making good, remedy, amends for injury or wrong-doing, then to the good, into the bargain, in addition, e.g., *dinner to boot* < ME. *bote*, AS. *bot*]; ***2.*** distantly: *better*
• **büßen** (vt & vi)	= to atone for, expiate	
• **Büßer** (m)	= one penitent	
• **Einbuße** (f) ['that in remedy,' orig.: a making good after a loss, then loss itself]	= loss, damage	
• **einbüßen** (vt)	= to forfeit, lose; suffer loss	
• **verbüßen** (vt) [*ver*, perfective prefix + *büßen*]	= to complete one's sentence, serve one's time	
• **bußfertig** (adj) ['penitence-ready']	= penitent, contrite	
• **Lückenbüßer** (m) ['repair (making good) of a hole (*Lücke*)']	= stopgap	
Bussole (see **Büchse**)		
Butt (m)	= a kind of flatfish, plaice	*butt¹* [a kind of flatfish] and *-but* in *halibut*
• **Heilbutt** (m) [lit.: 'holy butt,' bec. it was eaten on a holy day]	= halibut	
Butzen (m)	= clump; core (of a fruit or tumour)	*butt²* [thick end or stump of anything (e.g., rifle, cigarette)]

D		
Dach (n) [cf. AS. *thaec*]	= roof, shelter	*thatch* [< AS. *thaec*]
• **Dachfenster** (n)	= dormer window, skylight	
• **Dachgeschoß** (n)	= attic, the story below the roof	
Dachs (m) [> Ital. *tasso*, badger]	= badger	*dachs-* in *dachshund* ['badger hound']
dämmern (vi) [bs: to be dim, not clear < OHG. *demar*, cogn. *dinstar*, dark < IE. **teme-*, dark]	= to dawn (be in dimness)	distantly: *teme-* in *temerity* [rashness < L. *temere*, at random (blindly) < IE. **teme-*, dark]
• **Dämmerung** (f)	= dusk, dawn	
• **dämmerig** (adj)	= dusky	

GERMAN WORD	MEANING	ENGLISH COGNATE
Dampf (m) • **Dampfer** (m) • **dampfig** (adj) • **dämpfen** (vt) ―――――――――― • **dunkel** (adj)	= steam, vapor = steamship, steamer = steamy, sultry = to cause to steam ―――――――――― = dark, murky	*damp*
Darm (m), **Gedärme** (n)	= entrails, intestines, gut	*tharm, tharms* [dial.: intestines]
darren (see **dorren**)		
Dattel (f) [< Ital. *dattilo* (now *dattero*) < Gk. *dactylon*, finger (the date so-named because it is long and fingerlike)]	= date (fruit)	*1. date* [a fruit < OFr. *date* (Fr. *datte*; Ital. *dattilo*, now *dattero*) < Gk. *dactylon*, finger]; *2. dactylogram* [fingerprint]
dauern[1] (vi) [cogn. L. *durare*, to last] • **Dauer** (f)	= to continue, last, require (time) = duration, period, length	*duration* [< L. *durare*, to last]
dauern[2] (vt) [bs: to affect one dearly (cf. G. *teuer*, dear) < MHG. *turen*] • **bedauern** (vt) • **bedaurlich** (adj)	= to cause sorrow in = to pity, feel sorry for, lament, deplore = regrettable, deplorable	*dear*
Daumen (m) • **Daumenabdruck** (m)	= thumb = thumbprint	*thumb*
decken (vt) • **Decke** (f) • **Deckel** (m) • **entdecken** (vt) • **Entdecker** (m)	= to cover = blanket, covering; ceiling = lid, cover (box, book) = to discover, disclose = discoverer	*deck*
Degen[1] (m) (poet.) [cf. AS. *thegan*]	= warrior, fighter, hero	*thane* [a freeborn man of medieval England < AS. *thegan*, attendant]
Degen[2] (m)	= sword	*dagger*
dehnen (vt) [< IE. **ten-*, pull, stretch, whence L. *tendere*, to stretch, strain] • **Dehnung** (f) • **dehnbar** (adj) ―――――――――― • **gedunsen** (adj) [past p. of older *dinsen*, to pull < *dehnen*]	= to extend, stretch = tension, stretching = extensible, elastic, ductile ―――――――――― = bloated	*1. tend; 2. tension; 3. tent*
Deichsel (f) [bs: extended pole < OHG. *dihsala* < Gmc. **thinh-slo* < IE. **ten(gh)-*, stretch]	= pole, shaft, drawbar (for hitching horses to a wagon)	distantly: *tens-* in *tension, tense* [< L. *tendo, tendere, tensum*, to stretch out < IE. **ten(gh)-*, stretch]

GERMAN WORD	MEANING	ENGLISH COGNATE
Dekan, Dechant (m) [< L. *decanus*, an official over ten persons < *decem*, ten (whence Fr. *doyen;* Eng. *dean*)]	= dean (univ., eccl., etc.)	*dean* [< ME. *deen,* OFr. *deien* < LL. *decanus,* an official over ten persons < *decem,* ten]
Delle (f) [bs: valley < MHG. *telle* (cogn. G. *Tal,* valley)]	= dent, depression	*dale*
denken (vt & vi) [*dachte, gedachte*] • **Denker** (m) • **Andenken** (n) • **erdenken** (vt) • **Andacht** (f) • **bedacht** (adj) • **Verdacht** (m) [bs: evil thought < *ver,* neg. prefix]	= to think = thinker, philosopher = remembrance, souvenir = to conceive, invent = devotion = thoughtful = suspicion	*think, thought*
deuten (vt) [bs: to put to people, make understandable < MHG. *diet,* people; cogn. OHG. *diutisc,* the people (whence *Deutsch,* 'the people,' Germans > Ital. *tedesco,* German)] • **deutlich** (adj) • **andeuten** (vt) • **bedeuten** (vt) • **bedeutsam** (adj) • **umdeuten** (vt) [*um-,* around again, anew + *deuten*] • **zweideutig** (adj) ['of two interpretations']	= to interpret, read; point = clear, distinct, plain = to imply, intimate = to signify, mean; be important = important = to give a new interpretation to = ambiguous, suggestive	*words* < MHG. *diet,* OHG. *diutisc,* the people: *1. Dutch; 2. Teuton, Teutonic; 3. Diet-* in names *Dietrich, Dietz*
Devise (f) [< heraldry: coats of arms divided into compartments, often with mottos < Fr. *devise* < *deviser,* to divide] • **Devisen** (f/pl.)	= motto, maxim, device = foreign currency (foreign coins bear conspicuous mottos and arms)	*1. devise; 2. device; 3. divide*
dicht (adj) [< IE. **tenk-,* to become firm, curdle, thicken] • **dichten**[1] (vt) • **Dichtung** (f)	= close, dense, thick, tight = to make tight = sealing, tight seal	distantly: *words* < IE. **tenk-,* to become firm, curdle, thicken: *1. tight; 2. tangle*
dichten[2] (vt & vi) [< L. *dictare,* to prescribe, freqtv. < *dicere,* to say] • **Dichter** (m) • **Dichtung** (f) • **erdichten** (vt) • **erdictet** (adj)	= to compose (literature), write (poetry) = poet, author, writer = poetry, fiction = to invent, feign = fictitious	*1. to dictate* [to recite, give information orally]; *2. dictum* [an authoritative statement]; *3. to dight* [obs.: to arrange, order < L. *dictare,* to prescribe, freqtv. < *dicere,* to say]

GERMAN WORD	MEANING	ENGLISH COGNATE
dick (adj) • **Dicke** (f)	= thick, bulky = thickness, bulkiness	*thick*
Dieb (m) • **Dieberei** (f)	= thief = thievery	*thief*
Diele (f) [< OHG. *dilla* (cf. MDu. *dele*, whence Fr. *dalle*, stone slab)] • **dielen** (vt)	= board, plank; hence floor, vestibule = to lay boards, to floor	*deal*[1] [a board or plank < MDu. *dele*]
dienen (vi) [< OHG. *dionon* < Gmc. root **thiwa-*, serve] • **Diener(in)** (m, f) • **Dienst** (m) • **verdienen** (vt) _____ • **Dirne** (f) • **bedienen** (vt & refl) [bs.: to make serve]	= to serve = servant, domestic = service, duty = to deserve _____ = harlot; hussy = to operate, service; to make use of, employ	*1.* distantly: *dirndl* [a dress with a close-fitting bodice and full skirt, worn by a servant < G. *Dirne*, maid < Gmc. **thiwairna* < root **thiwa-*, serve]; _____ *2. tern* [a small gull, sea bird, believed < ON. *therna*, female servant]
Ding (n) • **bedingen** (vt) [bs: to make it legal, make it a case < *be* + *Dinge*, thing, legal case (= L. *causa*, case, matter)] • **bedingt** (adj) • **Bedingung** (f) • **unbedingt** (adj)	= thing, object, matter = to stipulate, fix by contract = conditional = condition, clause, stipulation = unconditional, absolute	*thing*
Dirne (see **dienen**)		
Distel (f)	= thistle	*thistle*
Docht (m) ['something woven,' perh. cogn. L. *texere*, *textum*, to weave]	= wick	perh. distantly: *textile*, *text*
Docke (f) • **Dockengeländer** (n)	= doll, stump, baluster, something cut short = balustrade	*1. to dock* [to cut short]; *2. docket* [an abridged list]; *3. dock* [the solid fleshy part of an animal's tail]
Dolch (m) • **erdolchen** (vt)	= dagger = to stab with a dagger	*? dirk* [< old form *dork*, var. of *dolk*, a dagger] and *to dolk* [to stab]
Donner (m) • **donnern** (vi)	= thunder = to thunder	*thunder*
Dorf (n) • **dörflich** (adj)	= village = of village life, rustic	*thorp* [arch.: village, hamlet]
Dorn (m) • **dornig** (adj)	= thorn = thorny	*thorn*

GERMAN WORD	MEANING	ENGLISH COGNATE
dorren (vi) [cogn. L. *torrere*, to dry up; *torridus*, parched]	= to wither, dry up	*torr-* in *torrid* [< L. *torrere*, to dry up; *torridus*, parched]
• **verdorren** (vi)	= to wither thoroughly	
• **dörren** (vt)	= to dehydrate, dessicate	
• **dürre** (adj)	= dry, arrid, barren	
• **Dürre** (f)	= dryness, drought	
• **Darre** (f), **Darrofen** (m) [*darr-* + *Ofen*, oven]	= drying kiln	
• **darren** (vt)	= to kiln dry	
Dose (f) ['holder of a portion' < L. < Gk. *dosis*, a giving, amount given]	= can, tin container	*dose* [< L. < Gk. *dosis*, a giving, amount given]
Dotter (m, n) [bs: trembling, quivering thing; cogn. Norw. *dudra*, to tremble]	= yolk of an egg	*1. totter* [to be unsteady]; *2. to doddle* [to tremble, shake]
Draht (see **drehen**)		
Dreck (m)	= dirt, filth, mud	*dregs*
drehen (vt & vi) [< OHG. *draen* (cf. AS. *thrawan*) < Gmc. root *thrae-*, to turn]	= to turn, twist; revolve	*1. throw* [orig.: to turn, twist, then to release by turn of wrist; original meaning still preserved in Eng. *throwing* (i.e., 'turning') *wheel* in pottery, and *thrown* (i.e., 'twisted') *silk* < AS. *thrawan*];
• **drehbar** (adj)	= rotating, revolving	
• **andrehen** (vt)	= to turn on (light)	
• **ausdrehen** (vt)	= to turn off (light)	
• **drechseln** (vt & vi)	= to turn (on a lathe)	
• **Drechsler** (m)	= turner, lathe worker	
• **Draht** (m) ['something twisted']	= wire	*2. thread* ['something twisted' < AS. *thrawan*]
Dreifuß (m) [< *drei*, three + *fuß*, foot]	= tripod	*three* + *foot*
dreistig (adj) [bs: pressing boldly, pushing < distant cogn. of *dringen*, to press]	= bold, audacious, impudent	intensification of *thro-* in *throng* [a pressing crowd]
• **Dreistigkeit** (f)	= audaciousness, impudence	
Drillich (see **Litze**)		
Drilling(e) (m) [< *dreiling* < *drei*, three + dim. suffix *-ling*]	= triplet(s)	*three* + dim. suffix *-ling* as in *darling*

GERMAN WORD	MEANING	ENGLISH COGNATE
dringen (vi) [*drang, gedrungen* (cf. AS. *thring-an,* to press)]	= to press, urge	*throng* [a pressing crowd < AS. *(ge)thrang < thringan,* to press, pinch] and *to throng*
• **dringend** (adj)	= pressing, urging [*urgent* < L. *urg-ere,* to press hard]	
• **dringlich** (adj)	= urgent	
• **durchdringen** (vi)	= to penetrate through	
• **eindringen** (vi)	= to intrude, invade	
• **vordringen** vi) ['to press forth']	= to advance	
• **vordringlich** (adj)	= pressing, urgent	
─────────	─────────	
• **Drang** (m)	= pressure, stress	
• **drängen** (vt & vi)	= to push, urge; be pressing, throng	
• **Gedränge** (n)	= a crowding, throng; difficulties	
• **bedrängen** (vt)	= to press s.o. hard, oppress	
• **Bedrängnis** (f)	= distress	
• **verdrängen** (vt)	= to push aside, displace, repress	
drohen (vi) [cf. AS. *threan*]	= to threaten, menace	*threa*- in *threat* [< AS. *threan*]
• **Drohung** (f)	= threat	
• **bedrohlich** (adj)	= threatening	
Drossel (f) [what uses the throat or windpipe]	= thrush, song-thrush	*1. throstle* [European song-thrush]; *2. throttle; 3. throat*
• **(er)drosseln** (vt) [whence Ital. *strozzare,* to throttle, strangle]	= to throttle, choke (fig. and for motors)	
drücken (vt)	= to press, squeeze	*to thrutch* [dial.: to press, squeeze, crowd]
• **drucken** (vt) [at first meaning 'to press,' *drucken* became restricted to mean 'to print.' An umlauted *drücken* was thus employed to assume the original meaning 'to press']	= to print	
• **Druck** (m)	= pressure, stress, print	
• **Ausdruck** (m)	= expression, phrase	
• **ausdrücken** (vt)	= to squeeze out, express	
• **bedrücken** (vt)	= to oppress, persecute	
• **Eindruck** (m)	= impression, effect	
• **eindrücken** (vt)	= to impress	
Dübel (m)	= peg, dowel	*dowel* [< ME. *duvel*]
• **verdübeln** (vt)	= to dowel	
dudeln (vi) [< Turk. *duduk,* a flute]	= to play the bagpipes, strum or hum monotonously	*doodle* [orig.: to play the bagpipe, then to move or scribble aimlessly]
• **Dudelsack** (m)	= bagpipes	
Duft (m) [< MHG. *dimpfen;* cogn. G. *Dampf,* steam, vapor]	= haze, pleasant smell, whiff	distantly: *damp*
• **duften** (vi)	= to exhale fragrance, give off scent	
• **duftend, duftig** (adj)	= fragrant	

GERMAN WORD	MEANING	ENGLISH COGNATE
dulden (vt & vi) [< OHG. *dulten* (cf. AS. *tholian*; Goth. *thulan*); root *dul-, thol-, thul-* believed cogn. with L. *tol-* in *tolerare*]	= to bear, endure, suffer, tolerate	*1. to thole* [arch. and dial.: to suffer, endure, tolerate < AS. *tholian*]; *2.* distantly: *tol-* in *tolerate* [< L. *tolerare*, cogn. Gmc. *dul-* and *thul-*]
• **duldsam** (adj)	= tolerant	
• **Duldsamkeit** (f)	= tolerance	
• **Duldung** (f)	= tolerance, sufferance	
• **Geduld** (f)	= patience	
• **geduldig** (adj)	= patient	
• **Ungeduld** (f)	= impatience	
Düng (m)	= dung, manure	*dung*
• **düngen** (vt)	= to cover with manure, fertilize	
• **Dünger** (m)	= fertilizer	
dünken (impers.) [ult. < *denken*, to think (cf. AS. *thyncan*)]	= to seem or appear (to s.o.)	*1. methinks* ['it seems to me' < AS. *thyncan*, to seem (to one)]; *2. think*
• **Dünkel** (m) [< *denken*, but with negative force]	= conceit, arrogance	
dünn (adj)	= thin, delicate, sheer	*thin*
• **Dünne, Dünnheit** (f)	= thinness, fineness	
• **verdünnen** (vt)	= to dilute, thin	
Dunst (m)	= fume, mist, haze, vapor	*1. dust; 2. dun* [a dull brown color]
• **dunstig** (adj)	= fumy, misty, haze	
• **dünsten** (vt & vi)	= to steam; give off smoke	
• **Ausdünstung** (f)	= exhalation, odor, perspiration	
Durst (m)	= thirst	*thirst*
• **durstig** (adj)	= thirsty, dry	
• **dürsten** (vi)	= to thirst	
Dusche (f) [< Fr. *douche;* Ital. *doccia* < L. *ducta*, conducted (water)]	= shower (bath)	*1. duct; aqueduct; 2. douche* [< Fr. *douche;* Ital. *doccia* < L. *ducta*, conducted (water)]

E

Ebbe (f)	= low tide	*ebb*
• **ebben** (vi)	= to ebb	
• **verebben** (vi)	= to ebb, subside	
eben (adj)	= even, plain, level	*even*
• **Ebene** (f)	= plane, plain	
• **ebenmäßig** (adj)	= harmonious, symmetrical	
• **ebnen** (vt)	= to level, smooth	

GERMAN WORD	MEANING	ENGLISH COGNATE
Eber (m)	= boar	*1. boar; 2. Ever-* in names: *Ever-ard*, 'strong as a boar'
echt (see **Ehe**)		
Ecke (n) [cf. AS. *ecg*] • **eckig** (adj)	= corner = angular; clumsy, awkward	*edge* [< AS. *ecg*]
edel (adj) [cf. AS. *aethele*] • **Adel** (m) • **adelig** (adj) • **Edelmann** (m) • **Edelmüt** (m) • **veredeln** (vt) • (see also **Adler**)	= noble; (of gems:) precious; (of body organs:) vital = nobility = noble = nobleman = generosity = to ennoble; (of goods:) to purify, refine	*1. Adel-, Edel-, Ethel-,* in names *Adelaide, Ethel* [noble]; *2. edelweiss* [lit.: 'precious (noble) white flower,' a flower with white blossoms, of the Swiss Alps]; *3. atheling* [a noble-man or prince of the Anglo-Saxons < *aethele*, noble]
Efeu (m)	= ivy	*ivy*
Egel, Blutegel (m) [< IE. **egh-, *eck-*, to stick, prick]	= leech ('blood leech')	*1. to egg* [to goad]; *2. edge*
Ehe (f) [bs: eternity, what is lawful < MHG. *ewe* < OHG. *ewa*, eternity (cf. AS. *ae, aewe*); cogn. L. *aevum*, age, a time of life] • **ehelich** (adj) • **verehelichen** (refl) • **echt** (adj) [< *ehacht* for *ehaft*, lawful, legitimate] • **Echtheit** (f)	= matrimony, marriage = matrimonial = to get married = genuine, true, legitimate, authentic = genuineness, authenticity	*1. e-* in *ever* [< AS. *a, aye*, always]; *2. -eval* in *coeval, medieval* [< L. *aevum*, age]
ehern (adj) [cogn. L. *aes, aeris*, copper, brass, money]	= of brass, brazen; firm	*aer-* in *aeruginous* [bluish-green, like oxidized copper < L. *aes, aeris*, copper]
Ehre (f) • **ehrbar** (adj) • **(be)ehren** (vt) • **verehren** (vt) • **ehrlich** (adj) • **Ehrgeiz** (m) ['desire for honor' < *ehre*, honor + *geiz*, avidity, greed < OHG. *git* (cogn. G. roots *gei-, geiz-, gier-, gehr-*, having strong sense of avidity)] • **ehrgeizig** (adj)	= honor = honorable, respectable = to honor, esteem = to revere, venerate = honest = ambition = ambitious	*Ehr-, Er-* in names: *Eric* + distantly: *to yearn* [< AS. *gyrnan* < *georn*, eager. See also **gern**, **Gier, Geier**]
Ei (n)	= egg	*egg*

GERMAN WORD	MEANING	ENGLISH COGNATE
Eiche (f) • **eichen** (adj)	= oak = oaken, of oak	*oak*
Eichel (f) [cf. AS. *aecern*]	= acorn	*ac-* in *acorn* [< AS. *aecern*]
eichen (vt) [< LL. *aequare*, to equalize]	= to gage, adjust, standardize (weights)	*eq-* in *equal*
Eid (m) • **Eidgenoß** (m) ['companion in oath' < *Eid* + *Ge-noß*, companion] • **Eidgenossenschaft** (f) • **vereidigen** (m) _____ • **Meineid** (m) [bs: of mean trust or oath; believed < root *maina* (cogn. *gemein*, common, base) + *Eid*, oath]	= oath = confederate = league = to swear s.o. into office _____ = perjury	*1. oath; 2. Huguenot* [any French Protestant of the 16thc.]; _____ *3. mean* (i.e., base) + *oath*
Eidechse (f) [bs: reptile-shaft < OHG. *egidehse* < IE. *angwhi* or *eghi-*, snake + *dehsa*, shaft, spindle < IE. *ten(gh)-*, stretch]	= lizard	*echi-* in *echidna* [Australian spiny anteater < Gk. < IE. *eghi-*, snake] + *tens-* in *tension, tense* [< L. *tendo, tendere, tensum*, to stretch out < IE. *ten(gh)-*, stretch]
eigen (adj) • **Eigenschaft** (f) • **eigentlich** (adj) • **Eigentum** (n) • **eigentümlich** (adj) • **eignen** (refl) (+ **für**) [bs: to match oneself to or for] • **aneignen** (vt) ['to make to one's own']	= own = quality, characteristic = actual = property = peculiar = to be suited (for) = to adopt, appropriate	*own*
Eile (f) [bs: striving; suffixed root *ei-* < IE. *ei-*, to go, whence L. *eo, ire, itum*, to go, and Gk. *ienai*, to go > *ion*, that going] • **eilen** (vi) • **eilends** (adv)	= haste, hurry = to hasten, hurry = speedily, quickly	distantly: words < IE. *ei-*, to go: *1. ion* [that going, pres. p. of Gk. *ienai*, to go]; *2. exit* [a going out < L. *ex*, out + *it-* < L. *eo, ire, itum*, to go]; *3. itinerant* [one journeying < *iter*, journey, going < L. *eo, ire, itum*, to go]
Eimer (m) [< L. < Gk. *amphora*, container for liquid]	= bucket, pail	*amphora*

GERMAN WORD	MEANING	ENGLISH COGNATE
ein (adj) • **Einheit** (f) • **einheitlich** (adj) • **einsam** (adj) • **einig** (adj) • **(ver)einigen** (vt) • **vereinbar** (adj) ['that can be joined with'] • **vereinbaren** (vt)	= one = unit = uniform = lonesome = united = to unite = compatible, capable of fitting in = to agree upon, stipulate, arrange	*one*
Einöde (f) [bs: solitude < *ein*, one]	= desert, solitude [< L. *solus*, alone]	*one* [cogn. G. *ein*]
Eintracht (see **tragen**) ·		
Eisen (n) [< OHG. *isan, iser*; Goth. *eisarna* < Gmc. *isarna*, whence AS. *iren*]	= iron	*iron* [< AS. *iren* < Gmc. *isarna*]
eitel (adj) • **Eitelkeit** (f) • **vereiteln** (vt) [bs: to render idle]	= empty, vain, futile = vanity, futility = to frustrate, foil, thwart	*idle*
Eiter (m)	= pus	*atter* [pus]
Ekel (m) [< MHG. *erklich*, disagreeable] • **ekeln** (refl) • **ekelhaft** (adj) • **verekeln** (vt)	= disgust, loathing, aversion = to be disgusted at = loathsome = to spoil	*irk* [< ME. *irken*, to loathe, be weary of]
Elch (m)	= elk, moose	*elk*
elend (adj) [lit.: 'in foreign land,' i.e., unfortu- nate < OHG. *elilenti*, in foreign land, banished < *eli*, other (cogn. L. *alius*, other; Eng. *else*) + *lant*, land] • **Elend** (n) • **verelenden** (vi)	= miserable, wretched = misery, wretchedness, poverty = to be reduced to misery	*el-* in *else* [distant cogn. L. *alius*, other, whence *alien, alias*] + *land*
elterlich, Eltern (see **alt**)		
empfehlen (see **Fell**)		
empfinden (vt) ['to find out by senses' < *emp* < *ent*, away from, out of (cogn. L. *ante*, Gk. *anti*) + *finden*, to find] • **empfindlich** (adj) • **Empfindung** (f)	= to perceive, feel = sensitive, susceptible = perception, sensation	*ante* [L. prefix meaning before, fac-ing, forward] + *find*

GERMAN WORD	MEANING	ENGLISH COGNATE
empor (adv) (poet.) [bs: aloft, carried up < OHG. *in-bore*, 'in upper space' < *bor*, height, where s.t. is carried up < IE. **bher-*, to carry (up)]	= upwards; aloft	words < IE. **bher-*, to carry (up), lift, raise: *1. to bear; 2. born; 3. bier; 4. bar-* in *wheelbarrow; 5. burden* [anything carried]
• **Empore** (f) [< *Emporkirche*, upper part of a church]	= gallery, loft (eccles.)	
• **empören** (vt) ['to make rise or flare']	= to rouse anger in, shock	
• **empören** (refl)	= to rise up, rebel	
• **Empörer** (m)	= rebel, insurgent	
• **Empörerung** (f)	= rebellion	
• **Bürzel** (m) [bs: raised rear end, as seen in game birds < *bor*, height]	= rump (ornith.), tail end	
• **purzeln** (vi) ['to go back-end up' < *bor*, height]	= to tumble, trip	
• **Purzelbaum** (m) [a flip 'back-end up,' then straight again as a tree, *Baum*]	= somersault	
• (see also **Bahre**)		
Ende (n)	= end	*end*
• **(be)enden, beendigen** (vt)	= to finish, bring to an end to	
• **vollenden** (vt)	= to finish, complete	
eng (adj) [< L. *ango, -ere*, to choke, distress]	= narrow	*ang-* in *anxiety* and *anxious* [< L. *ango, -ere*, to choke, press together, distress]
• **Enge** (f)	= narrowness; (pl.:) straits	
• **beengt** (adj)	= narrow, confined, cramped	
• **verengern** (vt & refl)	= to narrow	
• **Angst** (f)	= anxiety, anguish, fear	
• **ängstigen** (vt & refl)	= to frighten, alarm; be frightened	
• **ängstlich** (adj)	= anxious, uneasy, nervous	
• **bang(e)** (adj) [bs: in anguish < *bi* + *ang-*]	= anxious	
• **bangen** (+ **um**) (vi)	= to be anxious, worried about	
• **Banglichkeit** (f)	= anxiety, uneasiness	
• **bänglich** (adj)	= anxious, uneasy	
entlarven (vt) [< *ent*, away + L. *larva*, mask, ghost]	= to unmask, expose (e.g., of fraud)	*larva* [an insect's first stage of development being a mask or disguise of its ultimate one < L. *larva*, mask, ghost]
• **Entlarvung** (f)	= unmasking, exposure	
Erbe (m) [< IE. **orbh-*, to separate, whence Gk. *orphan*]	= heir (one left by death)	*orphan* [< Gk. *orphanos* < IE. **orbh-*, to separate]
• **erben** (vt)	= to inherit	
• **erblich** (adj)	= heriditary	
• **Erbschaft** (f), **Erbteil** (n)	= inheritance	
Erbse (f) [< OHG. *araweiz*, the legume]	= pea	*-arbanz-* in *garbanzo* [a legume, the chick pea]

GERMAN WORD	MEANING	ENGLISH COGNATE
Erde (f) • **beerdigen** (vt)	= earth, ground = to bury, inter	*earth*
• **Erdenge** (f) ['earth narrowing' < *Erd* + *Enge*, narrowness, cogn. L. *angustia*, tightness] • **irden** (adj) • **irdisch** (adj)	= isthmus; (pl.:) straits = earthen = earthly, worldly, mortal	*earth* + *anguish*
ereignen (see **Auge**)		
ergötzen (vt) [bs: to make forget (troubles, etc.), cause diversion < OHG. *irgezzen*, causative of *irgezzan*, var. of *ver-gezzan*, to forget] • **ergötzlich** (adj)	= to delight = delightful	*-get* in *forget* (i.e., forgetting troubles for delight)
erinnern (see **inner**)		
Erker (m) [orig.: place at a wall for an archer to defend against assault < L. *ar-carius*, bowman < *arcus*, bow] • **Erkerfenster** (n)	= alcove, bay window, oriel (archtr.) = oriel, bay window	*archer* [ME. < OFr. *archier* < L. *arcarius*, bowman < *arcus*, bow]
erkiesen (vt) [poetic irreg. verb < *er* + obs. *kiesen*, *kor*, *gekoren*, to choose (cf. AS. *ceosan*)] • **erkoren** (adj) from preterite tense **kor**: • **küren** (vt) • **Kurfürst** (m) prefix /suffix **kür-** in compounds: • **Kürlauf** (m) • **Willkür** (f) ['spontaneous choice,' at will] • **willkürlich** (adj) • **unwillkürlich** (adj)	= to choose, select = chosen, elect = to choose, elect = elector (of old Germany) = by individual choice, voluntary = freestyle skating = arbitrariness = arbitrary, random = involuntary, instinctive	*choose* [< AS. *ceosan*, whence Fr. *choisir*, to choose]
erlauben (vt) [cogn. *lieb*, dear, kind] • **Erlaubnis** (f) • **Erlaubnisschein** (m) • **Urlaub** (m) • **Urlauber** (m) • **Verlaub** (m) • (see also **glauben**, **lieb**, **Lob**)	= to allow, permit = permission, authority = permit, license = leave of absence, vacation, furlough = vacationer, one on leave = leave of absence, permission	*1. -lough* in *furlough* [a leave granted to military personnel]; *2.* distantly: *live-* in *livelong* (*day*) [entire, tediously long, lit.: 'dear long' < ME. *lefe* < AS. *leof*, dear]
ernten (vt) • **Erntrag** (m)	= to harvest = harvest	*earn*

GERMAN WORD	MEANING	ENGLISH COGNATE
erobern (vt) ['to come out on top' < *er*, thoroughly + *ober* < *über*, above] • **Eroberer** (m) • **Eroberung** (f)	= to conquer, capture = conqueror = conquest	*over*
erwähnen (vt) [bs: to speak; *er* + *wäh-*, cogn. *voc-* in L. *vocare*, to call, summon]	= to mention, refer to	distantly: words < L. *vocare*, to call: *vocal, evoke, convoke*
Erz (n) [< MHG. *erze*, OHG. *aruzzi*; OLG. *arut*; etym. uncert. but theorized < Sumer. *urud*, copper. But possib. ? < ML. *aeruta*, pl. < *aerutum*, of metal < L. *aes, aeris*, copper, brass, money. Or ? < L. *eruta*, things dug out < *eruere*, to dig out < *e*, out + *ruo, ruere, rutum*, to upturn, throw down, collapse; cf. L. *ruta et caesa*, things of an estate, that dug out (minerals) and that cut down (timber)] • **Erzbruch** (m) • **Erzblager** (n) • **erzen** (adj)	= ore; brass (poet.) = mine = ore bed = brazen, of bronze	? *aeruginous* [bluish-green, like oxidized copper, cogn. ML. *aerutum*, of metal < L. *aes, aeris*, copper] Or ? *ruin* [< Fr. < L. *ruo, ruere, rutum*, to upturn s.t., throw down, collapse]
Esel (m) [< L. *asellus*, dim. of *asinus*, ass, donkey]	= ass, donkey	*easel* [a structure to hold a painting < Du. *ezel*, ass (cf. apparatuses named for animals suited to a task: *sawhorse, crane, ram*)]
Esse (f) [< OHG. *essa* < IE. *as-*, to burn, glow]	= chimney, flue, forge	distantly: *ash* [ult. < IE. *as-*, to burn, glow]
essen (vt & vi) [cf. AS. *etan*] • **fressen** (vt & vi) ['to eat thoroughly'] • **fressgierig** (adj) • **Fraß** (m) • **Aas** (n) [bs: what is eaten away < *essen*]	= to eat = to devour; gorge (said of beasts of prey) = gluttonous, voracious = food, prey = carrion, carcass	*1. eat* [< AS. *etan*]; *2. to fret* [to be devoured by worry]
Essig (m) [< OHG. *ezzih* < L. *atecum*, metathesis of *acetum*, vinegar]	= vinegar	*acetic acid* [acid in vinegar]
Estrich (m) [bs: paved flooring < OHG. *astrih* < ML. *astricus, astracus*, plaster (whence Fr. *âtre*, hearth that is stone, plastered or tiled) < Gk. *ostrakon*, fragment of earthenware or shell reduced to make plastered or paved surfaces]	= pavement or flooring made of stone, plaster, asphalt, cement, etc.	*ostrac-* in *ostracize* [bs: to impose exile, orig. by casting votes using broken pieces of pottery < *ostrakon*, fragment of shell or earthenware]

GERMAN WORD	MEANING	ENGLISH COGNATE
Etat (m) [< Fr. < L. *status*, situation, state]	= budget	words < L. *status*, situation, state: *1. status; 2. state*
Eule (f)	= owl	*owl*
ewig (adj) [< OHG. *ewa*, eternity, cogn. L. *aevum*, age, a time of life] • **Ewigkeit** (f) • **verewigen** (vt)	= perpetual, eternal = eternity = to perpetuate	*1. e-* in *ever* [< AS. *a*, *aye*, always]; *2. -ev-* in *coeval, medieval* [< L. *aevum*, age]
Euter (n)	= udder	*udder*

F

Fach (n) [bs: bound or joined part < MHG. *vach*, OHG. *fah* (cf. AS. *faec*, interval, division) < IE. **pag-, pak-*, to fasten (whence L. *pango, pactum*, to fasten, fix)] prefix /suffix **-fach** in compounds: • **hundertfach, vielfach** • **Fachschule** (f) • **fachlich** (adj) • **Fachwerkhaus** (n) [bs: house frame built in divisions]	= division, compartment, cell; shelf, bay, specialization (profession) = -fold, division of: = hundredfold, manifold = specialized school = professional = half-timbered house (style of Germanic Europe, tudor style)	*1. faik* [Scot.: a fold (e.g., of cloth)] and *to faik* [to make folds (in s.t.)]; *2. fake*[2] [one of the 'divisions,' windings, or circles of a cable or hawser as it lies in a coil] and *to fake*[2] [to coil, lay a rope in *fakes*, prob. < AS. *faec*, interval, division]; *3.* distantly: *pact* [something fixed, set down < L. *pango, pactum*, to fasten, fix]; *4. page* [leaf of book, column of writing built up, constructed of parts < L. *pango*]
fachen (vt) [bs: to work a hearth < ML. *focare* < L. *focus*, hearth] • **anfachen** (vt) • **entfachen** (vt) [< *ent*, start of + *fachen*] • **Fächer** (m) • **fächeln** (vi)	= to fan or blow into a flame; (fig.:) to stir, incite, inflame = to kindle = to kindle; (fig.:) to arouse, provoke = fan, device to move a current of air = to give fan, use a *Fächer*	*1. foyer* [orig.: hearth, later entrance hall or lobby < Fr. < LL. **focarium* < L. *focus*, hearth]; *2. focus* [point where rays of light or heat come together, as from a hearth]
Fackel (f) [< L. *facula*, dim. of *fax, facis*, torch]	= torch	*facula* [astron.: one of the bright spots on the surface of the sun < L. *facula*, dim. of *fax, facis*, torch]
fade (adj) • **Fadheit** (f)	= stale, insipid = staleness, insipidity	*to fade* [to lose strength]

GERMAN WORD	MEANING	ENGLISH COGNATE
Faden (m) [orig.: the length of outstretched arms, esp. as a unit of measure, then the thread stretched to this length < OHG. *fadam* (cf. AS. *faethm*)]	= thread	*1. fathom* [a unit of measure equaling six feet, the length of thread held by outstretched arms < AS. *faethm*] and *2. to fathom* [orig.: to embrace, then measure the depth of, understand]
fähig (see **fangen**)		
fahl (adj)	= pale, sallow, dun	*fallow* [pale yellow]
fahnden (vi) (+ **nach**) [< *finden*, to find]	= to be in search after	*find*
Fahne (f) [< OHG. *fano* (cf. AS. *fana*)] • **Fahneid** (m) ['oath (*Eid*) to a flag'] • **Fahnflucht** (f) ['fleeing the flag'] • **Fähnchen** (n)	= flag, banner = oath of allegiance = desertion (milit.) = pennant, streamer	*1. (weather)vane* [flat piece of metal or cloth < AS. *fana*, flag]; *2. fanon* [narrow band worn by priests over the left arm; also a capelike vestment worn by the pope at mass]
fahren (vi) [*fuhr, gefahren*] • **Fahrt** (f) • **abfahren** (vi) • **Abfahrt** (f) • **erfahren** (vt) [bs: to thoroughly (*er-*) undergo (*fahr-*)] • **hochfahren** (vi) [bs: to go or start up] • **Hoffart** (f) [assimil. < MHG. *hochvahrt* < *hoch*, high + *fahr-*, a manner of going] • **hoffärtig** (f) • **hochfahrend** (adj) • **fahrlässig** (adj) • **Fahrlässigkeit** (f) • (see also **führen**, **fertig**)	= to travel, go, drive = ride, drive, journey, trip = to depart = departure = to experience = to start up, flare up = haughtiness, arrogance, pride = haughty, vainglorious = high-handed, haughty, arrogant = careless, negligent, reckless = carelessness, negligence	*1. fare; 2. wayfarer*
falb (adj)	= fallow, pale	*fallow* [pale yellow]

GERMAN WORD	MEANING	ENGLISH COGNATE
fallen (vt)	= to fall	*fall*
[*fiel, gefallen*]		
• **abfallen** (vi)	= to fall off or away, secede	
• **Abfall** (m)	= defection, secession; (pl.:) waste, rubbish	
[bs: a falling away; things fallen]		
• **auffallen** (vi)	= to be striking	
• **Beifall** (m)	= approbation, applause	
[bs: a falling near, approval < *bei*, of nearness + *Fall*]		
• **beifällig** (adj)	= approving, favorable	
• **gefallen** (vi)	= to please, be pleasing	
[bs: to fall before, or befall, esp. with pleasing effect]		
• **Gefallen** (m)	= favor, pleasure	
• **gefällig** (adj)	= pleasing, agreeable, kind	
• **Gefälligkeit** (f)	= kindness, favor, complaisance	
• **mißfallen** (vi)	= to be displeasing	
• **mißfällig** (adj)	= displeasing, disagreeable	
• **Unfall** (m)	= accident	
• **Zufall** (m)	= chance	
['what falls to' < *zu*, to + *fallen*]		
• **zufällig** (adj)	= casual, accidental [cf. *casual* < L. *casualis* < *casus*, chance event < *cadere*, *casum*, to fall; and *accidens* < *accidere*, to fall to]	
[bs: at chance, as it falls]		
• **fällen** (vt)	= to fell	
[bs: to cause to fall]		
falten (vt)	= to fold	*fold*
• **Falte** (f)	= fold, pleat, crease	
• **einfältig** (adj)	= simple	
[bs: of one fold]		
• **vielfältig** (adj)	= manifold, various, abundant	
fangen (vt)	= to catch, seize, capture	*1. fang* ['what catches,' a long tooth < AS. *fon* < Gmc. **fanhan*];
[< OHG. *fahan* < Gmc. **fanhan*]		
• **anfangen** (vt & vi)	= to take up, begin, start	*2. -fang-* in *newfangled* [fond of novelty, taking to what is new < *new* + *fangel* < AS. **fangol*, inclined to sieze]
[bs: to take up, start]		
• **befangen** (adj)	= biased, prejudiced; self-conscious, embarrassed	
[bs: seized, held by an opinion]		
• **unbefangen** (adj)	= impartial; unaffected	
• **empfangen** (vt)	= to receive, welcome	
[bs: to take from and in < *emp* < *ent*, away from, out of (cogn. L. *ante*, Gk. *anti*) + *fangen*]		
• **Empfang** (m)	= receipt, reception	
• **empfänglich** (adj)	= susceptible (i.e., that can receive)	
• **fähig** (adj)	= capable, able, fit, competent	
[orig.: able to seize, then able for anything < OHG. *fahan*]		
• **Fähigkeit** (f)	= capability, ability, competence	
Fant (m)	= dandy, fop	*infant* [< L. *infans*, baby, that not able to speak < *in*, not + *fans*, *-antis*, pres. p. of *fari*, to speak]
[< Ital. *fante*, youth < L. *infans*, baby]		

GERMAN WORD	MEANING	ENGLISH COGNATE
Farbe (f) [cf. Frk. *farwidon, farwijan,* to color ult. < IE. **perk-,* speckled] • **färben** (vt) • **Färbung** (f)	= color, paint, dye = to color, dye, tint = coloring, shade	*1. fard* [obs.: paint for the face < Fr. *farder* < Frk. *farwidon, farwijan,* to color]; *2.* distantly: *perch* [spotted fish < L. *perca* < Gk. *perknos,* spotted]
Farn (m), **Farnkraut** (n)	= fern	*fern*
fassen (vt) [< OHG. *fazzon* (cf. AS. *faetian*)] • **faßlich** (adj) • **Faß** (n) [bs: what holds] • **Gefäß** (n) • **umfassen** (vt) ['to hold all around'] • **umfassend** (adj) • **verfassen** (vt) [bs: to hold or tie together] • **Verfasser** (n) • **Verfassung** (f) • **Fetzen** (m) [orig.: cloth that holds, enwraps < MHG. *vetze* < OHG. *fazzon*] • **zerfetzen** (vt)	= to hold, contain, catch, grasp, apprehend = comprehensible, conceivable = cask, barrel, vat = vessel = to embrace, include = comprehensive, extensive = to compose, write (one's thoughts) = author, writer = constitution, composition, condition = rag, shred, tatter = to tear to pieces, shred	*1. vat* [a container that holds < earlier *fatte, fats* < AS. *faet* < *faetian,* to catch hold]; *2. fetch*
fatal (adj) [orig.: fated, destined, then mitigated to mean unpleasant < L. *fatalis,* fated, destined]	= unfortunate, awkward, embarrassing	*fatal*
faul (adj) • **faulig** (adj) • **faulen** (vi) • **Faulnis** (f) • **Faulheit** (f)	= idle, indolent; rotten = rotten, putrid = to rot, decay = rottenness, decay = laziness	*faul*
Faultier (n) [< *faul,* offensive; lazy + *tier,* animal]	= sloth (zool.)	*foul + deer*
Faust (f)	= fist	*fist*
Fazit (n) [< L. *facit,* it makes]	= result, total, sum	*1. fact; 2. feat*
fechten (vi) • **anfechten** (vt) • **anfechtbar** (adj) • **verfechten** (vt)	= to fight, fence = to contest, dispute = contestable = to defend, advocate	*fight*
Feder (f)	= feather, plume, writing pen; also (bec. of the feather's resiliency) a spring (of carriages, mechanisms)	*feather*

GERMAN WORD	MEANING	ENGLISH COGNATE
Fee (f) [< MHG. *feie* < ML. *Fata*, one of the fates]	= fairy	*fay* [alt. form of fairy]
fegen (vt) [< MHG. *vëgen*, to clean < Goth. *fagrs*, apt, fit] • **Fegefeuer** (n) ['cleaning fire']	= to sweep, clean with a broom = purgatory	*1. to feak* [of a hawk: to wipe the beak clean after feeding]; *2. to feigh*, or *fay* [to clean, clear away filth < ON. *faegja*]; *3. fair¹* [< AS. *faeger*, beautiful]
Fehde (f) • **befehden** (vt & refl)	= feud, quarrel = to make war upon; feud	*feud*
Fehl (m) • **fehlen** (vi) • **Fehler** (m) • **fehlerhaft** (adj) • **unfehlbar** (adj) • **verfehlen** (vt)	= blemish, flaw, fault = to be lacking, missing = mistake, flaw, defect = faulty, defective = infallible = to miss, mistake, fail to	*fail*
Feier (f) [< LL. *feria* < L. *feriae*, festival] • **feiern** (vt) • **feierlich** (adj) • **Feiertag** (m) • **Ferien** (pl)	= ceremony, celebration, festival, cessation of work = to observe (feast, etc.), celebrate = ceremonial, solemn = holiday, festival day = vacation, holidays	words < L. *feriae*, festival: 1. *ferial* [orig.: of a festival day other than Sunday, then weekday]; 2. *fair²* [a trade exposition, orig. held on festival days < OFr. *feire* < LL. *feria*]
feig (adj) [cf. AS. *faege*] • **Feigheit** (f) • **Feigling** (m)	= cowardly = cowardice = coward	*fey* [arch.: fated to die, doomed; in an excited state, formerly believed to portend sudden death < AS. *faege*, afraid]
feil (adj) [*f-l* cogn. *p-l* in Gk. *polein*, to sell] • **feilbieten** (vt) • **feilschen** (vi) • **Feilscher** (m)	= for sale, to be sold, mercenary = to offer for sale = to bargain, haggle, dicker = bargainer, haggler	distantly: *pol-* in *monopoly* [a market controlled or sold by one person or entity < Gk. *monos*, alone + *polein*, to sell]
Feile (f) · • **feilen** (vt)	= file = to file, polish, finish off	*file*
Feind (m) • **feindlich** (adj)	= enemy, opponent = hostile, inimical	*fiend*
feist (adj) [orig.: past p. of OHG. *feizzen*, to make fat]	= fat, stout	*fat*
Feld (m) • **Feldheer** (n) • **Feldherr** (m)	= ground, soil, land; (archt:) compartment, panel = army, field forces = general, strategist	*field*

GERMAN WORD	MEANING	ENGLISH COGNATE
Fell (n) [cf. AS. *fell*]	= hide, skin, coat, fur, pelt	*1. fell[1]* [skin, pelt < AS. *fell,* skin]; *2. fellmonger* [dealer in sheepskins]; *3. film* [a thin skin < AS. *filmen,* membrane < *fell*]
• **befehlen** (vt & vi) [bs: to cause to be carried out, lit.: 'entrust to another's protection,' < *be* + *fehlen* (unrelated to *fehlen,* to lack, fail), cogn. Goth. *filhan,* to provide with cover, conceal, cogn. G. *Fell,* skin, covering]	= to command, order	
• **Befehl** (m)	= command, order	
• **befehligen** (vt)	= to command	
• **empfehlen** (vt) [original sense: to entrust, confide, deliver with protection < *emp* < *ent,* away from (cogn. L. *ante,* Gk. *anti*) + *fehlen* (unrelated to *fehlen,* to lack, fail) < Goth. *filhan,* to provide with cover, bury]	= to recommend, commend	*ante* [L. prefix meaning before, facing] + distantly: *fell*
Fels, Felsen (m) [< OHG. *felis,* whence Fr. *falaise,* cliff]	= rock, boulder	*fell[2]* [a rocky, barren hill]
Fenster (n) [< L. *fenestra,* window]	= window	*fenestration* [the arrangement of windows in a building < L. *fenestra,* window]
Ferkel (n) [< OHG. *farhilin,* dim. of OHG. *farah,* pig (cf. AS. *fearh;* Du. *varken*)]	= young pig, piglet	*1. to farrow* [of a sow: to deliver piglets] and *farrow* [a litter of pigs < AS. *fearh,* pig]; *2. -vark* in *aardvark* [< Du. 'earth pig' < *aard,* earth + *varken,* pig]
fern (adj)	= distant, remote	*far*
• **Ferne** (f)	= distance, remoteness	
• **Fernglas** (n)	= binoculars	
• **entfernen** (vt & refl)	= to remove, withdraw	
fertig (adj) [orig.: ready for journey < *Fahrt,* journey < *fahren,* to go, ride]	= ready, finished	*1.* distantly: *fer-* in *ferry;* *2.* distantly: *to fare*
• **fertigmachen** (vt)	= to finish, settle	
• **anfertigen** (vt)	= to make, manufacture	
• **abfertigen** (vt) ['to send off what is ready']	= to dispatch	
• **Fertigkeit** (f) [bs: skill of readying, putting finishing touches on s.t.]	= dexterity, skill	
Fessel (f)	= shackle, chain, fetter	*fetter*
• **fesseln** (vt)	= to fetter, shackle; (fig.:) to fascinate, captivate	
• **fesselnd** (adj)	= fascinating, captivating, absorbing	

GERMAN WORD	MEANING	ENGLISH COGNATE
fest (adj) • **(be)festigen** (vt) • **Festung** (f)	= firm, solid, fixed = to strengthen, fortify = fortress	*fast* [firm, not easily moved, e.g., *fast* asleep, color*fast*]
Fetzen (see **fassen**)		
feucht (adj) • **Feuchtigkeit** (f) • **befeuchten** (vt)	= damp, moist = dampness, humidity = to dampen, moisten	*1. foughty* [dial.: musty]; *2.* perh. distantly cogn.: *fog*
Feuer (n) • **feuern** (vt & vi) • **feurig** (adj)	= fire; ardor = to hurl, release; shoot = fiery, ardent	*fire*
finden (vt) [*fand, gefunden*] • **erfinden** (vt) • **erfinderisch** (adj)	= to find = to invent = inventive	*find*
Finger (m) • **Fingerhut** (m) [lit.: 'finger hat']	= finger = thimble	*finger*
fingieren (vt) [< L. *fingo, fingere, finxi, fictum,* to shape, imagine, invent] • **fingiert** (adj)	= to fabricate, invent, feign = fictitious, feigned	words < L. *fingo, fingere, finxi, fictum,* to shape, imagine, invent: *1. fiction; 2. feign*
Fink (m)	= finch	*finch*
Finne (f)	= fin (of fish); blotch (medic.)	*fin*
finster (adj) [dissimil. < OHG. *dinstar* < IE. **teme-*, dark] • **Finsternis** (f) • **verfinstern** (vt)	= dark, obscure, gloomy = darkness, gloom = to darken, obscure	*teme-* in *temerity* [rashness < L. *temere,* at random (blindly) < IE. **teme-*, dark]
Finte (f) [< Ital. *finta,* pretense, fake < L. *fingere, fictum,* to shape, contrive]	= ruse, trick; feint (fencing)	*feign; feint*
Fisch (m)	= fish	*fish*
Fitze (f)	= skein (of yarn); trifle	*fit* [archaic: a short section of a poem or song < ME. *fitte* < ON. *fitja,* to knit together]
flach (adj) • **Fläche** (f) [bs: what is flat] • **Oberfläche** (f) • **abflachen** (vt)	= flat, level = flatness, plane, area, expanse, surface = surface = to level	*1. fluke* [flatfish, esp. flounder]; *2. flat*
flackern (vi)	= to flicker, waver (of light, flame)	*flicker*

GERMAN WORD	MEANING	ENGLISH COGNATE
Fladen (m) [< OHG. *flado,* whence OFr. *flaon*]	= flat cake	*flan* [a European custard]
Flamme (f)	= flame	*flame*
flattern (vi) • **flatterhaft** (adj)	= to flutter, flit; flap, wave = fickle, flighty	*flutter*
flau (adj) [< OFr. *flau* (whence Fr. *flou,* soft, hazy) < Frk. *hlao,* tepid; cf. cogn. OHG. *lao* > G. *lau,* tepid)] • **Flauheit** (f) • **Flaute** (f)	= weak, faint, feeble, listless, stale = weakness, faintness, staleness = dead calm, slack period	distantly: *lu-* in *lukewarm*
Flaum (m) [< OHG. *pfluma* < L. *pluma,* feather]	= down, fluff, fuzz	*plume*
flechten (vt) [cogn. L. *plectere, plexus,* to weave, twine] • **Flecte** (f) • **Flechtwerk** (n) • **verflechten** (vt) • **Verflechtung** (f)	= to weave, twist, plait = braid, plait, twist = wickerwork = to interweave, entangle = entanglement, interlacing	distantly: *plexus* [parts interwoven; network of nerves (anat.) < L. *plectere, plexus,* to weave]
Fleck (m) • **flecken** (vt) • **flicken** (vt) [bs: to work with patches < *Fleck,* shred, patch] • **Flicken** (m)	= flaw, spot, patch = to stain, speckle, patch = to mend, patch, repair = patch, repair (dress, shoe, roof)	*fleck*
Fledermaus (f) [lit.: 'fluttering mouse' < *flattern,* to flutter + *Maus,* mouse]	= bat (zool.)	*flutter + mouse*
Flegel (m) [< OHG. *flegil* < L. *flagellum,* flail, whip]	= flail	*flail* [< L. *flagellum,* whip]
flehen (vi) [etym. unclear; orig.: to flatter, coax, then to press for (cogn. Goth. *gathlaihan,* to cherish, caress). Perh. bs: to coax, caress, ult. make smooth, flat < IE. **plak-1,* be flat, even, whence *placate,* and *flake*] • **Flehen** (n) • **flehentlich** (adj) • **erflehen** (vt)	= to emplore, entreat = prayer, supplication = urgently, beseechingly = to obtain by entreaty, beg for	? words < IE. **plak-1,* be flat, even: *1. placate* [< L. *placare,* to calm (as of a flat sea)]; *2. flake*
Fleisch (n)	= meat, flesh	*flesh*

GERMAN WORD	MEANING	ENGLISH COGNATE
Fleiß (m) [< OHG. *flizan*, to strive (cf. AS. *flitan*)] • **fleißig** (adj) • **befleißigen** (refl) • **beflissen** (adj) • **geflissen** (adj) • **geflissentlich** (adj)	= diligence, industry = diligent, industrious = to apply or devote o.s. to = assiduous, studious = diligent, industrious = intentional, deliberate	*to flite* [obs.: to strive, contend < AS. *flitan*]
flicken (see **Fleck**)		
fliegen (vt & vi) [ult. < *fließen*, to be fleet, flow, run quickly (cf. AS. *fleogan*)] • **Flug** (m) • **Flügel** (m) • **Geflügel** (n) • **Fliege** (f)	= to fly = flight = wing, blade = fowl, poultry = fly (zool.); bow tie	*1. flight* [< AS. *fleogan*, to fly]; *2. to fly* [< ME. *fleien*; AS. *fleogan*]
fliehen (vt & vi) • **Flucht** (f) • **Zuflucht** (f) ['place to which one flees'] • **flüchten** (vi) • **flüchtig** (adj) • **Flüchtling** (m)	= to flee, avoid; escape = fleeing, flight = shelter, refuge [< L. *re*, back + *fugere*, to run away] = run away, escape = fleeting, fugitive = refugee	*flee*
Fliese (f) [< LG. *vlise* < OHG. *vlins*, flint] • **Fliesboden** (m)	= tile (for wall or floor), facing stone, flagstone = flagged floor	*flint* [stone splinter]
fließen (vi) • **fließend** (adj) • **Fluß** (m) • **Fließband** (n)	= to be fleet, flow, run = running, fluent = fluency = conveyor belt	*fleet*
Flocke (f) • **flocken** (vi) • **flockig** (adj)	= flake (snow), flock (wool) = to form flakes or flocks = flocky, fluffy	*flock*
Floh (m)	= flea	*flea*
Flor[1] (m) [< L. *flos, floris*, flower] • **Floskel** (f) ['flower of speech' < L. *flosulus*, dim. of *flos*, flower]	= bloom, blossoming; prime of life = flower of speech; (pl.:) empty phrases	*floral* [< L. *flos, floris*, flower]
Flor[2] (m) [< Fr. *velours*, velvet < OFr. *velous* < L. *villosus*, shaggy] • **Trauerflor** (m) • **umfloren** (vt)	= gauze, crape; pile, nap = mourning crape = to cover with crape, veil	*velure*, also *velours* [< Fr. *velours*, velvet < OFr. *velous* < L. *villosus*, shaggy]

GERMAN WORD	MEANING	ENGLISH COGNATE
Floß (n) • **flößen** (vt) • **flößbar** (adj)	= raft, float = to raft, float = floatable	*float*
Fluch (m) [bs: a strike in words < OHG. *fluo-han* (Goth. *flokan*) < IE. *plak-²*, to strike (whence L. *plango*, to beat the breast, lament; Eng. *fling*)] • **fluchen** (vi) • **verfluchen** (vt)	= curse, anathema, malediction = to curse, swear = to curse, cuss	words < IE. *plak-²*, to strike: *1. flick* [a light, quick stroke or blow] and *to flick*; *2.* distantly: *fling*; *3. plague* [anything that afflicts troubles]
flüchten (see **fliehen**)		
Flur (f) • **Flur** (m)	= field, meadow = entrance hall, corridor	*floor*
Flut (f)	= flood	*flood*
Fohlen (n)	= foal	*foal*
Föhre (f)	= pine tree	*fir*
folgen (vi) • **Folge** (f) • **folgsam** (adj) • **Erfolg** (m) [bs: what follows, result] • **erfolgreich** (adj) • **verfolgen** (vt) • **infolge** (prep) + *gen.* • **zufolge** (prep) + *gen.*	= to follow = sequence, result = obedient = success = successful = to pursue, persecute = in consequence of = following, according to	*follow*
Folter (f) [rack for putting one to torture < ML. *pulliter, pulletrus* < L. *poledrus*, 'horse,' rack for torture < L. *pullus*, young animal < Gk. *polos*, colt, any young animal; cf. other structures named for animals to perform functions like carrying, lifting, e.g., *sawhorse, crane, ram, easel* (lit.: 'little ass')] • **foltern** (vt) ['to put to the *Folter*,' the 'horse']	= torture = to torture, torment	*1. bollard* [orig.: a post for securing ropes on a ship or dock, assoc. with ON. *bolr*, LG. *polder*, wooden framework < OFr. *poldre, poltre* (whence Fr. *poutre*, beam, girder) < ML. *pulliter, pulletrus* < L. *poledrus*, 'horse' or wooden frame < L. *pullus*, colt, any young animal]; *2. pullet* [a young chicken]; *3. foal* [young animal, esp. horse]
foppen (vt) • **Fopperei** (f)	= to tease, kid, hoax, fool = teasing, leg-pulling	*to fob* [to cheat, trick]

GERMAN WORD	MEANING	ENGLISH COGNATE
fordern (vt) [bs: to have come forth < *vorder*, fore, of the front < *vor*, before]	= to demand, claim	*forth, further*
• **erfordern** (vt)	= to require, demand	
• **erforderlich** (adj)	= required, necessary	
• **Erfordernis** (n)	= requirement, exigency	
• **herausfordern** (vt) [to demand one to come out here (*heraus*, out here) over a conflict]	= to challenge, provoke [< L. *provocare*, to call forth < *pro*, forth; *vocare*, to call]	
• **herausfordernd** (adj)	= challenging, provoking	
• **fördern** (vt)	= to further, advance, promote	
• **förderlich** (adj)	= promotive, conducive, beneficial	
• **befördern** (vt)	= to convey, transport	
Forelle (f) [bs: spotted fish < MHG. *forhele* < IE. **perk-*, speckled]	= trout	distantly: *perch* [spotted fish < L. *perca* < Gk. *perknos*, spotted < IE. **perk-*, speckled]
forsch (adj) [< Fr. *force*, strength < L. *fortis*, strong]	= vigorous	*1. force* [< Fr. *force*, strength < L. *fortis*, strong]; *2. fortitude*
forschen (vt) [bs: to seek after < IE. **prek-*, to ask, entreat, whence L. *prex*, prayer, and *precari*, to entreat]	= to investigate, search	distantly: words < L. *precari*, to entreat < IE. **prek-*, to ask, entreat: *1. imprecate*; *2. prayer* [< Fr. *preiere* < L. *precarius*, obtainable by entreaty]; *3. precarious* [< L. *precarius*, obtainable by entreaty, dependent upon the will or favor of another person, hence dependent upon circumstances, insecure]
• **(Er)Forscher** (m)	= researcher, explorer	
• **Forschung** (f)	= research, exploration	
Fracht (f)	= freight, goods, cargo	*1. freight; 2. fraught*
Frage (f) [bs: a seeking after < IE. **prek-*, to ask, entreat, whence L. *prex*, prayer, *precari*, to entreat]	= question, problem	distantly: words < L. *precari*, to entreat < IE. **prek-*, to ask, entreat: *1. imprecate*; *2. prayer* [< Fr. *preiere* < L. *precarius*, obtainable by entreaty]; *3. precarious* [< L. *precarius*, obtainable by entreaty, dependent upon the will or favor of another person, hence dependent upon circumstances, insecure]
• **fragen** (vt & vi)	= to ask, question	
• **fraglich** (adj)	= questionable, problematic	
• **fragwürtig** (adj) [lit.: 'worthy of question']	= questionable, dubious	
• **Umfrage** (f) [bs: an asking around]	= public opinion poll	
frankieren (vt) [orig.: to exempt, allow to pass free of charge < OFr. *franc*, LL. *francus*, free, a Frank (free people)]	= to pay the postage or carriage	*1. to frank* [to mark (mail) to be sent free < LL. *francus*, free]; *2. frank* [free of reserve]; *3. franchise* [right, privilege]
frech (adj)	= impudent, insolent	*fresh*
• **Frechheit** (f)	= impudence, insolence	

GERMAN WORD	MEANING	ENGLISH COGNATE
fremd (adj) [bs: what is away from one < OHG., Goth. *fram*, away, distant] • **fremdeln** (vi) • **Fremde** (f) • **Fremder** (f) • **Fremdverkehr** (m) • **befremden** (vt, impers.) • **Befremden** (n) • **entfremden** (vt)	= strange, foreign, alien = to act strange, act shy = foreign country = foreigner, tourist = tourism, tourist traffic = to appear strange to, astonish, create an unfavorable impression on = surprise, astonishment, displeasure = to alienate, estrange	*from* [away, removed]
fressen (see **essen**)		
freuen (vt) • **freuen** (refl) (+ **über**) • **Freude** (f) • (see also **froh**)	= to cause gladness in s.o. = to be pleased about = joy, gladness, pleasure	*fro-* in *frolic*
Freund (m) • **freundlich** (adj)	= friend = friendly, nice, kind	*friend*
Frevel (m) [bs: aggressive or bold move for- ward; origin obscure: < OHG. *fravali* (cf. OSax. *frabol;* AS. *fraefel*) < Gmc. *fra*, forward, forth (cf. G. *ver, vor*) + *aval-* (uncert.)] • **freveln** (vi) • **Frev(e)ler** (m) • **freventlich** (adj)	= wanton offense, misdeed = to commit a crime, offense = criminal, outrager, transgressor = criminal, offensive, wicked	*(to and) fro* [away, forth] and *for-* in *forward, forth* + (*aefel* = ?)

Friede(n) (m)
[< OHG. *fridu* < Gmc. *frith*, peace
(cf. Frk. *fridu* > ML. *fredum*, 'peace
fine,' fine for breach of peace,
whence Fr. *frais*, costs)]
• **friedlich** (adj)
• **befrieden** (vt)
• **befriedigen** (vt)
 	
• **befriedigend** (adj)
• **zufrieden** (adj)
	= peace, tranquility
	
	= peaceful, peaceable
	= to pacify
	= to satisfy, appease [*appease*, lit.: 'to
	    put to peace' < OFr. *apaisier* < *a*
	    + *pais*, peace]
	= satisfactory, satisfying
	= content, pleased
		-fray, -frai- in: *1. affray* [breach of
		peace, disturbance < ME. < OFr. *es-
		fraer*, to frighten, lit.: 'remove from
		peace' < LL. **exfridare* < *ex*, out +
		Gmc. *frith*, peace] and *to affray* [to
		frighten]; *2. afraid* ['put out of
		peace,' past p. of *affray*]; *3. to de-
		fray* [to pay costs < Fr. *de*, away +
		frais, costs < ML. *fredum*, fine for
		breach of peace < Frk. *fridu*];
		4. Fred- in names: *Frederick* [<
		Friederich, 'rich in peace' or
		'peaceful ruler']

Friedhof (m) [< OHG. *vrithof*, space enclosed by a hedge < *vrit*, hedge (prob. cogn. AS. *writhan*, to twist, wind about, whence *wreath, writhe*) + *hof*, court] • **einfrieden** (vt) ['to hedge in']	= cemetery; churchyard = to enclose, fence in	*1. frith* [enclosure, forest, wood] and *to frith* [obs.: to wattle or fence in]; *2.* perh. distantly: *wreath, writhe* [< AS. *writhan*, to twist, wind about]

GERMAN WORD	MEANING	ENGLISH COGNATE
frieren (vi) [*fror, gefroren*] • **gefrieren** (vi) • **Frost** (m) • **frostig** (adj)	= to freeze over = to freeze, congeal = frost, chill = frigid, icy	*freeze, frost*
frisch (adj) • **erfrischen** (vt)	= fresh = to refresh	*fresh*
Frist (f) • **fristen** (vt) • **fristgerecht** (adj) [lit.: 'term-reckoned'] • **langfristig** (adj) • **befristen** (vt) • **Sperrfirst** (f) [< *sperren*, to bar, restrict]	= space of time, time allowed, term = to fix a term for, grant delay = in time, within the term = long-term, long-range = to set a time limit = restrictive period of time	*frist* [obs. exc. dial.: a space of time; a respite, delay]
froh, frohlich (adj) • **Frohlichkeit** (f) • (see also **freuen**)	= joyful, glad, cheerful = joyfulness, gladness	*frolic*
fromm (adj) [now restricted to religious meaning, original sense meant useful, able < MHG. *vrum* < OHG. *fram*, forward (cf. AS. *fram*)] • **Frömmigkeit** (f)	= pious, devout = piousness, devoutness	*1. frim* [obs. or dial.: vigorous, flourishing; full of sap, abundant < AS. *fram*, forward]; *2. to frame* [to make ready for use, to fit, construct < AS. *fram*]
Fron(arbeit) (f), **Frondienst** (m) [bs: service to a lord < OHG. *frono*, gen. pl. of *fro*, lord (feminine form: *frouwe*, mistress, whence G. *Frau*)] • **fronen** (vi) • **frönen** (vt) ———————— • **Frau** (f) • **Fräulein** (n)	= forced or compulsory service, drudgery = to do hard labor = to indulge in; be addicted or a slave to ———————— = woman, lady, wife = young woman	*vrouw* [woman < Du. *vrouw*, cogn. G. *Frau*]
Frosch (m)	= frog	*frog*
Fuchs (m) • **Füchsin** (f)	= fox = vixen	*1. fox; 2. vixen* [a female fox; also an ill-tempered woman < AS. *fixen*, fem. of *fox*]
Fug (m) [bs: seemliness, order; disposing or submitting to authority (only in *mit Fug und Recht*, 'with full right') < MHG. *vuoc*, propriety, seemliness (prob. via Norw. *faga*) ult. < *Fuge*?] • **befugen** (vt) • **befugt** (adj) • **Befugnis** (f) • **Unfug** (m) ['without authority']	= seemliness, authority, order = to authorize, empower = authorized = authority, right, power = mischief, disorder	*1. to fadge* [obs.: to suit, be suitable < Norw. *faga*, cogn. AS. *fegan*, to join together (see entry **Fuge**)]; *2. to fudge* [to make work, fit suitably]; *3.* distantly: *to fay in* [to join or fit together; (*shipbuilding:*) fit closely or exactly < AS. *fegan* (see entry **Fuge**)]

GERMAN WORD	MEANING	ENGLISH COGNATE
Fuge (f) [bs: fitting, adapting < MHG. *vüegen*, OHG. *fuogen* (cf. AS. *fegan*)]	= joint, seam, mortise, groove	*to fay in* [to join or fit together; fit closely or exactly (*shipbuilding*) < AS. *fegan* (also see entry **Fug**)]
• **fugen** (vt)	= to joint, point (masonr.)	
• **Gefüge** (n)	= structure, joints, articulation	
• **fügen** (refl)	= to dispose o.s. to; comply with, accommodate to	
• **fügsam** (adj) ['able to be fitted']	= (com)pliant	
• **gefügig** (adj)	= pliant	
• **anfügen** (vt)	= to attach, join to	
• **einfügen** (vt)	= to insert	
• **verfügen** (vt) ['to cause to adapt']	= to dispose; decree	
• **verfügbar** (adj)	= available, disposable	
• **zufügen** (vt)	= to add	
fühlen (vt & vi)	= to feel, be aware of; sympathize	*feel*
• **fühlbar** (adj)	= sensible	
führen (vt) [to make go < *fahren, fuhr, gefahren*, to travel, go]	= to lead (another)	*1. fare; 2. wayfarer*
• **Führer** (m)	= leader	
• **ausführen, durchführen** (vt)	= to carry out, execute	
• **Ausführung** (f)	= explanation	
• (see also **fahren**)		
füllen (vt)	= to fill	*fill*
• **erfüllen** (vt)	= to fulfill, perform fully	
• **erfüllbar** (adj)	= realizable	
fungieren (vi) [< L. *fungor, fungi, functus*, to perform]	= to officiate, act as, be in charge	words < L. *fungor, fungi, functus*, to perform: *1. function; 2. perfunctory*
furchen (vt)	= to groove	*furrow* [< AS. *furh*]
• **Furche** (f)	= groove, furrow, rut	
Furcht (f)	= fright, fear, dread	*fright*
• **furchtbar** (adj)	= dreadful, terrible	
• **furchtsam** (adj)	= timid	
• **furchten** (vt & refl)	= to fear, dread	
Furnier (m) [< Fr. *fournir*, veneer]	= veneer	*veneer*
• **furnieren** (vt)	= to veneer	
Fürst (m) ['foremost man' (cf. *prince* < L. *princeps* < *primus*, first + *capere*, to take)]	= prince, sovereign	*first*
• **fürstlich** (adj)	= princely, magnificent	
• **Fürstentum** (n)	= principality	
Furt (f)	= ford	*ford*

GERMAN WORD	MEANING	ENGLISH COGNATE
Fuß (m) • **fußen** (vi)	= foot = to be based, founded on	*foot*
Futter[1] (n) [< OHG. *fuotar* (cf. AS. *fodor*)] • **füttern**[1] (vt)	= feed, fodder = to feed (animals)	*fodder*
Futter[2] (n) [< OHG. *fuotar* (cf. Frk. **fodr*) < Gmc. *fodr*, whence Ital. *foderare*, to line, upholster, and Fr. *fourrure*, lining, fur, prized as lining] • **füttern**[2] (vt) • **Futteral** (n)	= lining, casing = to line, sheathe, pad, stuff = case, sheath	*1. fur* [< ME. *forre*, lining (prized when of fur), case, covering < OFr. *fuerre* < Frk. **fodr*, lining]; *2. to fother* [naut.: to stop a leak by forming a 'lining,' filling, plug, with oakum, rope yarn and sail cloth]

G

Gabel (f) • **gabelig** (adj) • **gabeln** (vt)	= forking, crotch of tree = bifurcated, forked = to bifurcate, divide	*gable*
gaffen (vi)	= to gape, stare	*gape*
gähnen (vi)	= to yawn	*yawn* [< ME. *yanen*]
Galgen (m)	= gallows, gibbet	*gallows* [< AS. *gealga*]
Gallert (n), **Gallerte** (f) [bs: congealed < ML. *gelatria* < L. *gelare*, to freeze]	= gelatin; jelly	*1. gelatin; 2. jelly*
Gans (f)	= goose	*goose*
Gardine (f) [< Fr. *cortine*; Ital., Sp. *cortina*; ult. 'of a court']	= curtain	*1. curtain; 2. court*
gären (vi) [bs: to bubble < MHG. *gern, jesen*] • **Gärung** (f)	= to ferment = fermentation	distantly: *1. gey-* in *geyser*; *2. yea-* in *yeast*
Garn (n)	= yarn, thread, cotton, net	*yarn*
Gasse (f) • **Gassenjunge** (m)	= lane, by-street = street urchin	*1. gat* [a narrow ship channel be- tween cliffs]; *2. gait* [orig.: a path between hedges, a street, then the manner of moving on foot < ON. *gata*]

GERMAN WORD	MEANING	ENGLISH COGNATE
Gast (m) • **gastlich** (adj) • **Gastfreundschaft** (f) • **Gaststätte** (f)	= guest, visitor, customer = hospitable = hospitality = restaurant	*guest*
Gatte (m), **Gattin** (f) [bs: one joined together with s.o.] • **Gattung** (f) [bs: a gathering of related things] • **begatten** (vt & refl)	= spouse, husband, wife = classification, sort, kind, species = to couple; mate	*1. -geth-* in *together; 2. gath-* in *gather*
• **Gatter** (n) [etym. uncert.; ? bs: to assemble railings together. Or ? what gathers (an area, things), as a fence < OHG. *gataro* < Gmc. **gaduron*, to bring together] • **ergattern** (vt) [bs: to 'net,' catch as in a lattice < *er-*, throughly + *gatt-*] • **vergattern** (vt)	= rail fence, grating, lattice = to get hold of, secure, bag = to enclose with a trellis or grating, assemble (milit.)	
• **Gitter** (n) [var. of *Gatter*] • **vergittern** (vt)	= grate, lattice = to enclose with a grate, lattice, or barrier	*3. gitter* [optics: a diffraction grating (i.e., assembled or 'gathered' lines)]
gaukeln (vi) [< MHG. *goukeln* < OHG. *goucal* (OFr. *jugler*) < LL. *goucalari* < *joculari*, to play joker] • **Gaukler** (m) • **gaukelhaft** (adj) • **umgaukeln** (vt) • **vorgaukeln** (vt)	= to juggle, do tricks; to flutter about = juggler, conjurer, charlatan = juggling, delusive = to flutter or hover around = to mislead one with blandishments	words < L. *jocus*, joke, game: *1. juggle* [< ME. *jogelen*; OFr. *jugler*]; *2. joke, joker*
Gaumen (m)	= palate, roof of mouth	*gum* [oral tissue]
Gauner (m) [< 15thc. *Joner*, cardsharp, *jonen*, to cheat < thieves' jargon and slur: a Greek < *y-v-n* in Heb. *yevon*, a Greek (cf. *y-w-n* in Arab. *yunani*, Greek) < Gk. *Ionos*, a Greek of *Ionia*] • **Gaunerei** (f)	= swindler, trickster, cardsharp = swindling, trickery, sharp practice	*1. Ionia* [ancient western Asia Minor]; *2. Ionian Sea; 3. Ionic* [style of classical column originated in Ionia]
gebaren, gebären (see **Bahre**)		

GERMAN WORD	MEANING	ENGLISH COGNATE
geben (vt)	= to give	*give*
• **Gabe** (f)	= gift, present	
• **angeben** (vt)	= to declare, state	
• **angeblich** (adj)	= declared, thus, alleged, pretended	
• **Angabe** (f)	= declaration, statement, assertion	
• **aufgeben** (vt)	= to give up	
• **ausgeben** (vt)	= to spend	
• **Begebnis** (n), **Begebenheit** (f)	= event, incident	
• **ergeben** (refl)	= to result, follow	
• **Ergebnis** (n)	= result	
• **Umgeben** (f)	= surroundings	
• **zugeben** (vt)	= to admit	
gedeihen (vi)	= to prosper, thrive, do well	*thigh* [swollen or fat part of the leg < AS. *theoh* < *theon*, to become vigorous; cogn. AS. *getheon*, to grow, flourish, prosper]
[*gedieh, gediehen* (cf. AS. *getheon*, to grow, flourish, prosper; cogn. AS. *theon*, to become vigorous)]		
• **gedeihlich** (adj)	= thriving, prosperous	
• **Gedeihen** (n)	= growth, prosperity	
————————	————————	
• **gediegen** (vi) [< MHG. *gedigen* (obs. var. participle of *gedeihen*), grown, solid]	= (esp. of metals:) pure, genuine, solid	
Gefahr (f) [< OHG. *fara*, ambush, deceit, danger]	= danger, peril	*1. fear* [orig.: sudden calamity, then anticipation of evil]; *2. ferly* [obs. and dial.: dreadful, strange; sudden; cf. *gefährlich*]
• **gefährlich** (adj)	= dangerous	
• **gefährden** (vt)	= to endanger	
• **gefährlos** (adj)	= without risk, safe	
gegen (adv)	= against	*-gain-* in *against*
• **begegnen** (vt)	= to encounter	
• **entgegen** (prep)	= opposite	
• **gegenwärtig** (adj) ['watching opposite']	= present	
• **Gegenstand** (m) ['what stands opposite']	= object ['what lies before' < L. *ob*, against + *jaceo*, lie]; topic, subject	
• **Gegner** (m)	= opponent	
• **Gegend** (f) [bs: adjoining land, what lies up against < *gegen*, against; loan transl. of ML. *contrata*, land lying against (touching) a city < L. *contra*, against, whence OFr. *contrée* > ME. *contre* > Eng. *country*]	= region, area	
Gehege (see **Hag**)		
geheim, Geheimnis (see **Heirat**)		

GERMAN WORD	MEANING	ENGLISH COGNATE
gehen (vi) [*gang, gegangen*]	= to go	*1.* go; *2.* gangplank, gangway
• **Gang** (m)	= corridor	
• **Aufgang** (m)	= rising (of sun)	
• **Untergang** (m)	= sunset	
• **Eingang** (m)	= entrance	
• **Ausgang** (m)	= exit	
• **Umgang** (m)	= ambulatory, gallery; procession	
• **umgehen** (vt)	= to cirumvent, bypass, go around	
• **umgehend** (adj) ['bypassing' = not into the middle]	= immediate ['with nothing in the middle' < L. *in*, not + *medius*]	
• **umgehen** (vi)	= to make a detour; be around; (+ *mit:*) keep company with	
• **umgänglich** (adj)	= sociable, companionable, affable	
• **vergehen** (vi)	= to elapse, pass away	
• **Vorgang** (m)	= process, event, incident	
• **vorausgehen** (vi)	= to precede	
• **Zugang** (m)	= approach, access	
• **zugänglich** (adj)	= accessible	
-gehr- (see gern)		
Gehre (f), **Gehren** (m) [bs: triangular figure, like a spearhead < OHG. *gero*, spear (cf. AS. *gara*, corner; *gar*, spear)] • **gehren** (vt) [to cut the end oblique or pointed]	= wedge, gusset, bevel, gore = to bevel, miter	*1.* gore [geogr.: a pointed, wedge-shaped section of a globe < AS. *gara*, corner, point]; *2.* gar- in *garlic* ['spear leek,' bec. of the 'spearhead' pod at top of stem of the garlic plant < *gar*, spear + *lic*, leek]
Geier (m) [bs: voracious or gaping bird < OHG. *gir* < IE. **ghai-*, to yawn or gape. Cogn. G. roots *gei-, geiz-, gier-, gehr-*, having strong sense of avidity]	= vulture	*1.* -geier in *lammergeier* and *lammergeyer* [a kind of vulture in Europe and Asia, lit.: 'vulture of lambs']; *2.* distantly: *to yearn* [< AS. *gyrnan* < *georn*, eager. See also **Geiz, gern, Gier**]
Geige (f) [< MHG. *gige*] • **Geiger** (m)	= violin = violinist	*1.* jig [a springy dance]; *2.* gigot [from its fiddle shape: a leg of lamb or veal; also, a sleeve close fitting at the arm but flaring at the shoulder]
geil (adj) • **Geilheit** (f)	= lascivious, wanton, randy; luxuriant = lasciviousness, lewdness; luxuriance	*galliard* [a lively dance of the l6thc.]
Geiß (f) • **Geißbock** (m)	= (nanny) goat = billy goat	*goat*
Geist (m) • **geistig** (adj) • **geistlos** (adj) • **geistvoll** (adj) • **geistlich** (adj) • **Geistliche** (m) • **begeistern** (vt)	= spirit, mind, intellect; ghost = intellectual, mental = spiritless, dull, stupid = ingenious, spirited = spiritual, clerical, sacred = clergyman = to enthuse, inspire [< L. *in*, in + *spiritus*; spirit; cf. *enthuse* < Gk. *en*, in + *theos*, god]	*ghost*

GERMAN WORD	MEANING	ENGLISH COGNATE
Geiz (m) [< OHG. *git*, cogn. G. roots *gei-*, *geiz-*, *gier-*, *gehr-*, having strong sense of avidity] • **geizen** (vi) • **geizig** (adj)	= avarice, greed = to be covetous = avaricious, covetous	distantly: *yea-* in *to yearn* [< AS. *gyrnan* < *georn*, eager. See also **gern**, **Gier**, **Geier**]
Geländer (n) [< MHG. *lander*, believed an alteration of *Latte*, narrow board]	= railing, banister, balustrade	*lath*
gelb (adj)	= yellow	*yellow*
Geld (n) [< *gelten*, to be worth]	= money, capital, coin	*yield*
Gelichter (n) [bs; what lies, spreads about < *liegen*, to lie]	= lot, rabble, riff-raff	*lie*
gelten (vi) [cf. AS. *gielan*] • **entgelten** (vt) • **unentgeltlich** (adj) • **vergelten** (vt) _____ • **gültig** (adj)	= to be worth, be valid = to compensate, pay for = free of charge = to repay, pay back _____ = holding its worth, valid	*yield* [< ME. *yeldan* < AS. *gielan*]
Gemach (see **machen**)		
gemein (adj) • **Gemeinheit** (f) • **Gemeinschaft** (f) • **verallgemeinern** (vt)	= mean, common, vulgar = vulgarity, vileness = community, intercourse = to generalize	*mean*
Gemse (f) [< LL. *camox*, chamois]	= chamois	*chamois* [a small goatlike antelope < LL. *camox*, chamois]
Gemüse (n) [< *ge-* + *Mus*, pap, stewed fruit, ult. mast, feed]	= vegetable	*mast* [food for hogs (chestnuts, acorns, etc.)]
genial (adj)	= endowed with genius, brilliant	*genius*
genießen (vi) [< OHG. *ginozo* (cf. AS. *neotan*), to enjoy, possess < *noz* (cf. AS. *neat*), cattle as possessions] • **Genosse** (m) [orig.: 'one with whom one has livestock (*noz*) in the same pasture'] • **Nießbrauch** (m)	= to enjoy (advantages, food, etc.) = companion, partner = usufruct (the right of using the property of another)	*1. neat* [obs.: any animal of the ox family < AS. *neat*, bovine possession]; *2. neatherd* [cowherd]; *3. neat's foot oil* [pale yellow oil obtained by boiling feet and shinbones of cattle, used in dressing leather]

GERMAN WORD	MEANING	ENGLISH COGNATE
genug (adj) • **genügen** (vi) • **begnügen** (refl) • **vergnügen** (vt) [bs: to give enough (*genug*), and so cause enjoyment] • **vergnügen** (refl) • **vergnügt** (adj) • **Vergnügen** (n), **Vergnügung** (f)	= enough = to be enough, suffice = to be contented with = to amuse, give pleasure = to enjoy o.s. = merry, gay = pleasure, amusement	*enough*
gerben (vt) [< OHG. *garawen*, prepare; *garwi*, preparation, whence Ital. *garbo*, fashion, grace] • **Gerber** (m)	= to prepare leather, tan = tanner	*1. garb* [preparations, now esp. clothing, coverings]; *2. gear* [< *gearwe*, preparation]
gering (adj) [orig.: light, fast (turning easily?), hence trifling, unimportant; etym. uncert., perh. < Gmc. *wrengh-*, to twist, ult. < IE. **wer-*, to turn, bend] • **geringfügig** (adj) ['of trifling fit'] • **geringachten** (vt) • **verringern** (vt) • **Verringerung** (f)	= little, trifling, slight, inferior = insignificant, trifling = to think little of = to lessen, diminish, reduce = reduction, diminution, cut	*? distantly: to wring*
gerinnen (vi)	= to curdle, congeal, coagulate, clot	*rennet* [a preparation used to curdle milk in making cheese]
gern (adv) [< OHG. *geron*, to long for, cogn. G. roots *gei-, geiz-, gier-, gehr-*, having strong sense of avidity] • **begehren** (vt) • **begehrlich** (adj)	= willingly, gladly = to demand, require, desire, crave = desirous, covetous	*to yearn* [< AS. *gyrnan* < *georn*, eager. See also **Geiz, Gier, Geier**]
Gerte (f)	= switch, rod, twig	*yard(stick)* [< ME. *yerde, gerde*]
Gerücht (see **rufen**)		
geruhen (see **ruchlos**)		
Geschirr (see **scheren**)		
Geschlecht (see **schlagen**)		
Geselle (see **Saal**)		
Gesinde, Gesindel (see **senden**)		

GERMAN WORD	MEANING	ENGLISH COGNATE
Gespenst (n) [bs: enticing < OHG. *spanan*. Etym. disputed: ? 'what pulls, stretches.' Or 'at will,' theorized cogn. L. *sponte*, of own accord] • **gespensterhaft** (adj) • **abspenstig** (adj) ['enticed away']	= spectre, ghost, apparition = spectral, ghostly = alienated	? *span* and *to span* Or ? *spont-* in *spontaneous* [< L. *sponte*, of own accord, unaided]
Gestalt (see **Stelle**)		
gestern (adv)	= yesterday	*yester(day)*
gesund (adj) • **Gesundheit** (f) • **gesunden** (vi)	= sound, healthy = health = to recover, get sound	*sound*
Getreide (see **tragen**)		
Gewähr (see **wahren**)		
Geweih (see **weigern**)		
Gewinn (m) • **gewinnen** (vt & vi) • **überwinden** (vt) [bs: to win over an opponent < *über*, over, above + *gewinnen*]	= gain, profit = to win, gain = to subdue, overcome	*win*
Giebel (m) [bs: forked branch (cf. Frk. *gibb*)]	= gable, pediment, fronton	*gibbet* [a gallows < OFr. < Frk. *gibb*]
Gier (f) [cogn. G. roots *gei-, geiz-, gehr-*, having strong sense of avidity] • **gieren** (vi) • **gierig** (adj) • **begierig** (adj) • **Begier, Begierde** (f) • **Neugier** (f), **Neugierde** (f) • **neugierig** (adj)	= greed(iness), avidity = to lust after = greedy, covetous = covetous, desirous, eager = desire, greed for, craving = curiosity = curious	*1. to yere* [obs.: to desire, long for]; *2.* distantly: *to yearn* [< AS. *gyrnan* < *georn*, eager. See also **Geiz, gern, Geier**]
gießen (vt) [*goß, gegossen*] • **Gießer** (m) • **Gießerei** (f) • **abgießen** (vt) • **vergießen** (vt) • **Abguß** (m) • **Gosse** (f)	= to pour = founder, one who casts metals = foundry = to pour off, cast = to pour out, spill = casting = sewer, gutter	*1. geyser; 2. gush; 3. gust; 4. -got* in *ingot*
Gipfel (m) [< MHG. *gupf*, cogn. *Kopf*, head]	= summit, peak, top ('head')	*cup* [< L. *cupa*, vat, cask, drinking cup]
Gischt (m) • **gischen** (vi)	= foam, spray, froth = to foam, spray, froth, effervesce	*yeast*

GERMAN WORD	MEANING	ENGLISH COGNATE
Glanz (m) • **glänzen** (vi) • **glänzend** (adj)	= brightness, luster = to glitter, shine = bright, brilliant	*glint* [< ME. *glinten, glenten*]
glatt (adj) • **Glätte** (f) • **glätten** (vt)	= smooth, sleek, glossy = smoothness, gloss = to smooth, burnish	*1. glad* [orig.: smooth, shining, then cheerful]; *2.* distantly: *glitter*
glauben (vt & vi) [< Gmc. **ga-laubjan*, to hold dear] • **Glaube** (m) • **glaubhaft** (adj) ['meriting (having) belief'] • **gläubig** (adj) • **Aberglaube** (m) [bs: excessive or superfluous belief < *aber*, believed a variant of *über*, over, added, repetition + *Glaube*] • **aberglaubisch** (adj) • (see also **erlauben, lieb, Lob**)	= to believe = faith, belief, creed = credible, authentic = believing, faithful = superstition [cf. L. *superstitio*, excessive fear < *super*, abundant, over + *stitio*, what stands] = superstitious	*-lieve* in *believe*
gleich (see **Leiche**)		
Gleis (see **List**)		
Gleisner (see **Leiche**)		
Gletscher (m) [< LL. *glaciarium* < *glacia* < L. *glacies*, ice]	= great ice field, glacier	*glacier* [< LL. *glaciarium* < *glacia* < L. *glacies*, ice]
Glied (n) [bs: part that moves freely < MHG. *gilit, ge* + *lit*, OHG. *lid* (cf. AS. *lith*)] • **gliedern** (vt) • **Gliederbau** (m)	= limb, member, joint = to articulate, dispose = articulation, structure	*lith* in expression *lith and limb* [Scot.: a division, section (e.g., of an orange) < AS. *lith*]
glimmen (vi)	= smolder, glimmer, glow	*glimmer*
glimpflich (adj) [< OHG. *gilimpf*] • **Glimpf** (m) • **Unglimpf** (m) • **verunglimpfen** (vt)	= mild, gentle, lenient = mildness, gentleness = harshness, affront = to disparage, slander	believed distantly: *limp*
glitzern (vi)	= to glitter, glisten	*glitter*
Glocke (f) [< LL. *clocca*, bell] • **Glockenspiel** (n) • **Glockenturm** (m) • **Glöckner** (m)	= bell; shade (of a lamp) = chimes = bell tower = bellringer	*1. clock* [mechanical timepiece named from the medieval practice of sounding the hours with a bell < LL. *clocca*, bell]; *2. cloak* [a bell-shaped outer garment]

GERMAN WORD	MEANING	ENGLISH COGNATE
glotzen (vi) • **glotzaugig** (adj) • **anglotzen** (vt)	= to stare, goggle = pop-eyed = to stare at, goggle at	*gloat* [to gaze or meditate with malicious pleasure]
Glück (n) • **glücklich** (adj) • **Unglück** (n)	= luck, happiness = happy = misfortune, accident	*luck*
glühen (vi) • **glühend** (adj) • **Glut** (f)	= to glow = glowing, ardent = heat, glow; (fig.:) ardor, fervor	*1. glow; 2. gleet* [a live coal]
gönnen (vt) [bs: to act with good use < OHG. *gi-unnan* (cogn. Gk. *onesimus*, useful)] • **Gönner** (m) • **Gunst** (f) [cf. *Kunst < können*] • **gunstig** (adj) • **mißgönnen** (vt) • **Mißgunst** (f) • **Ungunst** (f) _____ • **Gnade** (f) • **gnadig** (adj) • **begnad(ig)en** (vt)	= to wish well, to favor with; bestow, grant = well-wisher, protector = favor, grace, goodwill = favorable, gracious = to envy or begrudge s.o. s.t. = envy, jealousy = disfavor _____ = favor, grace, mercy = gracious, merciful = to pardon, grant favors to	*1. yonste* [obs. or rare: favor]; *2.* Greek-derived root *on-* in personal names in New Testament (writings of St. Paul): *Onesimus* [< Gk. for 'useful'] and *Onesiphorus* [< Gk. for 'profit-bearing']
Gott (m), **Göttin** (f) • **Gottheit** (f) • **Abgott** (m) [bs: godless < OHG. *ab-*, away + *got*, god] • **Götze** (m) [dim. of *Gott*]	= god, goddess = divinity = idol = idol	*god*
graben (vt) • **Grab** (n) • **Graben** (m) • **Grübchen** (n) • **begraben, vergraben** (vt)	= to dig = grave, tomb, sepulcher = ditch, trench = dimple = to bury	*1. grave; 2. groove; 3. graven; 4. engrave*
Gram (m) [< OHG. *gram* (cf. Frk. *gram*)] • **grämen** (vt) • **grämen** (refl) • **grämlich** (adj)	= grief, sorrow = to cause grief to s.o. = to grieve over = sullen	*-grin* in *chagrin* [disappointment or sorrow < Fr. *cha-*, intensive prefix + OFr. *graignier*, to sorrow < OFr. *graim*, sorrow < Frk. *gram*, affliction, grief]
Gras (n)	= grass	*grass*
grassieren (vi) [bs: to proceed violently < ML. < L. *grassor, grassari*, to go or prowl about, to attack < *gradior, gradi, gressus*, to go, step]	= (esp. of disease) to rage or be widespread	*aggression* [< L. *aggredior, aggressus*, to approach, approach hostilely < *ad*, to + *gressus*, past p. of *gradi*, to go, step]

GERMAN WORD	MEANING	ENGLISH COGNATE
gräßlich (adj), rarely **graß** [MDu. *grese*, shudder (cf. AS. *agrisan*, to shudder with fear)]	= horrible, atrocious	*grisly* [< ME. *grislich* < AS. *grislic* < *agrisan*, to shudder with fear]
• **Gräßlichkeit** (f)	= horribleness, atrocity	
grau (adj)	= gray	*gray*
• **grauen**[1] (vi) [bs: to turn gray (i.e., lighter, from darkness of night)]	= to dawn	
• **Grauen**[1] (n)	= dawn, daybreak	
grauen[2] (impers. + **mir**)	= to be filled with horror or dread	*grue-, grues-* in *gruesome* [causing fear < ME. *gruen*]
• **Grauen**[2] (n)	= horror, dread	
• **grauenhaft** (adj)	= horrible, dreadful	
• **grausen** (vi)	= **grauen**[2]	
• **Grausen** (n), **Graus** (m)	= horror	
• **grausam** (adj)	= dreadful, cruel	
• **Grausamkeit** (f)	= cruelty	
greifen (vt)	= to seize, grasp	*grip*
• **Griff** (m)	= grasp, grip, hold	
• **begreifen** (vt)	= to grasp, understand	
• **Begriff** (m)	= understanding, concept	
• **angreifen** (vt)	= to attack	
• **Angriff** (m)	= attack	
• **eingreifen** (vi)	= to intervene, encroach on	
• **Mißgriff** (m) ['wrong seize']	= mistake, blunder	
greinen (vi) [bs: pulling the mouth]	= to whine, cry	*1. groan; 2. grin*
Greis(in) (m, f) [bs: with gray or white hair < MHG. *gris* (OFr. *gris*, gray, prob. < OHG. *grao*, gray)]	= old man, old woman	*grizzled* [having become gray < OFr. *gris*, gray < OHG. *grao*]
• **greisenhaft** (adj)	= senile	
grell (adj)	= shrill, strident, loud, garish	*grill*[1] [obs. adj: rough, harsh, cruel]
• **Grellheit** (f)	= shrillness, glare, garishness	
Gremium (n) [< L. *gremium*, lap, bosom, 'heart']	= committee, corporation, board	*gremial* [of the lap, bosom < L. *gremium*, lap, bosom, 'heart']
Grenze (f) [ult. < IE. **ghre-*, orig.: to stand up, form an edge, then to grow]	= frontier, boundary, border, limit	distantly: words < IE. **ghre-*, orig.: to stand up, form an edge, then to grow: *1. green; 2. grow; 3. grass*
• **(an)grenzen** (vt & vi)	= to border (on), adjoin	
• **angrenzend** (adj)	= adjacent	
• **begrenzen** (vt & vi)	= to bound, limit	
Grieß (m)	= gravel, grit; semolina	*grit*
Grill (f) [< L. *grillus*, cricket < echoic]	= cricket; (fig.) whim, fancy	*grill*[2] [obs.: cricket < L. *grillus*, cricket < echoic]
• **grillenhaft** (adj)	= whimsical	

GERMAN WORD	MEANING	ENGLISH COGNATE
Grimm (m) [bs: anger, fury] • **grimmig** (adj)	= fury, rage = furious, fierce	*grimace* and *grim* [< IE. **ghrem-,* angry, to roar angrily]
grinsen (vi) • **Grinsen** (n)	= to grin, sneer = grin, sneer	*grin*
grob (adj) • **Grobheit** (f)	= coarse, crude, raw = coarseness, roughness	*gruff*
Groll (m) • **grollen** (vi) • **grollend** (adj)	= grudge, resentment = to be resentful, angry = resentful, cross	perh. distantly: *to growl*
gross (adj) • **Größe** (f) • **vergrößern** (vt)	= great, big = greatness, size = to magnify	*gross*
Gruft (f) [< LL. *grypta* (whence Ital. *grotta,* cave) < L. *crypta via,* underground passage < Gk. *kryptos,* hidden, covered]	= burial vault, tomb	*1. crypt* [< L. *crypta via,* underground passage < Gk. *kryptos,* hidden, covered]; *2. grotto* [Ital. *grotta,* cave < LL. *grypta* < L. *crypta* < Gk. *kryptos,* hidden, covered]
grün (adj) • **Grünspan** (m) ['green of Spain,' greenish rust on copper used in dye & medicine, produced in Spain < loan transl. of ML. *viride Hispanum*]	= green = verdigris ['green of Greece,' the greenish rust on copper, bronze or brass, produced in Mediter. lands < OFr. *vert de Grèce*]	*green*
Grund (f) • **grunden** (vt) • **grundsätzlich** (adj) • **aufgrund** (prep) + *gen.*	= ground, soil, bottom; reason, motive = to establish, promote = fundamental = on the basis of, on the grounds of	*ground*
Gruß (m) • **grüßen** (vt) • **begrüßen** (vt)	= greeting = to greet = to greet, welcome	*greet*
gültig (see **gelten**)		
Gurke (f) [< Czech *okurka* < Gk. *angourion,* cucumber]	= cucumber, pickle	*gherkin* [a kind of small cucumber < Du. dim. of *agurk* < Czech *okurka* < Gk. *angourion,* cucumber]
Gurt (m), **Gurte** (f) • **gürten** (vt) • **Gürtel** (m)	= girth, belt, strap, girdle = to gird = girdle, belt, sash	*1. to gird; 2. girdle*
gut (adj) • **Güte** (f) • **Gut** (n)	= good = goodness = possession, property	*good*

GERMAN WORD	MEANING	ENGLISH COGNATE
# H		
Haar (n)	= hair	*hair*
haben (vt) • **gehaben** (refl) • **vorhaben** (vt) • (for **erhaben** see **heben**)	= to have = to behave, conduct oneself = to purpose, intend, plan	*1. have; 2. behave*
• **Habe** (f) • **Habgier** (f), **Habsucht** (f) • **habgierig**, **habsuchtig** (adj) • (see also **Haft**)	= property, (personal) belongings, movables, personal estate = greed, covetousness, avarice = greedy, covetous, avaricious	
Habicht (m) [< OHG. *habuch* (cf. ME. *havec*)]	= hawk	*hawk* [< ME. *hauk, havec*]
hacken (vt) • **Hacke** (f) [that sharply angled, esp. to hack]	= to hack, mince, chop = hoe, mattock, pickax; heel	*1. hack; 2 hash* [a dish of chopped meat and vegetables < OFr. *hachier, t*o chop up]
Hader[1] (m) • **Haderlump** (m)	= rag = ragamuffin, scoundrel	*hood-* in *hoodlum* [rogue < Bavarian *hodalum* < *Haderlump*, 'rag-rag' < *Hader*, rag + *Lump*, ragamuffin < *Lumpen*, rag]
Hader[2] (m) • **hadern** (vi)	= dispute, quarrel, strife = to quarrel, be at strife with	distant cogn.: *hate* [seen in names *Hedda, Hedwig*]
Hafen (m)	= harbor, port	*haven*
Hafer (m)	= oats	*haversack* ['sack of oats,' a canvas bag with supplies, worn on the back or shoulder by soldiers and hikers]
Haft (f) [bs: catching, holding, cogn. *haben*] • **Häftling** (m) • **(an)haften** (vi) • **haftbar** (adj) • **verhaften** (vt) [bs: to make held] • **heften** (vt) [bs: to make caught] • **Heft** (n) • (see also **haben**)	= imprisonment = prisoner = to adhere, stick to = responsible, liable = to arrest = to fasten, affix, attach; stitch, sew, baste = haft, handle; stitched book	*1. haft* [handle or hilt of a knife or sword, cogn. *to have*]; *2.* distantly: *have*

GERMAN WORD	MEANING	ENGLISH COGNATE
Hag (m), **Hecke**[1] (f) • **Hagen** (m), **Hain** (poet.) • **Hagestolz** (m) [bs: person living on a defined plot of ground set up as too small to support a family but adequate for a single man < *Hag*, hedge + *stellen*, to place] • **behagen** (vt) [bs: to provide with a hedge, protect, fit up, please] • **behaglich** (adj) [bs: hedged in] • **Unbehagen** (n) • **Unbehaglichkeit** (f) ——————————— • **hegen** (vt) [bs: to keep in a hedge] • **Gehege** (n) • **heikel** (adj) [< *hegen*, cherishing + *ekel*, disgust]	= hedge = grove = bachelor = to please, suit = comfortable, peaceful = discomfort = displeasure ——————————— = to foster, cherish, harbor, tend = enclosure, preserve; fence, hedge = fussy, fastidious	*1. hedge; 2. hay-* in *hayward* [an officer having charge of fences and enclosures]
Hagel (m)	= hail (meteorol.)	*hail*
hager (adj) [cf. Frk. *hager*] • **Hagerkeit** (f)	= emaciated, gaunt, lean, thin = guantness, leanness	*-i(n)ger* in to *malinger* [to pretend to be ill or weak in order to escape work < Fr. *malingre*, sickly, puny < *mal*, bad + OFr. *haingre*, lean < Frk. *hager*, thin, lean]
Hagestolz (see **Hag**)		
Hahn (m) • **Huhn** (f) • **Henne** (f)	= rooster, cock; faucet, spigot (bec. of similarity to a cock's head) = chicken, hen = hen	*hen*
Hai (m)	= shark	*hoe*[2] [Scot.: dogfish; one of the families of small sharks]
Haken (m) • **haken** (vt & vi) • **hakig, hakenförmig** (adj)	= hook = to hook = hooked, hook-shaped	*hook*
halb (adj) • **Hälfte** (f) • **Halbinsel** (f) • **Halbkugel** (f) • **halbieren** (vt)	= half (of) = half = peninsula = hemisphere = to bisect	*half*
Halde (f) (poet.) [bs: what is inclined, sloping < OHG. *halda* < Gmc. **haltha-*, steep, inclined (cf. AS. *hieldan*, to tilt, slope)] • (see also **hold**)	= slope, declivity, hill-side; heap of rubbish	*to heel* [said of a ship; orig.: *to hield, heald*, to lean to one side, tilt (hence, *heeling error*, the error of the compass caused by the heeling of the vessel) < AS. *hieldan*]

GERMAN WORD	MEANING	ENGLISH COGNATE
hallen (vi) [< obs. *hellen* < IE. **kel-*, to shout, cry out]	= to (re)sound, echo	*to low* [to cry out, as a cow < ME. *lowen* < AS. *hlowan* < IE. **kel-*, whence L. *clamare*, to cry out or call > Eng. *clamor, claim*]
• **Hall** (m)	= sound, resonance	
• **verhallen** (vi) [< *ver*, exhaustive prefix + *hallen*]	= to fade or die away (of sound)	
• **Widerhall** (m) [< *wider*, counter, turned against]	= echo	
• **widerhallen** (vt & vi)	= to echo	
• **einhellig** (adj)	= unanimous	
• **mißhellig** (adj)	= dissentient; dissonant	
• (see also **hell**)		
Hals (m)	= neck; throat	*hawseholes* [holes for anchor cables at bow (neck) of a ship < ON. *hals*]
• **Halstuch** (n)	= neckerchief, scarf	
halten (vt & vi)	= to hold; stop, halt	*hold*
• **halten** (refl)	= to hold out, last, (of food:) keep	
• **Haltung** (f) ['one's holding of oneself']	= attitude	
• **anhalten** (vt)	= to stop, hold	
• **anhalten** (vi)	= to hold out, thus to last, continue	
• **anhaltend** (adj)	= continuous, persevering	
• **enthalten** (vt)	= to contain	
• **unterhalten** (vt)	= to entertain	
• **verhalten** (vt)	= to keep back, retain, act	
• **Verhalten** (n)	= action, conduct	
• **Verhältnis** (n)	= proportion, 'that held in'	
• **verhältnismäßig** (adv)	= in proportion, comparatively	
Hand (f)	= hand	*1. hand; 2. handle*
• **handeln** (vt) [< *Hand*, hand]	= to act, deal, trade	
• **Handel** (m)	= trade, commerce	
• **Händler** (m)	= dealer	
• **anhand** (prep) + *gen.*	= with the help of	
• **behend** (adj) [bs: with skilled hand (cf. Eng. *dexterity*, 'skilled use of the right hand' < L. *dexter*, right)]	= nimble, agile	
• **Behendigkeit** (f)	= nimbleness, agility	
hängen (vt & vi)	= to hang, suspend; to be hanging, be suspended	*hang*
• **Hang** (m)	= slope, declivity; (fig.:) propensity, inclination	
• **abhängen** (vt & vi)	= to take down, uncouple; to depend (upon)	
• **abhängig** (adj)	= dependent	
• **Abhängigkeit** (f)	= dependency	
• **Verhängnis** (n) [bs: what hangs in the balance for one, what is dispensed, esp. with negative result]	= destiny, fate, doom	
• **verhängnisvoll** (adj)	= fateful, fatal, disastrous	

GERMAN WORD	MEANING	ENGLISH COGNATE
hantieren (vi) [bs: to be habitually present at, hence to handle < OFr. *hanter*, to frequent]	= to work with, operate, wield	*to haunt* [< OFr. *hanter*, to frequent]
• **Hantierung** (f)	= operating, handling, occupation	
hapern (impers. + **bei**) [< Du. *haperen*, to falter, have difficulty, orig. to stutter, open and close the mouth < echoic *ap, ap*]	= to falter, have a hitch or shortness in	distantly: *yap* [echoic: opening and closing the mouth]
• **Happen** (m) [bs: goal of opening and closing the mouth, believed cogn. Du. *haperen*]	= mouthful, morsel, bite	
harren (vi) [? bs: 'remaining hard by'; *harren*, perh. alter. of *hart*, hard (cf. L. *durus*, hard, and *durare*, to bear, endure, hold out)]	= to wait or hope for, stay	*? hard by*
• **beharren** (vi)	= to be persistent, persist	
• **verharren** (vi)	= to persist in, stick to	
hart (adj)	= hard	*hard*
• **härten** (vi)	= to harden	
• **abhärten** (vt)	= to harden, toughen	
• **erhärten** (vt)	= to confirm, corroborate	
Harz (n) [early meaning: wax; cogn. Gk. *keros*, wax (*k-r-s = H-r-z*)]	= resin, rosin, gum	distantly: *kerosene* [a distillation of petroleum, paraffin oil, etc. < Gk. *keros*, wax]
haschen, erhaschen (vt) [< *hafskon < IE. *kap-, to seize, whence L. *capio, capere*, to seize]	= to snatch, seize	distantly: *capture* [< L. *captus, capere* < IE. *kap-, to seize]
Hase (m) [cf. AS. *hara*]	= rabbit	*hare* [< AS. *hara*]
Haß (m)	= hate, hatred	*hate*
• **hassen** (vt)	= to hate	
• **verhaßt** (adj)	= hateful, odious, hated	
• **häßlich** (adj)	= ugly, unpleasant	
Hast (f)	= haste	*haste, hasten*
• **hasten** (vi)	= to hurry, hasten, rush	
• **hastig** (adj)	= hasty, hurried	
Haube (f)	= cowl, hood	distantly: *hive*
Hauch (m) [echoic; cf. Eng. *whew!*]	= breath, whiff; (fig.:) trace, tinge	cf. echoic *whew*
• **hauchen** (vi)	= to respire, breathe	
• **hauchdünn** (adj) ['thin as breath' < *dünn*, thin]	= flimsy, sheer	
• **hauchzart** (adj) ['breath delicate' < *zart*, delicate]	= filmy, extremely delicate	

GERMAN WORD	MEANING	ENGLISH COGNATE
hauen (vt) • **Haue** (f) • **Bildhauer** (m) ['image (*Bild*) hewer']	= to hew, cut up, chop = hoe, pick = sculptor	*hew*
Haufen (m) • **häufen** (vt) • **Häufung** (f) • **häufig** (adj) ['by heaps'] • **häufig** (adv)	= heap, pile; (fig.:) crowd = to heap, accumulate = accumulation, heap(ing) = frequent = frequently	*heap*
Haupt (n) [cf. Goth. *haubith;* AS. *heafod*] • **Hauptmann** (m) • **behaupten** (vt) [bs: to regard an idea as head, chief] • **Behauptung** (f) • **enthaupten** (vt) • **überhaupt** (adv)	= head = captain = to assert, maintain = assertion, statement = to decapitate = on the whole, after all, whatever	*head* [< AS. *heafod*]
Haus (n) • **häuslich** (adj) • **Gehäuse** (n)	= house = domestic = casing, case	*house*
Haut (f) [cf. AS. *hyd, hid*] • **häuten** (vt)	= skin, hide = to strip off the skin	*hide* [< AS. *hyd, hid*]
Havarie (f) [< Fr. *avarie,* ult. < Arab. *awariya, awar,* damaged goods]	= damages or losses, orig. to a ship or its cargo	*average* [orig.: the reckoned damages to a ship or cargo, then a mean tariff, then any mean < Fr. *avarie* < Ital. *avaria* < Arab. *awar,* damaged goods]
Hebel (see **heben**)		
heben (vt) • **erheben** (vt) • **erheblich** (adj) [bs: of weight to be raised] • **unerheblich** (adj) • **Hebel** (m) [< *heben,* to raise] • **Hebelwirkung** (f) _____ • **erhaben** (adj) • **Erhabenheit** (f) • **Hefe** (f) ['what makes raised']	= to raise = to lift, elevate, raise = considerable, weighty = inconsiderable, irrelevant [< L. *in,* not + *relevare,* to lift again] = lever, handle, crank = leverage _____ = raised, elevated, embossed, sublime = protuberance; sublimity = yeast	*heave*
Hecke[1] (see **Hag**)		
hecken (vt & vi) • **Hecke**[2] (f)	= to hatch, bring forth young = hatching, breeding, brood	*hatch*

GERMAN WORD	MEANING	ENGLISH COGNATE
Heer (n) [< OHG. *heri, hari* (cf. Frk. *hari;* AS. *here*)]	= army	*1. to harry* [orig.: to raid, pillage, later to torment < AS. *here*, army]; *2. har-* in *harangue* [orig.: speech rousing a circle of soldiers < ML. < Frk. *hari hring,* a ring of warriors < Frk. *hari,* army]; *3. har-* in *harlot* [orig.: young male camp follower, then female camp follower < OFr. *herlot* < OHG. *heri, hari,* army + OHG. *lotar,* vagabond];
• **verheeren** (vt) [bs: to put the army to < *ver,* intens. prefix + *Heer*]	= to devastate, ravage	
• **Heereshaufen** (m)	= host, army	
• **Heerlager** (n)	= encampment	
• **Herzog** (m) ['army leader' < *Heer* + *zog* < *ziehen,* to pull, draw]	= duke [< L. *dux,* leader < *ducere,* to lead, pull; cf. Eng. *duct, ductile*]	
• **Herzogin** (f)	= duchess	
• **Herberge** (f) ['army shelter' < *bergen,* to shelter]	= shelter, lodging, inn	*4. harbor* ['army shelter,' then refuge, esp. for ships < AS. *here,* army + *beorg,* shelter]
• **herbergen** (vt)	= to shelter, lodge	
Hefe (see **heben**)		
hegen (see **Hag**)		
hehlen (vi) [< IE. **kel-,* to conceal, whence L. *celare,* to conceal]	= to receive stolen goods	*1. distantly: -ceal* in *conceal* [< L. *celare,* to hide, conceal < IE. **kel-,* to conceal];
• **Hehler** (m)	= receiver of stolen goods	
• **Hehlerei** (f)	= receiving of stolen goods	
• **Helm** (m) [what covers, hides]	= helmet; dome, cupola	*2. helmet*
hehr (see **Herr**)		
Heide (f)	= heath(land), moor	*1. heath; 2. heathen*
• **Heide** (m)	= heathen, pagan	
• **Heidentum** (n)	= heathenism	
• **heidnisch** (adj)	= heathen	
heikel (see **Hag**)		
heil (adj)	= unhurt, sound	*1. hail; 2. health; 3. whole*
• **Heil** (n)	= welfare, salvation	
• **Heiland** (m)	= savior	
• **heilen** (vt & vi)	= to heal, cure; heal up	
• **Unheil** (n)	= harm, mischief	
• **heillos** (adj)	= mischievous, wicked	
heilig (adj)	= holy, solemn	*holy*
• **heiligen** (vt)	= to sanctify	
• **Heilige** (m, f)	= saint	
• **Heiligkeit** (f)	= sanctity	
• **entheiligen** (vt)	= to desecrate	
Heim (see **Heirat**)		

GERMAN WORD	MEANING	ENGLISH COGNATE
Heirat (f) [< MHG. *hirat* < OHG. *hiwo*, master of a household (cogn. AS. *hiwa*, member of family) + *rat*, care, and so, provision]	= marriage, wedding	roots *hi-* and *ho-* in: *1. hind* [in Scotl. and northern England: a skilled farm worker or servant; peasant, rustic < AS. *hina*, earlier *hiwna*, gen. pl. of *hiwa*, member of a household]; *2. hide*, [an old English measure of land (bs: land to support a family)];
• **(ver)heiraten** (vt)	= to lead to altar, marry off	
• **verheiraten** (refl)	= to get married	
• **ungeheuer** (adj & adv) [bs: unusual, 'not household' < *un* + *geheu-* < *hiwo*, household]	= huge, enormous, monstrous, immense (adv: immensely, tremendously)	
• **Ungeheuer** (n)	= monster	
• **ungeheuerlich** (adj)	= monstrous, atrocious	
• **geheuer** (adj, adv) ['of the household,' guarded]	= secure, esp. against the ghostly	
esp.: **nicht geheuer**	= (+ neg.:) eerie, haunted, risky	
• **Heim** (n)	= home, hostel	*3. home*
• **Heimat** (f)	= own or native country	
• **heimatlich** (adj)	= native	
• **heimisch** (adj)	= local, native, domestic	
• **heimlich** (adj) ['trusted to the house,' guarded]	= secret, clandestine	
• **geheim** (adj)	= secret	
• **Geheimnis** (adj)	= secret, mystery	
• **heimsuchen** (vt) ['to visit esp. with harm']	= to afflict, strike, punish	
heiser (adj) [< OHG. *heis* (cf. AS. *has*)]	= hoarse	*hoarse* [< ME. *hors*; ON. **hars*, AS. *has*]
• **Heiserkeit** (f)	= hoarseness	
heiß (adj)	= hot	*hot*
• **heizen** (vt)	= to heat	
• **Hitze** (f)	= heat, passion, rage	
• **hitzig** (adj)	= rash, passionate, acute, violent	
• **erhitzen** (vt)	= to heat	
heißen (vt & vi) [cf. AS. **haitan*, to call, bid, whence *haes*, a command]	= to command, bid, direct (s.o. to do something); to call, name, denominate; be called, signify	*1. hest* [bidding, order < AS. *haes*, command, with unhistoric *t* < **haitan*, to call, bid]; *2. behest* [bidding, command]
• **Geheiß** (n)	= command, order	
• **verheißen** (vt)	= to promise	
heiter (adj) [bs: of a (bright) state < OHG. *heitar* < *heit*, state or manner, esp. a bright one (as suffix, *-heit* now means any state or manner, e.g., *Dunkelheit*, darkness)]	= bright, cheerful, serene	suffix *-hood* [orig.: a bright state, then any state determined by the qualifying noun, e.g., *childhood*, *knighthood*]
• **erheitern** (vt)	= to cheer up, amuse	

Easy Key to German Vocabulary

GERMAN WORD	MEANING	ENGLISH COGNATE
helfen (vt) [*half, geholfen*] • **Hilfe**, **Hülfe** (f) • **Gehilfe** (m) • **hilfreich, behilflich** (adj) • **Behelf** (m) [bs: what assists, helps] • **Behelfsmäßig** (adv) • **behelfen** (refl) • **unbeholfen** (adj) ['not well managed']	= to help = help, assistance = assistant = helpful = something makeshift, device = makeshift, improvised = to make do, manage = awkward, clumsy, heavy-handed	*help*
hell (adj) [orig.: assoc. with clear sound, then applied to matters of sight < IE. **kel-*, to shout, cry out] • **hellen** (vt) • **Helligkeit** (f) • (see also **hallen**)	= bright, clear, evident = to make clear, clarify = clearness, splendor, loudness	*1.* distantly: *to low* [to cry out, as a cow < ME. *lowen* < AS. *hlowan* < IE. **kel-*, to shout, cry out, whence L. *clamare*, to cry out or call > Eng. *clamor, claim*]; *2. to hell* [to burnish gold or silver < G. *hellen*]
Helm (see **hehlen**)		
Hemd (n) [< OHG. *hemidi*, undershirt (cf. AS. *hemethe*) < Gmc. **kamitja*] • **Totenhemd** (n) ['death shirt']	= shirt, undershirt = shroud	*chemise* [< Fr. < Gmc. **kamitja*, shirt]
hemmen (vt) • **Hemmung** (f)	= to check, stop, stem = inhibition	*to hem in*
Hengst (m) [cf. AS. *hengest*, male horse]	= stallion	*henchman* [orig.: horseman, then servant < AS. *hengest*, male horse]
Herberge (see **Heer**)		
Herbst (m)	= autumn	*harvest*
Herd (m)	= fireplace, cooking stove; focus	*hearth*
Herde (f)	= herd, flock; mass, crowd	*herd*
Herr (m) [< OHG. *her-ir-o*, elder, compar. of *her*, old (cf. AS. *har*)] • **herrisch** (adj) • **herrlich** (adj) • **Herrlichkeit** (f) • **verherrlichen** (vt) • **herrschen** (vt) • **Herrschaft** (f) • **hehr** (adj) (poet.) [bs: ancient, venerable < *her*]	= sir, mister; lord, master, gentleman [cf. Ital. *signore* and Sp. *señor* < L. *senior*, compar. of *senex*, old] = imperious, overbearing = magnificent, glorious = magnificence, glory = to glorify, exalt = to rule, govern = rule, dominance = exalted, august, sublime, lofty	*1. hoary* [gray or white, white with age, very old, ancient < ME. *hore*, AS. *har*]; *2. hoarfrost* [white, frozen dew]

GERMAN WORD	MEANING	ENGLISH COGNATE
Herz (n) • **herzhaft** (afj) • **herzig** (adj) • **herzlich** (adj)	= heart = courageous = lovely, charming = heartfelt, cordial	*heart*
Herzog (see **Heer**)		
Heu (n)	= hay	*hay*
Heuchler (see **hocken**)		
Heuer (f) [cf. AS. *hyre*] • **heuern** (vt)	= (naut.:) wages, pay (of seamen) = to charter, engage, hire (sailors)	*hire* [< AS. *hyre*]
Hexe (f) • **Hexerei** (f) • **behexen** (vt)	= witch = witchcraft = to bewitch	*1. hex; 2. hag*
Hinde, (poet.) **Hindin** (f)	= hind (female deer)	*hind* [female deer]
hindern (vt) • **Hinderung** (f) • **Hindernis** (n) • **hinderlich** (adj)	= to hinder, block = hindrance, obstruction = obstacle, barrier = hindering, obstructive	*hinder*
hinken (vi) [bs: to be deficient at the hip]	= to limp, hobble; be imperfect	*haunch* [hip < OFr. < Frk. **hanka*, hip]
Hirn (n), **Gehirn** (n) [< IE. **ker-1*, head, horn, cogn. Gk. *kranion*, cranium]	= brain(s)	distantly: *cran-* in *cranium* [< Gk. *kranion* < IE. **ker-1*, head, horn]
Hirsch (m)	= stag, hart	*hart* [a male deer]
Hirt(in) (m, f) [< *Herde*, herd, flock]	= shepherd(ess), herdsman	*herd*
hissen (vt) • **Hisse** (f)	= to raise, hoist = pulley, tackle	*hoist* [to raise aloft a flag, sail, etc., orig.: *hoise*, later with unhistoric *t*]
Hitze (see **heiß**)		
Hobel (m) • **hobeln** (vt)	= carpenter's plane = to plane	*howel* [a plane with a convex sole, used by coopers for smoothing the insides of casks]
hoch (adj) [< OHG. *hoh* (cf. AS. *heah*) < Gmc. **hauh-*, bent, arched, raised] • **Höhe** (f) ——— • **Hügel** (m) [< OHG. *houg* + suffix *-el*] • **hügelig** (adj)	= high = height, altitude ——— = hill, knoll = hilly	*1. high* [< AS. *heah*]; *2. height*

GERMAN WORD	MEANING	ENGLISH COGNATE
hocken (vi) [ult. < Gmc. *hauh-*, bent, arched, raised; cogn. *hoch*, high]	= to squat, crouch	words ult. < Gmc. *hauh-*, bent, arched, raised: *1. hawker* [peddler, orig.: one with a burden, crouching, arched]; *2. huckster* [peddler]; *3.* distantly: *high*
• **Höcke** (f)	= a squat position; a squat vault	
• **Hocker** (m)	= stool	
• **Höker** (m)	= peddler, hawker	
• **höken** (vi)	= to hawk about	
• **Heuchler(in)** (m, f) [bs: one who stoops, fawns after]	= hypocrite	
• **Heuchelei** (f)	= hypocrisy	
• **heucheln** (vt & vi)	= to be a hypocrite, to feign	
• **heuchlerisch** (adj)	= hypocritical	
Hof (m)	= court, yard, farm	distantly: *hive*
• **Hofmann** (m)	= courtier	
• **höflich** (adj)	= courteous, polite	
• **Gehöft** (n)	= farm(stead)	
• **hübsch** (adj) ['befitting a court' < *hövesch* < *Hof*]	= pretty, lovely	
Hoffart (see **fahren**)		
hoffen (vt & vi)	= to hope	*hope*
• **hoffentlich** (adv)	= it is to be hoped	
• **Hoffnung** (f)	= hope	
hohl (adj)	= hollow	*hollow*
• **Höhle** (f)	= hollow, cave	
• **aushöhlen** (vt)	= to hollow out, excavate	
Hohn (m) [< OHG. adj. *honi* (cf. Goth. *hauns* < Gmc. *hauni-*, contemptible; cf. Frk. *haunjan*, to mock > Fr. *honte*, shame)]	= scorn, disdain, derision	Eng. cogn. lacking, but found in *Hon-* of famous French motto of the Most Noble Order of the Garter: *Honi soit qui mal y pense*, 'Let him be shamed who thinks (shame)' [< Fr. *honnir* < Frk. *haunjan*, to mock]
• **höhnisch** (adj)	= scornful, derisive	
• **höhnen, verhöhnen** (vt)	= to mock, sneer or scoff at, taunt	
Höker (see **hocken**)		
hold (adj) [bs: inclined or tilted toward, showing graciousness or favor (cf. AS. *hieldan*, to incline; Goth. *hulths*)]	= (predicat.:) kind, gracious, well-disposed; (attribut.:) lovely, charming	*to heel* [said of a ship; orig.: *to hield, heald*, to lean to one side, tilt (hence, *heeling error*, the error of the compass caused by the heeling of the vessel) < AS. *hieldan*]
• **abhold** (adj)	= ill-disposed, averse	
• **unhold** (adj)	= ungracious, ill-disposed	
• **Unhold** (n)	= fiend, monster	
• **Huld** (f)	= graciousness, favor, clemency	
• **huldreich, huldvoll** (adj)	= gracious	
• **huldigen** (vi)	= to pay homage	
• **Huldigung** (f)	= homage	
• (see also **Halde**)		

GERMAN WORD	MEANING	ENGLISH COGNATE
holen (vt) • **einholen** (vt) • **erholen** (refl) [bs: to fetch back one's strength < *er*, thoroughly + *holen*] • **wiederholen** (vt) [*wieder*, again + *holen*]	= to fetch, go for, draw, get = to bring in, collect = to recover (from illness), relax = to repeat, reiterate; to fetch back	*to haul*
Holz (n) • **hölzern** (adj)	= wood[1], timber, lumber = wooden, (fig.:) clumsy, awkward	*holt* [arch.: a grove, copse, wooded hill]
hören (vt & vi) • **aufhören** (vi) [bs: attention (= hearing) causing one to stop] • **gehören, angehören** (vi) • **gehörig** (adj) • **gehorsam** (adj) ['giving ear to,' obeying] • **Gehorsam** (m) • **Behörde** (f) [bs: authority causing one to hear and obey, via *gehören*, to belong] • **verhören** (vt) • **Verhör** (n) • **zuhören** (vi)	= to hear = to cease = to belong to = belonging to; suitable = obedient [< Fr. obeir < L. *oboedire*, give ear to, obey < *ob* + *audire*, to hear] = obedience = authority, board, council = to try, examine = interrogation, examination = to listen to	*hear*
Horn (n)	= horn	*horn*
Horst (m) • **horsten** (vi)	= eyrie, eagle nest; copse = to nest	*horst* [a raised rock mass like an eyrie]
Hort (m) • **horten** (vt & vi)	= hoard, treasure = to hoard, stockpile	*hoard*
Hose (f)	= trousers	*hose, hosiery*
hübsch (see **Hof**)		
Huf (m)	= hoof	*hoof*
Hüfte (f)	= hip	*hip*
Hügel (see **hoch**)		
Huld (see **hold**)		
Hülle (f) • **hüllen** (vt) ['to furnish with a hull'] • **hüllenlos** (adj) • **enthüllen** (vt)	= cover, wrapper, case = to cover, wrap = uncovered, unclad = to uncover, reveal, expose	*hull*
Hülse (f)	= hull, husk, pod, shell; tube, socket case	*hull*

GERMAN WORD	MEANING	ENGLISH COGNATE
Humpen (m) [bs: a large container]	= tankard	*hump*
Hund (m) • **hundisch** (adj)	= dog = doggish, shameless, vile	*hound*
hüpfen (vi)	= to skip, gambol, frisk	*to hop*
Hürde (f)	= fold, pen (farmyard)	*hurdle* [wickerwork barrier]
Hure (f)	= whore, prostitute	*whore*
hurtig (adj) [orig.: bouncing in or from a hit, thus, quick < MHG. *hurt*, blow (cf. Frk. *hurt* > OFr. *hurter*, to push, hit > Fr. *heurter*, also ME. *hurten*, to hit, then to hurt by hitting)] • **Hurtigkeit** (f)	= quick, alert, agile = quickness, alertness, agility	*to hurt* [< ME. *hurten*, to hit and cause pain or damage < OFr. *hurter*, to push, hit quickly]
husten (vt & vi) [echoic (cf. AS. *hwostan*)] • **Husten** (m)	= to cough up; cough = cough	*to hoose* [dial.: to cough; cf. unrelated but similarly echoic *wheeze* < AS. *hwesan*]
Hut¹ (f) • **hüten** (vt) • **Hüter** (m) • **behüten** (vt) • **behütsam** (adj)	= care, charge; guard = to guard, keep, protect = guardian, keeper = to guard, keep, protect = cautious, careful	*heed*
Hut² (m)	= hat	*hat*
Hütte (f) • **Hüttenkunde** (f) and **Hüttenwesen** (n) [bs: iron works < the role of cabins in mining and metallurgy]	= cottage, hut, cabin = metallurgy	*hut*

I

impfen (vt) [bs: to implant; origins in horticulture < MHG. *impfeten* < OHG. *impiton*, to graft in (cf. AS. *impian*) < LL. *impotus* < Gk. *emphytos*, implanted < *emphyo*, to implant < *en*, in + *phyo*, to grow] • **Impfung** (f) • **Impfstoff** (m) • **Impfpflichtig** (adj)	= to vaccinate, inoculate = vaccination = vaccine = liable to vaccination	*1. imp* [orig.: a young shoot, sapling, implant, then offspring, child, little demon or spirit < AS. *impian*, to imp, engraft, start a growth < LL. *impotus* < Gk. *emphytos*, implanted < *emphyo*, to implant]; *2. phy-* in *phytology* [study of plants] and *neophyte* [lit.: 'new planting,' hence, convert, beginner, novice]

GERMAN WORD	MEANING	ENGLISH COGNATE
Ingwer (m) [< LG. *zingiberis*]	= ginger	*ginger* [< OFr. *gingibere*]
inner (adj) • **inne(n)** (adv) • **Innere** (n) • **innig** (adj) • **Innigkeit** (f)	= inner, interior, internal = within, inside = interior = intimate, close = intimacy	*in, inner*
• **erinnern** (vt) [bs: to stir within the mind < MHG. *(er)innern* < OHG. *innaron*, what is within] • **erinnern** (refl)	= to remind of = to remember	
Innung (f) [bs: a putting or getting in, incorporating < OHG. *innon*, to take in (cf. AS. *innian*, to put in)]	= guild, corporation	*inning* [a putting in, enclosing, esp. in a limited period of time, in sports (baseball) or politics < AS. *innian*, to put in]
Insasse (see **sitzen**)		
Inserat (n) [< journalism: insertion of an ad < L. *inserat*, let there be inserted, subjunctive of *inserere*, to insert]	= advertisement	*insert*
irden (see **Erde**)		
irren (vi & refl) [cogn. L. *errare*, to err] • **irre** (adj) • **irrig** (adj) • **Irrtum** (m) • **beirren** (vt) • **verirren** (refl)	= to err, wander; be mistaken = confused; insane, mad = erroneous = error = to confuse, mislead = to go astray	*to err, errant, error*

# J		
jagen (vt & vi) • **Jäger** (m) • **Jagd** (f) • **Jagdbeute** (f) • **Jagdschein** (m)	= to hunt, go on a chase = hunter = hunt(ing), chase = quarry, booty = hunting license	*1. yacht* [< Du. *jaghtschip*, pursuit ship]; *2. to yaw*, as in 'pitch and yaw' [of a ship: to turn or deviate, to swing right or left < ON. *jaga*, to sway < MHG. *jagen*, to hunt]
jäh (adj) [< OHG. *gahi*, rapid, impetuous] • **jählings** (adv)	= sudden, abrupt; steep, precipitous = all of a sudden, abruptly	*gay* [merry < OFr. *gai*, lively, impetuous < OHG. *gahi*, rapid, impetuous]

GERMAN WORD	MEANING	ENGLISH COGNATE
Jahr (n) • **Jahrhundert** (n) • **Jahrzehnt** (n)	= year = century = decade	*year*
Jammer (m) • **jammern** (vi) • **Jammern** (n) • **jämmerlich** (adj)	= misery, distress = to groan, lament = lamentation = lamentable, deplorable	*to yammer* [to whine, complain, yell]
jener (demon. pron.)	= that one	*1. yon; 2. yonder; 3. beyond*
Joch (n) [< L. *jugum*, joke]	= yoke; (archt.:) cross-beam, girder, bay division	*yoke*
Joppe (f) [< Fr. *jupe*, skirt < Ital. *giubba*, jacket < Arab. *al jubbah*, a loose outer garment]	= jacket	*jumper* [orig.: loose jacket or blouse worn by sailors; then sleeveless dress worn over a blouse < Fr. *jupe*, with unhistoric, intrusive *m*]
jucken (vi) [< OHD. *jucchen* (cf. AS. *giccan*)] • **jucken** (vt) • **jucken** (refl)	= to feel irritation on the skin, itch = to irritate, make itch = to scratch o.s.	*itch* [< ME. *yitchen*, AS. *giccan*]
jung (adj) • **verjüngen** (vt) • **verjüngen** (refl)	= young, new = to rejuvenate; make reduced = to grow young again; taper off	*young*
Junker (m) [< *junc*, young + *herre*, lord]	= young noble; squire, aristocrat	*young* + *Herr*

# K		
Kabeljau (m) [etym. uncert. < MDu. *cabeljau* (whence Fr. *cabillaud*) presumed a metathesis of Sp. *bacallao*]	= codfish	*cabilliau* [codfish < Fr. *cabillaud*]
Käfer (m)	= beetle, scarab	*chafer* [a group of related beetles that feed on plants]
Käfig (m) [< MHG. *kevje* < OHG. *chevia* < L. *cavea*, a hollowed area]	= cage	*cave*
kahl (adj) [cf. AS. *calu*] • **Kahlheit** (f)	= bald, barren, bleak, naked, plain, blank = baldness, barrenness, bleakness	*callow* [unfledged, without feathers; inexperienced, immature < AS. *calu*, bare, bald]
Kai (m)	= quay, wharf	*quay*

GERMAN WORD	MEANING	ENGLISH COGNATE
Kalb (n)	= calf	*calf*
Kalk (m) • **kalken** (vt)	= limestone = to whitewash	*calcium, calcify*
kalt (adj) • **Kälte** (f)	= cold, frigid = cold, chill	*cold*
Kamin (m)	= fireplace, chimney	*chimney*
Kamm (m) • **kämmen** (vt & vi)	= comb; crest; ridge = to comb	*comb*
Kammer (f) [< L. *camera* < Gk. *kamara*, vaulted chamber] • **Kämmerer** (m)	= chamber, compartment, cabinet = chamberlain, treasurer	*1. chamber; 2. camera*
Kampf (m) [orig.: battlefield, then a battle < L. *campus*, field] • **kämpfen** (vi) • **Kämpfer** (m) • **Kämpe** (m)	= battle, combat = to contend, struggle = warrior, combatant = champion, seasoned warrior	*words < L. campus, field: 1. campus; 2. campaign [orig.: expedition in open country]; 3. champion [winner on the field]*
Kaneel (m) [< Fr. *cannelle*, Ital. *cannella*, cinnamon < L. *canna*, tube, cane (the form assumed by peeled cinnamon bark)]	= cinnamon	*cane*
Kaninchen (n) [< MHG. *kuniklin* < L. *cuniculus*, rabbit, whence Ital. *coniglio*]	= rabbit	*cony, coney [a rabbit < OFr. conil < L. cuniculus, rabbit]*
Kanne (f)	= pitcher, tea or coffee pot	*can*
Kante (f) [< LL. *cant(h)us*, iron tire, wheel edging] • **kanten** (vt) [bs: to work the edges] • **kantig** (adj) • **kentern** (vi) ['to go on its edge']	= edge, brim, corner = to set on edge, tilt; to square (stone), work a border = angular, edged, squared = to capsize, keel over	*words < LL. cant(h)us, iron tire, wheel edging: 1. canted, to cant [to turn the edge, make angled]; 2. canton [region, corner (edge) of land]; 3. canteen [military shop for provisions < Ital. cantina, 'wine corner,' nook, cellar]*
Kanzlei (f) [< L. *cancelli*, railing, lattice marking a restricted space] • **Kanzler** (m) • **Kanzel** (f) • **abkanzeln** (vt) ['to lecture s.o. as from a pulpit']	= chancellery, office = chancellor = pulpit; (milit.) cockpit = to reprimand, dress s.o. down	*words < L. cancelli, railing or lattice marking a restricted space: 1. chancellor; 2. to cancel [to mark out with crossed lines]; 3. chancel [restricted part of a church having the altar]*

GERMAN WORD	MEANING	ENGLISH COGNATE
karg (adj) [cf. AS. *cearig*] • **kärglich** (adj)	= scant, sparse, meager = scanty, meager, poor	*chary* [cautious, shy; frugal, stingy < AS. *cearig*]
kariert (adj) [< Fr. *carré*, square < L. *quadratus*]	= checkered	*1. square; 2. squadron; 3. quarry* [source of squares of stone]
Kartoffel (f) [dissimil. < OItal. *tartuffolo*, truffle < VL. *terrae tufer* for *terrae tuber*, tuber of the earth]	= potato	*1. truffle; 2.* distantly: *ter(rain) + tuber*
Kaserne (f) [bs: place for soldiers; orig. a rampart wall for four soldiers on watch < Fr. *caserne*, Ital. *caserma* < L. *quaternus*, group of four]	= barracks	*1. casern(e)* [orig.: a small hut for four, then any troop barracks near battlements of a fortified town]; *2. quaternary* [adj: in sets of four]; *3. quatrain*
Käse (m) [cf. AS. *ces;* < L. *caseus*, cheese, whence Sp. *queso*, cheese]	= cheese	*1. cheese* [< ME. *chese*, AS. *cese* < L. *caseus*]; *2. casein* [a constituent of milk and the basis of cheese]
kassieren[1] (vt) [bs: to collect money for the *Kasse*, money chest < Ital. *cassa* (Fr. *caisse*, *chasse*) < L. *capsa*, box, case] • **Kasse** (f)	= to cash, collect = money chest; teller's window	words < L. *capsa*, box, case: *1. case; 2. cash* [money kept in a *caisse*, money chest]; *3. cashier*[1]
kassieren[2] (vt) [bs: to empty out as pointless < L. *cassus*, empty, hollow]	= to annul, cancel	*to cashier*[2] [to dismiss with disgrace, discard < LL. *cassare*, to nullify < L. *cassus*, empty]
Kater (m) • **Katze** (f)	= tom cat = cat	*cat*
kauern (vi & refl)	= to squat, crouch down	*cower* [to crouch as from fear]
kaufen (vt) [< OHG. *koufon* (Goth. *kaupon;* AS. *ciepan*); L. *caupo*, shopkeeper, innkeeper] • **Kauf** (m) • **Kaufmann** (m) • **verkaufen** (vt) • **Verkauf** (m) • **Verkäufer(in)** (m, f)	= to buy, purchase = purchase, bargain = merchant, tradesman = to sell = sale = vendor, salesperson	*1. cheap* [< AS. *ceap*, a purchase, bargain]; *2. a chaffer; to chaffer* [a haggling over price; to bargain < *cheap*, a purchase + *fare*, journey]; *3. chapman* [peddler]; *4. Copenhagen* [*Köbenhavn*, 'merchant's port' (haven)]
kaum (adv)	= scarcely	*come-* in *comely* [delicate, but orig.: feeble < AS. *cymblic*, feeble, brittle]

GERMAN WORD	MEANING	ENGLISH COGNATE
Kebse (f) and **Kebsweib** (n) [bs: a woman for one's intimate space or lair < L. *cavea*, cave + *Weib*, woman, female] • **Kebsehe** (f) [< *Kebs* + *Ehe*, marriage] • **Kebskind** (n)	= concubine = concubinage = illegitmate child	*cave* (+ *wife*)
keck (adj) [cf. AS. *cwicu*]	= bold, audacious	*quick* [< AS. *cwicu*, lively, rapid]
Kegel (m) • **kegelig** (adj)	= skittle-pin (bowling), cone = conical	*kegler* [bowler]
Kehle (f) [< OHG. *kela* (cf. AS. *ceolu*); cogn. L. *gula*, throat] • **kehlen** (vt) [bs: to make a throat, channel] • **gekehlt** (adj)	= throat = to channel, flute = fluted	*1. jowl* [the fleshy part hanging under the lower jaw < ME. *cholle* < AS. *ceolu*, throat]; *2. gully* [ravine, channel < L. *gula*, throat]; *3. gullet* [throat, tube leading from the mouth to the stomach]
kehren[1] (vt) [< MHG. *keren* (cf. AS. *cierran*, *cyrran*, to turn) < IE. *ger-*, to twist, turn] • **Kehre** (f) • **bekehren** (vt) ['to turn' one's religion] • **Bekehrter** (m) • **verkehren** (vt) • **Verkehr** (m) • **Verkehrstraße** (f) • **verkehrt** (adj)	= to turn = sharp bend, turn = to convert (religion) = a convert = to convert s.t. to s.t.; run, ply; associate with ('to turn with s.o.') = traffic, transport, communication = thoroughfare = inverted, turned upside down	*1. chore*, also *chare* [a turn, piece of work, household task < AS. *cerr*, *cyrr*, a turn < IE. *ger-*, to twist, turn]; *2. char-* in *charcoal* [wood 'turned' to coal]; *3. -jar* in *ajar* [of a door: 'turned open' < ME. *on charr*, on a turn]
kehren[2] (vt) [etymology obscure; < MHG. *ker(e)n*; OHG. *kerien*] • **Kehricht** (m, n)	= to sweep, brush = sweepings, rubbish	cognates lacking; ? distantly assoc. with *kehren*[1], to turn
Keil (m) [bs: a widening, what makes wide or splits < MHG. *kil*; believed cogn. Goth. *keinan*, to burst open, split < root *kei-*, to burst, split] • **keilen** (vt) • **keilförmig** (adj) • **Keilschrift** (f) • **Keiler** (m) [bs: splitter, gasher] • **einkeilen** (vt)	= wedge, keystone, quoin = to wedge, fasten with wedges = wedge-shaped = cuneiform characters = wild boar = to wedge in, hem in	*kill*[1] [channel, creek, esp. in US. place names, e.g., *Schuylkill River* (Philad.) < Du. *kil*, channel, creek < root *kei-*, to split, burst]
Kelch (m) [< L. *calix* < Gk. *kylix*, cup]	= cup, goblet, chalice	*1. kylix* [an ancient Greek vase type]; *2. chalice* [< L. *calix* < Gk. *kylix*, cup]

GERMAN WORD	MEANING	ENGLISH COGNATE
Kellner(in) (m, f) [< ML. *cellenarius*, overseer of supplies, provisions < L. *cella*, store room]	= waiter, waitress	*cellar* [< L. *cella*, store room]
Kelter (f) [< OHG. *kelketra* < LL. *calctura*, trampling of grapes < *calcare*, to tread with the heel < *calx, calcis*, heel] • **keltern** (vt)	= winepress = to press wine	*1. calcaneum* [heel bone]; *2. recalcitrant* [disobedient, lit.: 'kicking back' < *re + calcitrare*, to kick, tread with the heel]
kennen (vt) [*kannte, gekannt;* < Gmc. *kne(w)-* (cf. AS. *cnawan*)] • **Kenner** (m) • **Kenntnis** (f) • **erkennen** (vt) • **bekannt** (adj) • **bekennen** (vt) • **Bekenntnis** (n) ———— • **kund** (adj) [< old participial form of *kennen*] • **Kunde** (f) • **Sternkunde** (f) • **Kunde** (m) [bs: one who, by frequenting, is known < OHG. *kund* < *kunnan* (G. *kennen*), to know (cf. AS. *cuth*)] • **kundig** (adj) • **kündigen** (vi) ['to make s.t. known'] • **ankünden, verkünden** (vt)	= to know = expert, connoisseur = knowledge = to recognize = familiar = to acknowledge, confess = confession; creed ———— = known = knowledge, science = astronomy = customer, client, patron = knowing, acquainted = to give notice = to announce	*1. know* [< AS. *cnawan*]; ———— *2. uncouth* [orig.: unfamiliar, strange, then awkward or uncultured < *un* + AS. *cuth* < *cunnan*, to know]
kerben (vt) • **kerbig** (adj) • **Kerbe** (f)	= to notch, indent = notched, jagged = notch, nick	*carve*
Kerker (m) [< L. *carcer*, prison]	= prison, jail	*incarcerate*
Kerl (m)	= fellow, chap, guy	*churl* [a rustic, boor] and *churlish*
Kern (m) • **Kernfächer** (n/pl) • **Korn** (n)	= kernel, nucleus, core, grain, pip, pith = basic subjects, core curriculum = corn, grain, seed	*1. kernel; 2. churn* [to remove the 'grain,' curds, out of milk]
Kerze (f) [from the use of paperlike peelings of bark twisted and oiled as wicks < OHG. *karza* < L. *charta*, leaf of papyrus or paper]	= candle	words < L. *charta*, leaf of papyrus or paper < Gk. *chartes*, leaf of papyrus, paper: *1. chart* and *charter; 2. carton* and *card*
Kessel (m)	= kettle, cauldron	*kettle*

GERMAN WORD	MEANING	ENGLISH COGNATE
Kette (f) [< OHG. *chetina* < L. *catena*, chain] • **ketten** (vt) • **Verkettung** (f) • **Bergkette** (f)	= chain = to chain = concatenation = mountain range	*catenary* [the curve made by a flexible chain suspended between two points < L. *catena*, chain]
Ketzer (m) [< Ital. *Gazari*, the Cathars, a heretical sect of Europe of the 11th and 12thc. < Gk. *Katharoi*, 'purified ones' < *katharos*, pure] • **Ketzerei** (f) • **ketzerisch** (adj)	= heretic = heresy = heretical	*1. Cathars* ['purified ones,' a heretical sect of Europe of the 11th and 12thc.]; *2. catharsis* [a doctrine of emotional purgation in dramatic art, lit.: 'cleansing' < Gk. *katharos*, pure, clean]; *3. cathartic* [medicine for purging the bowels]
keuchen (vi)	= to cough	*cough*
Keule (f) [< MHG. *kiule*, possib. var. of *Kegel*, cone]	= club, cudgel, pestle; drumstick, leg (club-shaped parts of meat or poultry)	distantly: *kegler* [bowler; see **Kegel**]
keusch (adj) [bs: aware of morals, values < L. *conscius*, cognizant, sharing knowledge] • **Keuschheit** (f)	= chaste, pure = chastity, purity	*conscious* [< L. *conscius*, cognizant, sharing knowledge < *con*, with + *scire*, to know]
kichern (vi) [< L. *cachinnare*, to laugh loudly]	= to giggle, titter	*to cachinnate* [to laugh loudly < L. *cachinnare*]
kieken (vi)	= to peep, have a look	*to keek* [Scot.: to peep, spy]
Kiel (m) • **Kielfeder** (f)	= quill = quill pen	*quill*
Kiepe (f)	= basket (worn on the back), dosser	*1. kipe* [dial.: basket, esp. for catching fish]; *2. coop* [pen of basketwork for confining poultry]
Kind (n) • **Kindheit** (f)	= child = childhood	*1. kindergarten; 2.* distantly: *a kind* ['of a family,' relation]; *3. kin*
Kinn (n)	= chin	*chin*
kippen (vt & vi) • **kippelig** (adj) • **Kippe** (f) • **Kippwagen** (m)	= to tip over, upset, tilt; lose balance = unstable, tottery = seesaw; (gymn.:) upward circle = tip-car, dump truck	*kip* [gymn: a performer's thrust to change or raise the center of gravity of the body]
Kirche (f) [< L. < Gk. *kyriakos oikos*, lordly house < *kyrios*, lord, master] • **kirchlich** (adj) • **Kirchenstuhl** (m)	= church = ecclesiastical, clerical = pew	*1. church* [< ME. *chirche* < AS. *cirice* < Gk. *kyriakos oikos*, lordly house < *kyrios*, lord, master]; *2. Kyrie eleison* ['Lord Have Mercy,' prayer sung in the Eastern and Western Churches]

GERMAN WORD	MEANING	ENGLISH COGNATE
Kirsche (f) [< LL. *ceresia*, cherries]	= cherry	words < LL. *ceresia*, cherries: *1. cerise* [bright red]; *2. cherry*
Kissen (n) [< OFr. *coissin* < LL. **coxinum*, support for the *coxa*, hip]	= cushion, pillow, pad	*1. cushion* [< OFr. *coissin* < LL. **coxinum*, support for the *coxa*, hip]; *2. coxa* [the hip or hip joint]
Kiste (f) [< L. *cista*, chest] • **Kistler** (m)	= box = maker of chests or trunks	*1. cist; 2. cistern; 3. chest*
Kitt (m) [< OHG. *kuti*] • **kitten** (vt)	= cement, putty, luting = to cement, putty, lute	*1. kit* [a composition of resin, pitch and tallow]; *2.* distantly: *cud*
kitzeln (vt & vi) • **Kitzel** (m) • **kitzelig** (adj)	= to tickle = a tickle = ticklish	*to kittle* [Scot.: to tickle; to puzzle]
Kladde (f) [bs: messy thing, clump; that done loosely; cogn. *Klotz*, block, log]	= rough or first draft; rough notebook, day book	*clut-* in *clutter* [jumble < var. of *clotter* < *clot*, round mass, cogn. G. *Klotz*, block, log]
klaffen (vi) [echoic: 'clap,' to break apart with sharp noise]	= to gape, split open, stand apart, fit loosely	echoic *clap*
klagen (vi) [bs: < IE. **gal-*, to call, shout] • **anklagen** (vt)	= to complain, lament = to accuse, charge	root *c-l-* in words < IE. **gal-*, to call, shout: *1. clatter; 2. call*
klamm (adj) • **klammen** (vt) • **Klammer** (f) • **Klamm** (f) [bs: clamping of terrain] • **ausklammern** (vt) ['to leave out of the fastening'] ──────────── • **klemmen** (vt) • **beklemmen** (vt) • **beklemmend** (adj) • **beklommen** (adj) • **Klempner** (m)	= tight, narrow, scarce, close = to clamp, fasten, brace = clamp, bracket, clasp = gorge, ravine, canyon = to leave out of consideration ──────────── = to jam, squeeze, pinch = to constrict, oppress = constricting = oppressed, anxious, uneasy = plumber, sheet-metal worker	*1. clamp; 2. clam*
(-)**klang** (see **klingen**)		
klappen (vt & vi) [echoic: sound of s.t. shifted] • **Klappe** (f)	= to tip up (or down); to clap, flap; to work out well (cf. Eng. 'to click') = flap, valve, dropleaf	*clap* [echoic]
klatschen (vi) [echoic] • **Klatsch** (m) • **Klatscherei** (f)	= to clap, crack, make sound; applaud; blab, gossip = smack, crack = gossiping, prattle	cf. echoic Eng. *clatter*

GERMAN WORD	MEANING	ENGLISH COGNATE
klauben (vt & vi) [bs: to separate, go through with fingertips, nails, or teeth, cogn. obs. *klieben*, to split, separate]	= to pick, cull, sort, gather	distantly: *1. to cleave²* [to split]; *2. cleaver;*
• **Kluft** (f) • (see also **Knoblauch**)	= crack, crevice, cleft, ravine, gorge	*3. cleft; 4. cloven*
Klaue (f)	= claw	*claw*
Klause (f) [< L. *clausus*, enclosure, past p. of *claudere*, to close]	= hermitage, cell	*1. cloister; 2. close; 3. clause* [a self-contained group of words]
kleben (vt & vi) • **klebend** (adj) • **klebrig** (adj) • **Klebstoff** (m)	= to glue, paste; adhere = adhesive = sticky, adhesive = glue, paste	*to cleave¹ to* [to adhere, cling; be faithful to]
Klee (m)	= clover	*clo-* in *clover*
Kleid (n) • **kleiden** (vt & refl) • **Kleidung** (f) • **ankleiden** (vt & refl) • **entkleiden** (vt & refl)	= garment, gown = to clothe = clothing = to dress = to undress	*1. cloth; 2. clothing; 3. clad, unclad*
klein (adj) [orig.: clean, then small (cf. AS. *claene*, pure)] • **Kleinheit** (f) • **verkleinern** (vt)	= small = smallness = to make smaller, reduce	*clean* [preserves original sense 'pure,' whereas G. cogn. *klein* shifted to mean 'small']
• **Kleinod** (n) [bs: delicate treasure; + suffix *-od* (variants *-at, -ut, -öde*), wealth, treasure (cf. AS. *ead*)]	= jewel, gem; (fig.:) treasure	+ *Ed-* in names *Edwin, Edmond, Edith* [< AS. *ead*, riches, prosperity]; also *-ud* in *feudal* [< ML. *feodum*, use of land in exchange for service < OHG. *fihu*, cattle + *od*, wealth]
Kleister (m) [bs: sticky < Gmc. **glei-*, to stick] • **kleistern** (vt) • **kleisterig** (adj)	= paste = to paste, size = sticky, pasty	*1. clay* [sticky substance < Gmc. **glei-*, to stick]; *2.* distantly: *glue*
• **Kleie** (f)	= bran	
klemmen (see **klammen**)		
Klette (f) [bs: what clings, hangs on < Gmc. root **glei-*, to stick] • **(er)klettern** (vi) ['to hang on firmly as a *Klette*'] • **Kletterei** (f)	= prickly burr, burdock = to climb, scale (up) = climbing	*1. clote* [the burdock, a prickly burr that clings]; *2.* distantly: *clay* [what sticks together < Gmc. **glei-*, to stick]

GERMAN WORD	MEANING	ENGLISH COGNATE
klimmen, (er)klimmen (vi)	= to climb	*climb, clamber*
klingen (vi) [echoic: sound of striking metal] • **verklingen** (vi) • **Klinge** (f) • **Anklang** (m) • **Einklang** (m)	= to ring, chime, sound, clink = (of sounds:) to fade away or die = blade (of knife, sword) = undertone, suggestion, approval = harmony, unison	*clink, clang* [echoic]
Klinke (f)	= latch, door handle	*clench*
Klippe (f)	= cliff, crag, reef	*cliff*
Klopf (m) • **klopfen** (vt & vi)	= blow, knock, clap = to beat, knock; throb	*clap*
Klöppel (m) [bs: small club < *Klöpfel*, knocker] • **klöppeln** (vt & vi) ['to work a bobbin']	= bobbin = to make lace	*clapper* [clublike form inside a bell]
Klotz (m) [cf. AS. *clott*] • **klotzig** (adj)	= block, log = in chunks, coarse, enormous	*1. clot* [< AS. *clott*, round mass]; *2. clod* [a lump, esp. of earth]; *3. cloud* [orig.: a mass of anything, then a mass of vapor in the sky]
Kluft (see **klauben**)		
klug (adj) [etym. uncert.; believed bs: sharp, to the point < Gmc. **klokk-;* ? ult. < IE. **glogh-*, thorn, point, whence Gk. *glossa*, tongue] • **Klugheit** (f) • **altklug** (adj)	= clever, prudent, shrewd = cleverness, good sense = precocious	? distantly: *glo-* in *glossary* [< Gk. *glossa*, tongue < IE. **glogh-*, thorn, point]
knabbern (vt & vi)	= to nibble, gnaw	*knap-* in *knapsack* [a sack to hold 'pinches,' small amounts]
Knabe (m) [bs: short stick, 'little one' < Gmc. *knab-*, short stick, peg] • **Knappe** (m) _____ • **Knebel** (m) [bs: an obstructing bar or stick] • **knebeln** (vt) [bs: to apply a bar or obstruction]	= boy, lad, younster = page, esquire _____ = crossbar, toggle; muzzle, gag = to muzzle, gag	*knave* [orig.: young boy < Gmc. *knab-*, short stick, peg]
Knall (m) [bs: any sudden sound; a report] • **knallen** (vi)	= clap; report = to crack, clap; give a report	*knell* [meaning limited to sound of a bell]
knapp (see **kneifen**)		
Knappe (see **Knabe**)		

GERMAN WORD	MEANING	ENGLISH COGNATE
Knäuel (m & n) [< MHG. *kniuwel*, dissimilated from OHG. *chliwelin, kliuwa* (cf. Du. *kluwen*)]	= skein, coil, ball of thread; (fig.:) tangle, snarl, throng	*1. clew (of yarn)* [ball of thread]; *2. clue* [a fact leading to discovery, from legend of Ariadne's thread leading out of a maze < *clew (of yarn)*]
Knebel (see **Knabe**)		
Knecht (m) [meaning has degenerated from a man originally of high station, to one in a lower station]	= farm laborer, servant, slave	*knight*
• **knechten** (vt)	= to enslave, tyrannize	
• **knechtisch** (adj)	= slavish, servile	
• **Knechtschaft** (f)	= slavery, servitude	
kneifen (vt & vi)	= to pinch, nip	*1. knife* [what pinches, cuts];
• **Kniff** (m)	= a pinch, fold, crease; trick; ruse (from cardsharps marking cards by a *Kniff*, crease)	
• **kniffen** (vt) [bs: to make a *Kniff*, crease]	= to fold down, crease	
• **kniffelig** (adj)	= tricky, puzzling	
• **knapp** (adj) [bs: pinching, tight]	= close-fitting, tight, scant, concise	*2. knapsack* [a sack to hold 'pinches,' small amounts]
• **knapp** (adv)	= barely, just (within)	
• **knappen** (vt & vi)	= to pinch off, nibble; be stingy	
Kneipe (f) [bs: a tight drinking space, var. of G. *kneifen*, to pinch, squeeze]	= public house, pub, tavern	*1.* distantly: *knife; 2. knapsack* [sack to hold 'pinches,' small amounts]
• **kneipen** (vi)	= to booze, carouse	
kneten (vt)	= to knead	*knead*
Knie (n)	= knee	*knee*
Kniff (see **kneifen**)		
knobeln (see **Knochen**)		
Knoblauch (m) ['cloven leek,' plant having a cloven bulb < dissimil. of MHG. *Klobe-louch*, OHG. *klovolouch* < obs. *klieben*, to cleave[2], split + *Lauch*, leek] • (see also **klauben**)	= garlic	*cloven (cleave) + leek*

GERMAN WORD	MEANING	ENGLISH COGNATE
Knochen (m) • **knochig** (adj) • **verknöchern** (vt & vi) • **Knöchel** (m) _____ • **knobeln** (vi) [< MHG. *knobel, knovel*, var. of *Knöchel*, knuckle < ancient game of chance using knucklebones as dice]	= bone = bony = to ossify = knuckle, ankle _____ = to throw dice; (fig.:) puzzle over	*knuckle*
Knolle (f) • **knollig** (adj)	= bulb, tuber = bulbous, tuberous	*knoll* [a hillock or mound]
Knopf (m) • **knöpfen** (vt) _____ • **knüpfen** (vt) • **anknüpfen** (vt & vi) _____ • **Knospe** (f) ['little button' < metathesis of MHG. *knofse, *knobze] • **knospen** (vi)	= button = to button _____ = to tie, knot, fasten = to tie, fasten; enter in, begin _____ = bud = to bud	*knob*
Knute (f) • **knuten** (vt)	= lash, whip, knout = to lash with a knout	*knout* [a whip]
Kobold (m)	= imp, gremlin, sprite	*goblin*
kochen (vt & vi) • **Kuchen** (m) • **Küche** (f) • **Küchenschrank** (m)	= to cook = cake, pastry = kitchen; cuisine, cookery = kitchen cabinet	*cook*
Köder (m) [< OHG. *querdar* < **kwer-thra* < IE. **gwere-*, to swallow, devour, whence L. *vorare*, to swallow up] • **ködern** (vt)	= bait, lure; enticement = to bait, lure; decoy	distantly: *vor-* in *voracious* [< L. *vorare*, to swallow up < IE. **gwere-*, to swallow, devour]
Kohl (m)	= cabbage; (fig.:) rubbish	*cole (slaw)*
Kohle (f)	= coal	*coal*
Kolben (m) [bs: a shaft large at one end]	= club, mallet; piston; flask, retort; rifle butt	*club*

GERMAN WORD	MEANING	ENGLISH COGNATE
kommen (vi)	= to come, arrive; happen	*come*
• **ankommen** (vi)	= to arrive, get to	
• **bekommen** (vt)	= to get, receive, obtain	
• **herkommen** (vi)	= to approach; be derived from	
• **herkommlich** (adj)	= traditional, conventional	
[bs: comming here from the past]		
• **vorkommen** (vi)	= to occur, be found [*occur* < L. *ob*,	
[bs: to come before one]	before + *currere*, to run]	
• **zuvorkommen** (vi)	= to prevent, anticipate	
• **zuvorkommend** (adj)	= obliging, polite, courteous	
[bs: anticipating against insult]		
• **Zuvorkommenheit** (f)	= politeness, courtesy	
• **künftig** (adj)	= future, to come	
[bs: what will come]		
• **Einkünfte** (f)	= income, revenue	
• **Herkunft** (f)	= descent, origin	
[< *herkommen*]		
• **Zukunft** (f)	= future, time to come	
Konjunktur (f)	= economic trend; boom; slump	*conjuncture* [a combination, esp. of events or circumstances]
[astrol.: 'conjuncture of conditions']		
Konkurrenz (f)	= competition	*concours* [a final competition in an art class in some American schools < Fr. *concours*, competitive test, a run against others < L. *con*, with + *curro*, -*ere*, *cursum*, to run]
[< Fr. *concours*, competitive test, a running against < L. *concurro*, -*ere*, *cursum* < *con*, with + *curro*, I run]		
• **konkurrieren** (vi)	= to compete	
Kontor (m)	= office	*1. counter; 2. compute*
[bs: where counting is done < Fr. *comptoir*, counter, bank, bar < L. *computare*, to reckon]		
• **Kontorist** (m)	= clerk	
Kopf (m)	= head	*cup*
[< L. *cupa*, vat, cup (cf. L. *testa*, earthenware pot, whence Ital. *testa*, head, and Fr. *tête*, head)]		
• **köpfen** (vt)	= to behead, decapitate	
Koppel (f)	= couple, coupling; pair of dogs (in hunting)	*1. copula* [something that links things together]; *2. couple*
[< L. *copula*, fastening, connection]		
• **(ver)koppeln** (vt)	= to couple, join	
Korb (m)	= basket, hamper, crate	*corbeil* [a sculptured basket of fruit, flowers, used as architectural ornament < Fr. *corbeille*]
[< L. *corbis*, wicker basket; dim. *corbicula*, whence Fr. *corbeille*]		
kosen (vt & vi)	= to fondle, caress	*1. cozy* [< Nor. *kose sig* (= G. *kose sich*), make oneself comfortable, lit.: 'caress oneself']; *2. to coze* [to have a friendly chat < Fr. *causer*, to chat]
[orig.: to talk, esp. of amorous things < OHG. *koson*, to treat, appeal, chat < *kosa*, talk < L. *causa*, legal case, pretext, whence L. *causari* > Fr. *causer*, to talk of small things, chat]		
• **liebkosen** (vi)	= to fondle, caress	

GERMAN WORD	MEANING	ENGLISH COGNATE
kosten (vt) [< L. *gustare*, to taste]	= to taste, sip, sample	*1. gustatory; 2. gusto*
Krabbe (f) • **krabbeln** (vi)	= crab = to move like a crab, crawl	*crab*
krachen (vi) • **Krach** (m)	= to crash, smash, crash, crack; quarrel = crash, racket	*crash, crack*
Kraft (f) • **kraftvoll, kräftig** (adj) • **kräftigen** (vt & vi) • **kraft** (prep) + *gen.*	= strength, vigor = strength, powerful = to strengthen = by power of	*craft* [skill as strength]
Kragen (m) [orig.: the neck or throat, then apparel around the neck (cf. Du. *kraag;* AS. **craga*)]	= collar; neck of a bottle	*craw* [of a bird: a sacklike enlargement in the gullet in which food is softened for digestion; also, the stomach of any animal < AS. **craga;* cogn. Du. *kraag,* neck]
Krähe (f)	= crow	*crow*
Kralle (f) [bs: something curved, twisted, curled < IE. **ger-,* to twist, turn]	= talon, claw; clutch	*c-r-l-* in words meaning curved, twisted < IE. **ger-* + suffix *-l:* *1. cruller* [a small twisted pastry < Du. *krullen,* to curl]; *2. curl*
Kram (m) [orig.: the covering over a booth selling small wares, then the wares themselves; theorized < *(s)kram* < Gmc. *skerm,* cover, shield, whence G. *Schirm,* screen] • **Krämer** (m) • **Kramladen** (m) • **Kramwaren** (f) • **kramen** (vi) • **auskramen** (vt)	= small wares, stuff, retail trade, odds and ends, rubbish = shopkeeper, grocer = small shop, grocer's shop = small wares, groceries = to rumage through = to dig up, trot out	distantly: *-crim* in *scrim* [covering, screen, loosely woven cotton, cogn. G. *Schirm,* screen]
krank (adj) [bs: twisted by illness < IE.**ger-,* to twist, turn] • **Krankheit** (f) • **Kranke** (m, f) • **erkranken** (vi) • **kränklich** (adj) • **kränkeln** (vi)	= ill = sickness, illness = sick person, patient = to fall sick = sickly = to be in poor health	*crank-* in words < IE. **ger-* meaning curved, twisted: *1. crank* [a twisted handle]; *2. crank* [an eccentric]; *3. cranky* [irritable]
Kranz (m) [< IE. **ger-,* to twist, turn]	= wreath, garland	words < IE. **ger-,* to twist, turn: *1. krantz, kranz* [a wall of rock encircling the base of a mountain; any steep wall of rocks < S. Afr. Du.]; *2. crank* [a twisted handle]
kratzen (vt & vi)	= to scratch	*scratch*

GERMAN WORD	MEANING	ENGLISH COGNATE
kraus (adj) [*k-r-* (cf. *kehren*, to turn; *Kralle*, claw) < IE. **ger-*, to twist, turn] • **Krausheit** (f) • **Krause, Kräuse** (f) • **kräuseln** (vt) • **Gekröse** (n)	= curly, frizzy; intricate = curliness, crispiness = frill, ruffle = to curl, crimp, plait, fold = mesentery (intestinal membrane), tripe	words of root *k-r-* < IE. **ger-*, to twist, turn: *1. cri-* in *crinkled* [full of twists]; *2. cri-* in *cripple* [one twisted, turned]; *3. curl* [via MDu.]
Kraut (n) • **krautartig** (adj) • **Unkraut** (n)	= plant, weed, cabbage = herbaceous = weeds	*-kraut* in *sauerkraut* [dish of fermented (sour) cabbage]
Krawall (m) [< ML. *charavallium, chalvaricum* (whence Fr. *charivari, chalivali*), original source obscure]	= riot, brawl, uproar	*charivari*, also *shivaree* [a noisy celebration, esp. a mock serenade for newlyweds made by beating on pans, etc. < Fr. *charivari*]
Kreide (f) [< L. *creta*, chalk, white clay, once thought < *creta*, Crete, as source for mineral chalk, but now held < *terra creta*, sifted earth < *cretum*, past p. of *cernere*, to sift, separate]	= chalk	*1. cretaceous* [having the nature of chalk < L. *creta*, chalk]; *2. crayon* [orig.: a marking tool made of chalk < Fr. *crayon* < *craie*, chalk < L. *creta*]; *3. secrete* [to sift out as fluid < *se* + *cretum* < *cernere*, to sift]
Kreis (m) [a circle scratched on the ground < OHG. *krizzon*, to scratch in < IE. **krat-* (*grat-*), to scratch]	= circle	words < IE. **krat-* (*grat-*), to scratch: *1. grate; 2. scratch*
Krempel (m) [commercial term < *crompare*, metathesis of Ital. *comprare*, to buy < L. *comparare*, to be of equal value]	= rubbish, stuff, things	*comprador* [in China, a native agent for a foreign business < Portug. *comprador*, buyer < L. *comparare*]
Kreuz (n) [< L. *crux, crucis*, cross] • **kreuzen** (vt) • **kreuzigen** (vt) • **Kreuzfahrer** (m)	= cross = to cross, intersect = to crucify = crusader	*1. cross* and *crucify; 2. cruiser* [what travels cross-wise < Du. *kruisen*, to move cross-wise]
kriechen (vi) [< IE. **ger-*, to twist, turn]	= to creep, crawl	*creep* [< AS. *creopan*, to go bent down < IE. **ger-*, curved, twisted]
Krieg (m) [bs: striving, resistance] • **Krieger** (m) • **kriegen** (vt) [bs: to strive and so obtain]	= war, armed conflict = warrior, combatant = to seize, catch, get	*blitzkrieg* [lightening war]
Krippe (f) [bs: what is woven or plaited]	= crib, manger	*crib*
Krone (f) [< L. *corona*, crown]	= crown	*coronation*

GERMAN WORD	MEANING	ENGLISH COGNATE
Kropf (m) • **kröpfen** (vt)	= goiter; excrescence; projecting part (of wall, ledge, etc.) = to cram, gorge (poultry); to make project at right angles (e.g., at top of a wall)	*1. crop* [of a bird: a sacklike enlargement in the gullet in which food is softened for digestion; synonym: *craw*]; *2. to crop out* [to project]
Krücke (f) [< IE. *ger-, to twist, turn]	= crutch	*1. crook; 2. crutch*
Krug (m)	= jug, pitcher, mug	*crock*
krumm (adj) [bs: not straight < IE. *ger-, to twist, turn] • **krümmen** (vt) • **Krümmung** (f)	= curved, crooked, bent, stooping (of stature) = to bend, curve = curvature, bend	*1. crump* [dial.: bent, crooked], *crumpled; 2. krummhorn* [an obsolete curved wind instrument < G., lit.: 'bent horn']; *3. crumpet* [a curled griddle cake]
Kübel (m) [< L. *cupa*, vat]	= bucket, pail; tub	*cup*
Kufe (f) [< L. *cupa*, vat] • **Küfer** (m)	= tub, vat = cooper, barrel maker; cellarman	*1. cup; 2. cooper* [person who makes or repairs barrels]; *3. coop* [area to confine poultry; to confine]
Kugel (f) • **kugelig** (adj) • **kugeln** (vt & vi) ['to go like a ball']	= ball, sphere, bullet, shot = spherical, globular = to make s.t. roll; to roll about	*cudgel* [orig.: a club with a rounded head, then a short, thick club]
Kuh (f)	= cow	*cow*
kühl (adj) • **Kühle** (f) • **abkühlen** (vt & refl)	= cool = coolness = to make cool, refrigerate; cool down	*cool*
kühn (adj) • **Kühnheit** (f) • **erkühnen** (refl)	= bold, audacious = boldness, audacity = to venture, dare to, make bold to	*keen* [orig.: bold, then sharp, acute]
Kulm (m) [< L. *culmen*, peak, top]	= mountain top	*culminate* [to reach the highest point < L. *culmen*, peak, top]
Kummer (m) [< MHG. *kumber*] • **kummervoll** (adj) • **kümmern** (vt) • **kümmern** (refl) (+ **um**) [bs: to accept as a worry] • **kümmerlich** (adj)	= trouble, worry, grief, sorrow = sorrowful = to bother, cause worry = to care for, look after = miserable, pitiable	*1. to cumber* [orig.: to burden in a troublesome way]; *2. cumbersome; 3. to encumber*
kund (see **kennen**)		

GERMAN WORD	MEANING	ENGLISH COGNATE
kunterbunt (adj) [orig.: many-voiced, then confused < ML. *contrapunctum* (music) < L. *contra*, against + *punctum*, pricked, marked by a point] • (see also **bunt**)	= higgedly-piggedly, pell-mell; gaudy	*contrapuntal* and *counterpoint* ['pointed against,' 'opposing notes,' of plainsong having accompaniment < L. *contra*, against + *punctum*, pricked, marked by a point]
Kuppel (f) [< L. *cupola*, dome]	= dome, cupola	*cupola* [< L. *cupola*, dome < *cupa*, vat, cask, drinking cup]
kurz (adj) • **kürzlich** (adv) • **abkürzen** (vt)	= short = recently = to shorten, abbreviate	*curt*
Kuß (m) • **küssen** (vt & vi)	= kiss = to kiss	*kiss*
Küste (f) [< L. *costa*, coast]	= coast, beach, shore	*coast*
Küster (m) [< L. *custos*, guard]	= sacristan, sextan (of a church)	*custodian*
Kutte (f) [< MHG. *kotte* < Frk. **kotta*]	= cowl, monastic cloak	*1. coat* [< Fr. *cotte* < ML. *cotta* < Frk. **kotta*]; *2. cotillion* [a formal ball, previously a kind of dance, named for the skirts (petti*coats*) which women wore]

L		
laben (vt & refl) [bs: to revive with drink < L. *lavare*, to wash, wet] • **labend** (adj) • **Labsal** (n)	= to refresh, restore = refreshing, reviving = refreshment; comfort	*lav-* in words < L. *lavare*, to wash, wet: *1. lavatory*; *2. lave*; *3. launder* [< OFr. < LL. *lavandarius* < *lavare*]; *4. lavender* ['wash scent,' plant used to scent the wash]
Lache (f)	= pool, puddle	*lake*
Lachs (m)	= salmon	*lox* [salmon salted and smoked]
laden[1] (vt) • **Ladung**[1] (f) • **entladen** (vt) • **entladen** (refl) • **Lade** (f) • **Schublade** (f) ['shove box' < *schieben*, to shove]	= to load = cargo, freight, load = to unload = to discharge, go off (of guns) = case, chest, drawer, box = drawer (what one draws, pulls out)	*1. laden* [loaded]; *2. to load*

GERMAN WORD	MEANING	ENGLISH COGNATE
laden[2] (vt) [disputed: theorized from a practice of an official carrying a board (lath) with insignia, to convey a summons < *Lad-*, distantly cogn. *Latte,* lath, strip of wood] • **Ladung**[2] (f) • **einladen** (vt) • **ausladen** (vt)	= to invite; summon, cite = summons, citation = to invite = to cancel invitation to s.o.	disputed: ? *lath* [a narrow strip of wood]
Laden[3] (m) [orig.: board(s) serving as window shutter, also booth or stall; distantly cogn. *Latte,* lath]	= window shutter; shop, stall, store	*lath*
lädieren (vt) [< L. *laedo, laedere, laesum,* to strike, hurt]	= to injure, damage	words < L. *laedo, laedere, laesum,* to strike, hurt: *1.* -*lide* in *collide* [< L. *con,* with + *laedo*]; *2.* *lesion* [wound, injury < L. *laesum*]
Lager (see **liegen**)		
lahm (adj) • **lahmen** (vi) • **lähmen** (vt) • **Lähmung** (f)	= lame = to be lame = to make lame, paralyze = paralysis	*lame*
Laib (m) [cf. Goth. *hlaifs,* bread; AS. *hlaf*]	= loaf (of bread, etc.)	*loaf* [< AS. *hlaf*]
Laich (m) [< OHG. *leih,* play, activity (cf. Goth. *laik,* dance; AS. *lac,* play, activity) < Gmc. **laik-* < IE. **leig-,* to leap, tremble, be active] • **laichen** (vi) • **Laichen** (n) • **Laichzeit** (f)	= spawn = to spawn = spawning = spawning time	*1.* -*lock* in *wedlock* [< *wed* + AS. -*lac,* suffix denoting activity, play < IE. **leig-,* to leap, tremble, be active]; *2.* *lark* [frolic < ON. *leika* (with intrusive *r*), to play]; *3.* *to lake* [dial.: to leap, play, sport]; *4.* *to lek* [of grouse: to gather]
Lakai (m) [< Fr. *laquais* < Sp. *lacayo,* servant]	= male servant of low rank, footman	*lackey* [< Fr. *laquais* < Sp. *lacayo,* servant]
Laken (n) [etym. disputed, believed 'loose,' 'drooped' < IE. **(s)leg-,* languid]	= sheet, bedcloth	distantly: words < IE. **(s)leg-,* to be languid, loose: *1.* *slack;* *2.* *lax;* *3.* *lake* [obs.: fine linen]
Lamm (n)	= lamb	*lamb*
Land (n) • **Ausland** (n) • **Ausländer** (m) • **landläufig** (adj)	= land, country = foreign country = foreigner = customary, current, widely known	*land*

GERMAN WORD	MEANING	ENGLISH COGNATE
lang (adj)	= long, tall	*long*
• **Länge** (f)	= length	
• **langen** (vi)	= to suffice, reach	
• **verlängern** (vt)	= to lengthen, prolong, extend	
• **anlangen** (vi)	= to reach the goal, arrive	
• **langsam** (adv)	= slow	
• **länglich** (adj)	= oblong	
• **hinlänglich** (adj)	= long enough, sufficient	
• **zulangen** (vt)	= to help o.s. (at table)	
[bs: to make a long reach to]		
• **unzulänglich** (adj)	= insufficient	
————————————	————————————	————————————
• **verlangen** (vt)	= to long for, demand, require	*to long for*
Lappen (m)	= rag	*l. lap* [orig.: a garment's loose part < AS. *laeppa*]; *2. lapel; 3. label*
[< OHG. *lappa* (cf. AS. *laeppa*)]		
läppern (vt & vi)	= to lap, sip	*to lap*
Lärm (m)	= noise	*alarm*
[< Ital. *allarme*, a call to arms]		
• **lärmen** (vi)	= to make noise	
• **lärmend** (adj)	= noisy	
lassen (vt & vi)	= to let, permit; leave, abandon	*1. to let* [< AS. *laetan*];
[< OHG. *lazzan* (cf. AS. *laetan*)]		
————————————	————————————	————————————
• **lässig** (adj)	= lazy, indolent, slack, careless	*2. lazy*
• **Lässigkeit** (f)	= laziness, indolence, carelessness	
• **anlassen** (vt)	= to set going, leave on (a garment]	
• **Anlaß** (m)	= motive (setting in motion), occasion	
['a letting on,' a starting]		
• **anläßlich** (adj)	= occasionally	
• **anläßlich** (prep) + *gen.*	= on the occasion of	
• **veranlassen** (vt)	= to cause, occasion	
• **entlassen** (vt)	= to dismiss, discharge	
['to let away']		
• **Entlassung** (f)	= dismissal, discharge	
• **Erlaß** (m)	= decree, proclamation	
• **erlassen** (vt)	= to promulgate, issue	
• **Nachlaß** (m)	= reduction, inheritance	
• **nachlassen** (vt & vi)	= to reduce, leave behind; abate, slacken	
['to let behind']		
• **nachlässig** (adj)	= negligent, careless	
• **verlassen** (vt)	= to quit, leave, abandon	
• **verlassen** (refl) (+ **auf**)	= to rely on	
['to abandon (let) o.s. to']		
• **Verlaß** (m)	= reliance	
• **verläßlich** (adj)	= reliable	
• **Zuverlässigkeit** (f)	= reliability, certainty	
• **unzuverlässig** (adj)	= unreliable	
• **zulassen** (vt)	= to admit, allow	
['to let to']		

GERMAN WORD	MEANING	ENGLISH COGNATE
Last (f)	= load, burden, weight	*1. -last* in *ballast* [anything heavy carried in a ship to give stability]; *2. last* [a large measure of weight]
• **lasten (auf)** (vi)	= to weigh on, press upon	
• **belasten** (vt)	= to load, burden; incriminate	
• **Belastung** (f)	= burden, debt; incrimination	
• **unbelastet** (adj)	= unencumbered, carefree	
• **vorbelastet** (adj)	= handicapped	
['preloaded,' esp. with difficulty]		
• **lästig** (adj)	= annoying, inconvenient	
[bs: burdensome]		
• **belästigen** (vt)	= to annoy, molest [< L. *molestare*, to be a burden to < *moles*, burden]	
[bs: to be burdensome to]		
• **Belästigung** (f)	= annoyance, nuisance	
• **entlasten** (vt)	= to unburden, ease; to free of charges, exonerate [< L. *ex* + *onus, -eris*, burden]	
• **Entlastung** (f)	= discharge, relief; exoneration	
Laster (n)	= vice, depravity	*1.* distantly: *locust* [< L. *locusta* < IE. **lêk-*, to leap, fly]; *2. lobster* [altered < L. *locusta*, a marine shellfish capable of leaps]
[bs: offense, aggressive leap < OHG. *lastar* < *lahan*, to rebuke < base **lah-* believed < IE. **lêk-*, to leap, fly (whence L. *locusta*, a marine shellfish)]		
• **lasterhaft** (adj)	= vicious, depraved	
• **lästern** (vt)	= to slander, revile, blaspheme	
• **Lästerer** (m)	= slanderer, blasphemer	
Laterne (f)	= lantern, street lamp	*1. lantern; 2. lamp*
[< L. *laterna, lanterna* < Gk. *lampter*, light, torch]		
Latte (f)	= paling, lath	*1. lattice; 2. lath*
Lattich (m)	= lettuce	*1. lettuce; 2. lactic* [< L. *lac, lactis*, milk]
[ult. < L. *lactuca*, lettuce, named because of the milky juice of its leaves < *lac, lactis*, milk]		
lau (adj)	= tepid; (fig.:) indifferent	distantly: *lu-* in *lukewarm*
• **Lauheit** (f)	= lukewarmness; indifference	
Laub (n)	= foliage, leafage	*leaf*
• **laubig, laubreich** (adj)	= leafy	
• **entlauben** (vi)	= to shed leaves	
Laube (f)	= arbor, portico	*1. lobby* [< ML. *lobium* < OHG. *laubja*, sheltered place]; *2. lodge*
[< OHG. *laubja*]		

GERMAN WORD	MEANING	ENGLISH COGNATE
laufen (vi)	= to run	*1. elope* [< ME. *alopen*, to run away]; *2. to lope*; *3. -lop* in *gallop*; *4. loafer* [bs: a person 'on the run,' vagabond, not working]
• **Lauf** (m)	= course, run, race, pace	
• **Laufbahn** (f)	= career	
• **ablaufen** (vi)	= to run off, drain, expire	
• **entlaufen** (vi)	= to run away, escape	
• **umlaufen** (vi)	= to circulate	
• **Umlauf** (m),	= circulation	
• **geläufig** (adj)	= current [lit.: 'running' < L. *currere*, to run, flow]	
[bs: running, on a run]		
• **gegenläufig** (adj)	= going countercurrent	
• **rückläufig** (adj)	= retrograde; recurrent	
• **vorläufig** (adj)	= preliminary, preparatory, tempo-rary	
['what runs before']		
Laune (f)	= mood, temper, caprice	*1. lunatic; 2. loony*
[< belief in moon's influence upon people < L. *luna*, moon]		
• **launig** (adj)	= humorous, whimsical	
• **launisch** (adj)	= moody, wayward	
Laus (f)	= louse	*louse*
lauschen (vi)	= to listen, strain one's ears	*listen* [< AS. *hlystan* < *hlyst*, hear-ing < IE. *kleu-*, to hear]
[< OHG. *(h)losen* < Gmc. **hlus-ti*, to hear (cf. AS. *hlyst*, hearing) < IE. **kleu-*, to hear]		
• **belauschen** (vt)	= to overhear, eavesdrop on	
laut (adj)	= loud, noisy	*loud*
• **lauten** (vi)	= to sound, read (as)	
• **läuten** (vt & vi)	= to ring, toll (of a bell)	
• **laut** (prep) + *gen.*	= according to, in accordance with	
lauter (adj)	= pure, clear, genuine	*1.* distantly: *cloaca* [sewer, privy, waste cavity in birds and fishes < L. *cluere*, to wash]; *2. clys-* in *cata-clysm* [deluge, cataclysm, lit.: 'a washing down,' < Gk. *kata*, down + *klyzo*, to wash < IE. **kleu-*, to wash, clean]; *3. clyster* [enema, what washes < Gk. *clyzo*, to wash]
[bs: cleansed; suffixed form (*-ter*) < IE. **kleu-*, to wash, clean (whence L. *cluere*, to wash > *cloaca*, sewer, canal; also Gk. *klyzo*, to wash > *cataclysmos*, deluge, cataclysm)]		
• **läutern** (vt)	= to purify, refine	
• **erläutern** (vt)	= to explain	
[bs: to refine in words]		
Lawine (f)	= avalanche	words < L. *labi, lapsus*, to slip: *1. labile* [subject to change, unsta-ble]; *2. avalanche* [metathesis of LL. *labina*, earth slippage]; *3. lapse* [a slip, fall, failure]; *4. collapse*
[< OItal. *lavina* < LL. *labina*, earth slippage (whence by metathesis Fr. *avalanche*) < L. *labi, lapsus*, to slip]		

GERMAN WORD	MEANING	ENGLISH COGNATE
leben (vi) • **lebendig** (adj) • **lebhaft** (adj) • **beleben** (vt) • **erleben** (vt) • **überleben** (vt) • **verleben** (vt) [bs: to live through]	= to live, reside = living = animated, vivacious = to enliven, animate, vivify = to experience = to survive, outlive = to spend, pass (time)	*1. to live;*
• **Leib** (m) • **leiblich** (adj) • **Leibwache** (f) • **Unterleib** (m)	= body; abdomen, stomach = bodily, corporeal = bodyguard = abdomen, belly	*2. life*
Leber (f) • **Leberfleck** (m)	= liver = mole	*liver*
lechzen (see **leck**)		
leck (adj) • **Leck** (n) • **lecken**[1] (vi) • **lechzen** (vi) [bs: leaked dry, parched < MHG. *lechezen*]	= leaky, leaking = leak(age) = to be leaking, run = to languish, long or yearn for s.t.	*leak*
lecken[2] (vt) • **lecker** (adj) • **leckerhaft** (adj) • **Leckerei** (f)	= to lick = tasty, savory, delicious; fastidious = fastidious = fastidiousness, daintiness; tidbit	*lick*
Leder (n) • **ledern** (adj)	= leather = of leather, leathery	*leather*
ledig (adj) [< MHG. *ledic*, free, sole] • **lediglich** (adv) • **erledigen** (vt) [bs: to thoroughly (*er*-) make free] • **entledigen** (refl) [*ent*, away + *ledig*]	= single, unmarried, exempt; (of offspring:) illegitimate = solely, merely = to free up, settle, dispatch = to rid (free) o.s. of s.t.	*liege* in *liege lord, liege man* [of disposable (free) service: *liege lord*, in medieval times, a lord choosen independently, freely, by a vassal < ME. *leyge* < OFr. *lige* < MHG. *ledic*, free]
leer (adj) • **Leere** (f) • **leeren** (vt) • **entleeren** (vt) • **leerstehend** (adj)	= empty, vacant, void, vain, blank = emptiness, vacuum, void = to empty, clear out = to empty = (dwelling:) vacant, unoccupied	*leer, leare* [arch.: empty, clear; (of a horse:) without a burden]

GERMAN WORD	MEANING	ENGLISH COGNATE
legen (vt)	= to put, place	*lay*
• **gelegen** (adj)	= well situated, opportune	
• **Gelegenheit** (f)	= opportunity	
• **gelegentlich** (prep) + *gen.*	= on the occasion of	
• **Beleg** (m)	= proof, evidence, documentation	
• **belegen** (vt)	= to prove, verify, document	
• **belegbar** (adj)	= provable, verifiable	
• **Ausleger** (m)	= cantilever; derrick, crane; expositor, commentator	
• **überlegen** (vt & vi) ['to put one's thought over s.t.']	= to think about, consider	
• **verlegen** (vt)	= to remove to another place; supply with (goods, money); mislay; bar	
• **Belag** (m)	= coating, covering, surface	
• **Gelage** (n) [bs: to lay down (food) < *ge* + *legen;* cf. colloq. 'a spread,' a meal with a variety of food]	= feast, drinking bout [cf. same sense in *mess, mess hall* < OFr. *mets,* courses placed on a table, past p. of *mettre,* to place]	
• **Verlag** (m)	= funds, capital (for an undertaking), place of publishing	
• **Verlager** (m)	= publisher	
• **verlegen** (adj) ['put in a bad spot']	= damaged by lying, spoiled; embarrassed	
• **Verlegenheit** (f)	= embarrassment	
• (see also **liegen**)		
legieren (vt) [< L. *ligare,* to bind, whence Ital. *legare,* to bind; Fr. *allier,* to bind, alloy]	= to bind (esp. metals), to alloy	*1. ligament* and *ligature* [< L. *ligare,* to bind]; *2. alloy, ally* and *alliance* [< Fr. *allier,* to bind, ult. < L. *ligare,* to bind]
• **Legierung** (f)	= alloy	
Lehm (m)	= loam, mud	*loam* [rich soil composed of clay, sand and organic matter]
lehnen (vt & vi)	= to make lean, prop; to lean	*to lean*
• **Lehne** (f)	= support, back or arm (of chair)	
• **anlehnen** (refl)	= to lean against	
lehren (vt)	= to teach, instruct	*lore, learn* [orig.: course of study as a track < IE. **leis,* track, furrow; *l-s* > var. of *l-r*]
• **Lehrer** (m)	= teacher, instructor	
• **Lehre** (f)	= doctrine, precept, moral	
• **gelehrsam, gelehrt** (adj)	= scholarly	
• **Gelehrte** (m)	= scholar	
• **lernen** (vt & vi)	= to learn	
Leib (see **leben**)		

GERMAN WORD	MEANING	ENGLISH COGNATE
Leiche (f), **Leichnam** (m) [< OHG. *lih*, body (cf. Goth. *lika*; AS. *lic*, body), whence G. suffix *-lich*, 'having the body of,' 'having the shape or nature of,' corresp. to Eng. suffix *-ly*]	= corpse	*1. lich* [Scot. and dial.: a corpse < AS. *lic*, body]; *2. lich gate* [a roofed gate at the entrance of a churchyard, where a coffin can be put down to await arrival of the clergyman];
• **Leichentuch** (n)	= shroud	
• **Leichenwagen** (m)	= hearse	
• **gleich** (adj) [bs: of same body < OHG. *gilih* < *ge* + *lih*, body]	= equal, like, same	*3. like* [similar, equal, lit.: 'of same body' < AS. *gelic* (= G. *gleich* < OHG. *gilih*)]; *4.* adverbial suffix *-ly* [having the shape, nature, 'body' of < AS. *-lic*]
• **gleichen** (vi)	= to be equal to, be comparable	
• **Gleichheit** (f)	= equality, parity; sameness, likeness	
• **Gleisner(in)** (m, f) [bs: one who 'acts like,' feigns < MHG. *gelichsenaere* < OHG. *gilih-hison* < *gilih*, like]	= hypocrite	
• **ähnlich** (adj) [bs: of close appearance < OHG. *analih*, of like form < *an*, on, near + OHG. *lih*, body]	= like, similar to	*on + like*
• **Ähnlichkeit** (f)	= likeness, resemblance	
• **ähneln** (vi) [< older *ähnlichen*]	= to look like, resemble	
leicht (adj)	= easy, light, slight	*light*
• **erleichtern** (vt)	= to facilitate	
Leid (n) [bs: suffering < OHG. *leid* (cf. AS. *lath*), whence Fr. *laid*, ugly; Ital. *laido*, ugly]	= injury, harm; grief (G. root *leid-* is used much as L. root *pass-* in *passus*, past p. of *pati*, to suffer)	*loath* [unwilling (e.g., 'to be *loath* to travel') < AS. *lath*, hateful, disagreeable]
• **leid tun**	= to cause (do) sorrow to	
• **leider** (adv)	= unfortunately	
• **leiden** (vi)	= to suffer	
• **leidlich** (adj)	= tolerable, sufferable	
• **Leiden** (n)	= suffering	
• **Leidenschaft** (f)	= passion	
• **leidenschaftlich** (adj)	= passionate	
• **beleidigen** (vt)	= to offend, insult	
• **mitleidig** (adj)	= compassionate	
• **Beileid** (n)	= condolence	
leihen (vt) (+ von) [< OHG. *lihan* (cf. AS. *laenan*)]	= to lend out, loan; borrow	*1. le(n)-* in *lend* [< ME. *lenen*, with unhistoric *d*]; *2. loan*
• **beleihen** (vt)	= to grant a loan on	
• **Anleihe** (f)	= loan, advance	
• **verleihen** (vt)	= to lend or bestow	
Leim (m) [bs: wet and binding]	= glue	*lime* [substance used in making mortar for binding bricks]
• **leimen** (vt)	= to glue, size	

GERMAN WORD	MEANING	ENGLISH COGNATE
leise (adj) [< OHG. *liso* (whence Ital. *liscio*, smooth, gentle) < IE. **leie-*, to waste away > Gk. *limos*, famine]	= (of sound:) low, faint, gentle	*li-* in *bulimia* [a continuous, wasting hunger < Gk. *bous*, ox + *limos*, famine, hunger < IE. **leie-*, to waste away]
Leiste (f) [cf. AS. *liste*]	= border, strip	*list* [a narrow strip of cloth or wood, also a series of names whose order forms a strip < AS. *liste*, hem, border]
leisten (vt) [bs: to stay on the track < Gmc. **lais-*, to know, have skill < IE. **leis*, track, furrow; *l-s* > var. of *l-r*]	= to perform, do, fulfill, afford (a cost)	*1. to last; 2. a last* [shoemaker's form; bs: footstep < IE. **leis*, track]; *3. lore, learn* [course of study as a track]
• **List** (f) [bs: careful track < Goth. *lists* < Gmc. **lais-*, to know, have skill]	= cunning, craft, artifice, ruse, trick	
• **listig** (adj)	= cunning, crafty, sly	
• **Gleis** (n)	= track (railway)	
leiten (vt) • **Leiter**[1] (m) • **Leitspruch** (m)	= to lead, guide, conduct = leader, conductor, head, manager = motto	*to lead*
• **begleiten** (vt) [conflated < two MHG. forms: *beleiten*, and *geleiten* < *leiten*]	= to accompany	
Leiter[2] (f)	= ladder	*ladder*
Lend (f) • **Lendentuch** (n)	= loin = loincloth	*lends* [the loins; also buttocks]
lenken (vt & vi) [< OHG. *hlank-*, bend] • **Lenkung** (f) • **Lenker** (m) • **ablenken** (vt) • **Gelenk** (n) • **gelenkig** (adj) • **ungelenk** (adj)	= to direct, conduct, guide; turn, bend, steer = guidance, control = ruler, governor = to turn away, divert, deflect = joint, articulation; hinge, link = flexible, supple = stiff, clumsy	*1. link* [a section that allows bending]; *2. flinch* [< OFr. *flenchir*, to bend aside < Gmc. *hlank-*, bend]
lernen (see **lehren**)		
Lettner (m) [< ML. *lectionarium*, liturgical book of readings, hence the place in a church where readings were delivered < L. *lectus*, past p. of *legere*, to read]	= rood screen separating the choir (sanctuary area) from nave in a church	*1. lectionary* [liturgical book of readings]; *2. lectern* [a stand from which a reading or speech is delivered < L. *lectus*, past p. of *legere*, to read]

GERMAN WORD	MEANING	ENGLISH COGNATE
letzt (adj) [< obs. *laß*, weary, slack < MHG. *laz*, tardy (Goth. *lats*, slow, weary)] • **verletzen** (vt) ['to render weary, slow, late' < *ver* + MHG. *letzan*, to injure < *laz*, tardy] • **Verletzung** (f) • **verletzend** (adj) • **verletzbar, verletzlich** (adj)	= last, final, extreme = to injure, harm, hurt; to offend (hurt mentally) = injury, hurt, violation = offensive, cutting = vulnerable, violable	*late, last*
Leuchte (see **licht**)		
leugnen (vt) [< OHG. *laugna*, secret; cogn. G. *lügen*, to lie] • **unleugbar** (adj) • **verleugnen** (vt)	= to deny, contest = undeniable = to renounce, disown	distantly: *to lie*
Leumund (m) [< Gmc. *hleumon*, hearing < IE. *kleu-*, to hear] • **verleumden** (vt)	= reputation, repute, character = to slander, defame	*loud* [< AS. *hlud* < IE. *kleu-*, to hear]
Leute (pl.) [bs: growth, a populus < OHG. *liuti* < IE. *leudh-*, to mount up, grow] ——————— • **Lode** (f) [bs: growth, release < Goth. *liudan* < IE. *leudh-*, to mount up, grow] • **lodern** (vi) [bs: to grow, release, esp. as flame]	= people, persons, servants, hands ——————— = young shoot, sprig, sapling = to flare, blaze freely	*1. Leo-* (orig. *Liut-*) in name *Leopold* ['the people's bold one' < *Liutpold* < *Liutbalt* < *liut*, people, free men + *balt*, bold, strong]; *2.* distantly: *li-* in *liberate* and *liberty* [< L. < IE. *leudh-*, to mount up, grow, find release]
licht (adj) • **Licht** (n) • **Lichtung** (f) • **belichten** (vt) ——————— • **Leuchte** (f) • **leuchten** (vi) • **beleuchten** (vt) • **erleuchten** (vt)	= light, bright, shining = light, candle = clearing = to expose, bring to light ——————— = light, lamp = to give off light, shine = to throw light on = to illuminate, enlighten	*light*
Lid (n)	= eyelid	*lid*
lieb (adj) [cf. AS. *leof*] • **Liebe** (f) • **lieben** (vt & vi) • **lieblich** (adj) • **Liebling** (m) • **liebenswert, -würdig** (adj) • (see also **erlauben, glauben, Lob**)	= dear, kind, nice = love = to love, be fond of = lovely, charming, delightful = darling, pet, favorite = lovable	*1. lief* [valued, dear < AS. *leof*]; *2. live-* in *livelong (day)* [entire, tediously long, lit.: 'dear long' < ME. *lefe* < AS. *leof*, dear]; *3.* distantly: *love*
Lied (n) • **Liederdichter** (m)	= song, tune, air, melody = song-writer, lyric poet	*lied* [a German lyric or song]

GERMAN WORD	MEANING	ENGLISH COGNATE
liederlich (see **lotter**)		
liefern (vt) [< Fr. *livrer*, to deliver < L. *liber-are*, to free up] • **Lieferung** (f) • **(an-, aus-)liefern** (vt) • **überliefern** (vt) • **Überlieferung** (f)	= to deliver, furnish, supply, afford = delivery, shipment = to deliver up = to transmit, hand down = tradition	*-liver* in *deliver* [< Fr. < L. *liberare*, to free up]
liegen (vi) [*lag, gelegen*] • **Lage** (f) • **erliegen** (vi) [*er*, totally + *liegen*] • **überlegen** (adj) ['to come out lying above'] • **Überlegenheit** (f)<hr>• **Lager** (n) • **lagern** (vt & vi) • **belager** (vt) • (see also **legen**)	= to lie, be situated = site, situation = to succumb to = superior = superiority<hr>= den, lair; encampment = to store; camp = to lay siege, beleaguer	*1. lie;* <hr>*2. lair* ['lying-place' < AS. *leger*]; *3. beleaguer* [to besiege by encircling, surround]
lind (adj) [< OHG. *lindi* (cf. AS. *lithe*) < IE. *lento-*, flexible] • **lindern** (vt) • **Linderung** (f)	= soft, gentle, mild = to soften, mitigate, ease, soothe = easing, mitigation [< L. *mitis*, soft]	*lithe* [flexible, supple < AS. *lithe* < IE. *lento-*, flexible]
Lippe (f)	= lip	*lip*
List (see **leisten**)		
Litze (f) [< L. *licium*, thread] • **Litzendraht** (m)<hr>• **Drillich** (m) [< OHG. < OFr. *treliz* < L. *trilix* < *tre*, three + *licium*, thread]<hr>• **Zwilch** (**Zwillich**) (m) [< OHG. *zwi-*, two + *lih*, thread]	= cord, lace = stranded wire<hr>= ticking, heavy cloth <hr>= ticking, coarse cloth	*1. -lis* in *trellis* [wood strips like weave of threads < OFr. *treliz* < L. *trilix* < *tre*, three + *licium*, thread];<hr>*2. drill* [heavy cloth with a diagonal weave bec. of third thread < G. *Drillich*];<hr>*3. twill* [< ME. *twi*, two + *lich*, thread < L. *licium*]
Lob (n) [< OHG. *lob* (cogn. *lieb-* in *lieben*, to love)] • **loben** (vt) • **geloben** (vt) • **Gelübde** (n) • **verloben** (vt & refl) • **Verlobte** (m, f) • (see also **erlauben**, **glauben**, **lieb**)	= praise, commendation = to praise = to promise, vow = promise, vow, pledge = to engage (in marriage) = fiancé(e)	distantly: *love*

GERMAN WORD	MEANING	ENGLISH COGNATE
Loch (n) [cogn. G. *Lücke*, gap, opening] • **lochen** (vt) • **löcherig** (adj)	= hole, opening, gap = to perforate, pierce = full of holes; porous	*lock* [a part of a canal that has been 'loosened,' freed, separated out as an enclosure]
Locke (f) • **locken**[1] (vt) • **lockig** (adj) ───── • **locken**[2] and **anlocken** (vt) [believed < use of tufts of leaves or locks of hair to lure animals] • **Lockung** (f) • **verlocken** (vt) • **Lockvogel** (m)	= tuft, lock, curl = to curl, make curly = curly ───── = to entice, allure, decoy = enticement, allurement = to allure, entice, tempt = decoy	*lock* [of hair]
locker (adj) [bs: with a gap, not tight; < *lokker, lucker* < *Lücke*, gap, opening] • **lockern** (vt & refl) • (see also **Lücke**)	= loose, slack = to loosen, make slack; become loose, give way	*lock* [a part of a canal that has been 'loosened,' freed, separated out as an enclosure]
Lode (see **Leute**)		
Löffel (m)	= spoon	*to lap* [to take up with the tongue]
Lohe (f) • **lohen** (vi)	= blaze, flame = to blaze, be in flame	*low* [dial.: a flame]
Lohn (m) [< OHG. *lon* (cf. AS. *lean*) < IE. **lau-*, gain, profit] • **lohnen** (vt) • **belohnen** (vt) • **Belohnung** (f)	= wages, reward = to compensate, reward = to recompense = reward	direct cogn. lacking; distantly: *lu-* in *lucre, lucrative* [< L. *lucrum*, gain, profit < IE. **lau-*, gain, profit]
Lokal (n) [bs: public locality] ───── prefix **Lokal:** • **Lokalbahn** (f) • **Lokalverkehr** (m)	= restaurant, pub ───── = local = local railway = local traffic	*locality*
Los (n) • **losen** (vi)	= lot; destiny, fate = to cast or draw lots	*lot, lottery*
los (adj) • **lösen** (vt) • **ablösen** (vt) ['to free from'] • **erlösen** (vt) • **Erlöser** (m) ───── prefix **los-:** • **losarbeiten** (vi)	= loose, free = to loosen, untie = to relieve = to redeem, deliver = the Redeemer, Saviour ───── = to start to = to start work(ing)	*loose, -less,* as in *careless*

GERMAN WORD	MEANING	ENGLISH COGNATE
Lot (n) [cf. AS. *lead*] • **loten** (vt) • **löten** (vt) • **verlöten** (vt)	= small weight, plumb(line), solder; (fig.:) perpendicular = to plumb, sound = to solder = to solder up	*lead* [a gray metal < AS. *lead*]
Lotse (m) [believed bs: 'man who leads' < Du. *lootsmann* < AS. *ladmann*, guide < AS. *lad*, way (cogn. *to lead*); yet perhaps: a sounder, 'he who sounds water depths with lead weight' < MDu. *loot*, lead] • **lotsen** (vt) [bs: to serve as a *Lotse*]	= pilot (mar.) = to pilot (a ship, barge)	? words < AS. *lad*, way (cogn. *to lead*): *1. lodesman* [pilot]; *2. lode-*in *lodestar* [star that leads < AS. *lad*, way, course, (cogn. *to lead*) + *star*]; *3. to lead* Or ? *lead* [minerol. < AS. *lead*]
lotter, lotterig (adj) [< MHG. *lotter, loter*, useless < OHG. *lotar*, vagabond] • **Lotterbube** (m) • **verlottern** (vi) • **verlottert** (adj) ———————— • **liederlich** (adj) [distant cogn. of *lotter*] • **Liederlichkeit** (f)	= vagrant, slovenly, loose, dissolute = lazy fellow, vagabond = to go to ruin, go down = dissolute, ruined ———————— = careless, negligent, slovenly = carelessness, slovenliness	*-lot* in *harlot* [orig.: young male vagabond, camp follower, then female camp follower < OFr. *herlot* < OHG. *heri, hari*, army + OHG. *lotar*, vagabond] ———————— *lither* [obs. adj: bad, wicked, ill-tempered, then lazy, sluggish]
Löwe (m) [< L. *leo, leonis*, lion]	= lion	*lion*
Luchs (m) [< IE. *lu(n)k-*]	= lynx	*lynx* [< Gk. *lynx* < IE. *lu(n)k-*]
Lücke (f) • **lückenhaft** (adj) • **lückenlos** (adj) • (see also **locker**)	= gap, void, blank = full of gaps; incomplete, defective = without a gap; complete, unbroken	*lock* [a part of a canal that has been 'loosened,' freed, separated out as an enclosure]
Luder (n) [bs: bait < MHG. *luoder* (cf. Frk. *loder*)] • **Luderleben** (n)	= carrion = dissolute (rotted) life	*lure* [< OFr. *leurre* < Frk. *loder*, bait]
Luft (f) • **lüftern** (vt & vi) • **Luftaufnahme** (f), **Luftbild** (n)	= air, breeze = to put in the air, raise, lift; expose to view, disclose; to air = aerial photograph	*1. aloft; 2. loft*
lugen (+ **nach**) (vi) • **lugen** (+ **aus, von**) (vi)	= to look out for = to peer or peep	*look*
lügen (vi) • **Lüge** (f) • **Lügner** (m)	= to lie, speak falsely = lie, falsehood = liar	*lie*

GERMAN WORD	MEANING	ENGLISH COGNATE
Lümmel (m) [< obs. *lumm*, slack (cogn. G. *lahm*, lame, weak, sluggish)] • **lümmeln** (vi)	= lout, boor, ruffian = to loll, lounge	distantly: *lame*
Lumpen (m) • **lumpig** (adj) • **Lump** (m)	= rag; (pl.:) tatters = ragged, shabby, paltry = ragamuffin, scoundrel	*-lum* in *hoodlum* [rogue < Bavarian *hodalum* < *Haderlump*, 'rag-rag' < *Hader*, rag + *Lump*, ragamuffin < *Lumpen*, rag]
Lunge (f)	= lung	*lung*
Lunte (f)	= fuse, slowmatch (milit.)	*lunt* [a slow-burning match; to kindle or smoke]
Lust (f) • **lustig** (adj) • **belustigen** (vt) • **lüstern** (adj)	= pleasure, delight = jolly = to amuse, entertain = desirous or greedy of, lewd	*lusty*

# M		
Maat (m) [theorized: 'with whom one shares food' < Gmc. **mati*, meat]	= (naut.:) mate	*1. mate* [officer of navy or merchant ships (cf. *companion* < OFr. *compaignon* < L. *con*, with + *panis*, bread)]; *2. meat*
machen (vt & vi) • **Gemach** (n) [orig.: convenience, made to suit] • **gemächlich** (adj) • **gemach** (adv) • **allmählich** (adv) [orig.: made easy < *all + ge-mäch-lich*]	= to do, make, produce, cause = room, apartment, chamber = easy, comfortable = slowly, gently, by degrees = gradually, little by little	*1. make; 2. match* [to suit one to another, bring together as equal or corresponding < AS. *gemaecca*, match, mate]
• **Makler** (m) [origin in commerce: 'he who makes or strikes a deal' < *machen*] • **mäkeln** (vi) [orig.: to dicker at trading, then fault over anything] • **mäkelig** (adj) • **Mäkelei** (f)	= broker, middleman = to find fault with, carp = fussy, carping, finicky = fault-finding, criticism	

GERMAN WORD	MEANING	ENGLISH COGNATE
Macht (f) [< OHG. *maht* < *mögen*, to be able] • **mächtig** (adj) • **ermächtigen** (vt)	= power, might, authority = powerful, mighty, immense = to authorize	*1. might;*
• **mögen** (vt & vi) • **möglich** (adj) • **Möglichkeit** (f) • **Vermögen** (n) ['what makes one able' < *vermögen*, to be able to do]	= to wish, want; to be able, be willing = possible, practicable, feasible = possibility = capability, power, means	*2. may* [aux. verb expressing potentiality]
Mädchen (see **Magd**)		
Made (f) • **madig** (adj)	= maggot, worm, mite = maggoty, worm-eaten	*mite* [a small insect]
Magd (f) [< MHG. *maget*, OHG. *magad*, virgin girl (cf. AS. *maeg(e)d*)] • **Mädchen** (n)	= maid-servant, dairy-maid = girl, maid-servant	*maid* [< AS. *maeg(e)d*] and *maiden*
Magen (n) [cf. AS. *maga*]	= stomach	*maw* [stomach of an animal; gaping mouth of a voracious animal < AS. *maga*]
mahlen (vt) [cogn. L. *molere*, to grind] • **Mehl** (n) • **Mühle** (f) • **Müller** (m)	= to grind = flour, meal = mill = miller	*1. meal* [ground grain]; *2. mill;* *3. molar* [< L. *molere*]
• **zermalmen** (vt)	= to crush	
Mähne (f)	= mane	*mane*
mahnen (vt) [cogn. L. *monere*, to warn, serve as reminder] • **ermahnen** (vt)	= to remind, admonish = to admonish	*1. admonish; 2. monitor; 3. monument*
Mähre (f)	= mare	*mare*
Makel (m) [< L. *macula*, spot] • **makellos** (adj)	= stain, flaw, blemish = stainless, unblemished	*macul-* in *immaculate* [without stain < L. *in*, not + *macula*, spot]
Makler (see **machen**)		

GERMAN WORD	MEANING	ENGLISH COGNATE
Mal¹ (n) • **malen** (vt) ['to depict with marks'] • **Maler** (m) • **Gemälde** (n) • **Denkmal** (n) [bs: sign, marker of remembrance (*Denk-*)]	= mark, sign, spot, stain = to paint, portray = painter, artist = painting, picture = monument, memorial	*mole* [a congenital spot on the skin < AS. *mal,* spot]
Mal² (n) • **Mahl** (n) • **Gemahl(in)** (m, f) ['one to share a meal with' (cf. *companion* < OFr. *compaignon* < L. *con,* with + *panis,* bread). See also **Genosse, Gefährte**]	= point, point in time = meal, repast, banquet = consort, husband, wife	*1. -meal* in *piecemeal* [suffix: (a measure, piece at a) time]; *2. meal* [food eaten at a specific point in time]
In adverbs: • **einmal** • **diesmal** • **manchmal** • **nochmal** • **zweimal** • **vielmal(s)** • **zumal** ['to that point']	 = for once, one day = this time = sometimes = once more = twice = many times = particularly, especially	
mangeln (vi, impers.) [uncert. but theorized cogn. L. *mancus,* crippled, defective, whence Ital. *mancare,* Fr. *manquer,* to be lacking] • **Mangel** (m) • **mangels** (prep) + *gen.* • **bemängeln** (vi) [bs: to find failings]	= to be wanting, be lacking = want, lack, deficiency = for lack of, in the absence of = to criticize, cavil at	*manqué* [that falls short, a would-be in an endeavor, e.g., *poet manqué* < Fr. *manquer,* to be lacking < L. *mancus,* crippled, defective]
Mann (m) • **männlich** (adj) • **Mannschaft** (f) • **übermannen** (vt) • **Mensch** (m) • **Menschheit** (f) • **entmenscht** (adj)	= man; husband = male, masculine = body of men, crew, team, squad = to overpower = human being = human race, mankind = barbarous, cruel	*man*
Mappe (f) [orig.: a map painted on cloth, *mappa mundi,* map (lit.: 'cloth') of the world, later the casing in which the map was stored, then any case for papers < L. *mappa,* cloth napkin] • **Aktenmappe** (f) [< *acta,* acts, records + *Mappe*]	= briefcase, portfolio, file = file, briefcase	*map*

GERMAN WORD	MEANING	ENGLISH COGNATE
Märchen (n) [bs: fantastic fable, legend, dim. of obs. **Mär(e)**, rumor, fame, glory < OHG. *mari*, glory, ult. < IE. **me-*, big, great] • **märchenhaft** (adj) • **Märchenwelt** (n)	= fairy tale; fantastic story, fib = fabulous, fictitious = wonderland, world of romance	*1. mar-* in *maraud* [to raid, seek plunder < OFr. *marault*, vagabond, but orig.: one wielding glory or fame, prob. < OHG. *mariwald*, glory-wielder < OHG. *mari*, glory + *walt-*, wield]; *2. -mar* in names: *Dagmar*, day's glory]; *3.* distantly: *more* [< IE. **me-*, big, great]
Mark[1] (n) [< OHG. *mar(a)g* (cf. AS. *mearh*)] • **markig** (adj) • **ausmergeln** (vt) ['to remove the marrow or substance' < *aus* + *Mark*]	= pithe, pulp, marrow = marrowy, pithy = to emaciate, exhaust	*marrow* [< ME. *merowe* < AS. *mearh*]
Mark[2] (f)	= boundary, borderland	*march(es)* [frontier, borderland]
Marke (f) • **markieren** (vt)	= mark, sign, stamp, brand = to mark, brand	*mark*
Marmor (m) [< L. *marmor* < Gk. *marmaros*, marble]	= marble	*marble* [< OFr. < L. *marmor* < Gk. *marmaros*]
Maser (f) • **maserig** (adj) • **Masern** (pl.)	= mark, spot, scar; (in wood:) vein, streak = veined, mottled, streaky = measles	*mazer* [obs.: a drinking bowl usually made of spotted or streaked maple-wood]
Maß (n) [bs: right proportion < *messen, maß, gemessen*, to measure (cf. AS. *gemaet*, fitting, measured)] • **Maßstab** (m) • **mäßig** (adj) • **mäßigen** (vt) • **Mäßigkeit** (f) • **ermäßigen** (vt) [bs: to moderate thoroughly (*er-*)] • **gemäß** (adj) • **gemäß** (prep) + *gen.* • **Ebenmaß** (n) • **unmäßig** (adj) _____ • **anmaßen** (refl) ['to find meet (measured) to o.s.'] • **anmaßend** (adj) • (see also **messen**)	= measure, proportion, (right) quantity = measure, ruler, standard = moderate, reasonable = to moderate, temper = moderation, temperance = to reduce, abate, cut (price) = appropriate = according to, in agreement with = symmetry = immoderate, unreasonable _____ = to arrogate, usurp = arrogant, presumptuous	*1. meet* [fitting, e.g., 'it is *meet* that he...' < AS. *(ge)maet*, fitting, made to fit < AS. *metan*, to measure]; *2. to mete out* [to apportion, allot < AS. *metan*, to measure]
Masse (f) [< L. *massa*, lump, mass] • **massig** (adj) • **massenhaft** (adj)	= mass, bulk, multitude = massy, bulky solid = numerous, in large measure, abundant	*mass* [< L. *massa*, lump, mass]

GERMAN WORD	MEANING	ENGLISH COGNATE
Matrose (see **Matte**[2])		
matt (adj) • **Mattheit** (f) • **Mattigkeit** (f) • **ermatten** (vi) [< *er* + *matt*]	= dim, subdued, feeble, tired = dimness, dullness = exhaustion, feebleness = to grow tired, weary	*mat*
Matte[1] (f)	= meadow	*meadow* [< ME. *medewe*]
Matte[2] (f) [< L. *matta*, straw mat] ──────────── • **Matrose** (m) [bs: bunkmate of a mat or 'sleeper,' < Du. *matroos*, sailor < early forms *mattennoot*, *matghenot* (whence Fr. *matelot*, sailor)]	= (door)mat ────────── = sailor (milit.)	*1. mat;* ────────── *2. matross* [a soldier next in rank below a gunner]
Mauer (f) [< L. *murus*, wall] • **mauern** (vt & vi) • **untermaueren** (vt)	= wall = to build a wall, to wall = to underpin, substantiate	words < L. *murus*, wall: *1. mural;* *2. immure*
Maul (n) [< IE. **mu*-, imitative of inarticulate sounds, whence L. *muttire*, to mut- ter, and *mutus*, silent] • **maulen** (vi)	= muzzle, mouth = to sulk, pout	distantly: words < IE. **mu*-, imita- tive of inarticulate sounds: *1. mutter* [< L. *muttire*, to mutter]; *2. mute* [< L. *mutus*, silent]
Maus (f)	= mouse	*mouse*
Mauser (f) [< OHG. *muzzon* < L. *mutare*, to change] • **mausern** (refl)	= moulting = to moult	*moult* [to shed hair or skin < L. *mu- tare*, to change, with unhistoric *l*]
Meer (n)	= sea, ocean	*1. mere* [arch.: sea; lake, pond; marsh]; *2. mer-* in *mermaid*
mehr (adv) • **vermehren** (vt)	= more = to increase, augment	*more*
meiden (vt) [bs: to move away < IE. **mei-t(h)* < **mei*-, to change, go, move (whence L. *mutare*, to change, and *meare*, to pass)] • **vermeiden** (vt) • **Vermeidung** (f)	= to avoid, shun, keep away from = to avoid, shun = avoidance	distantly: *mut-*, *meat-* in *1. mutate* [< L. *mutare*, to change]; *2. per-* *meate* [< L. *per*, through + *meare*, *meatus*, to pass < IE. **mei-t(h)* < **mei*-, to change, go, move]
Meier (m) [bs: one in charge, 'greater man' < L. *major domus*, one in charge of an estate < *major*, greater] • **Meierei** (f), **Meierhof** (m)	= steward (of an estate) = (dairy-)farm	*1. major; 2. major-domo* [chief steward of a large household < ML. *major domus* < *major*, elder, greater + *domus*, genit. of *domus*, house]

GERMAN WORD	MEANING	ENGLISH COGNATE
Meineid (see **Eid**)		
meinen (vt & vi) • **Meinung** (f) [but: *Bedeutung,* meaning] • **vermeintlich** (adj) [of an opinion even wrong]	= to mean; be of the opinion = opinion, belief = supposed, putative	*to mean*
Meißel (m) [< OHG. *meizil* < *meizan,* to cut (Goth. *maitan*) < IE. **mai-,* to cut] • **meißeln** (vt)	= chisel = to chisel	*1.* distantly: *mite* [biting insect < IE. **mai-,* to cut]; *2. emmet* [arch.: ant, a biting insect < AS. *aemette*]
Meister (m) [< Ital. *maestro* < L. *magister,* mas- ter]	= master; boss	*maestro* and *master* [< L. *magister,* master]
melden (vt) • **Meldung** (f) • **abmelden** (vt)	= to announce, report, register = announcement, registration = to withdraw, resign	*to meld* [(in card game of pinochle:) to announce or declare one's cards for a score]
Memme (f) [bs: one at mother's breast < infan- tile *mamma*]	= coward, poltroon	*mamma*
Menge (f) [cf. AS. *mengan*] • **mengen** (vt) • **einmengen** (vt & refl) • **Gemenge** (n)	= quantity, amount, crowd, multitude = to mix, blend = to intermix; meddle, interfere = mixture, medley; scuffle, melee	*1. mingle* [< AS. *mengelen,* freqtv. of *mengan,* to mix]; *2. among* ['mixed in' < AS. *gemang,* a crowd]; *3. mongrel* [a mixed breed]
Mesner (m) [< OHG. *mesinari* < ML. *mansion- arius* < *mansio,* lodging (whence Fr. *maison*) < past p. *mansum* < *manere,* to dwell, remain]	= sacristan, sexton (one in charge of maintenance of church property)	*mansion* [< ML. *mansio,* lodging < L. *mansum,* past p. of *manere,* to dwell, remain]
Messe (f) [< L. *missum,* past p. of *mittere,* to send, let out] • **Buchmesse** (f)	= (commerce:) trade fair, market; mass (Roman Catholic service) = book fair	words < L. *missum,* past p. of *mit- tere,* to send: *1. Mass* [a Catholic service]; *2. mission; 3. mess hall* [milit.: room for meals set out]
messen (vt) [*maß, gemessen* < OHG. *mezzan* (cf. Goth. *mitan;* AS. *metan*)] • **meßbar** (adj) • **Durchmesser** (m) • **Maß** (n) (also see entry **Maß**) • **ermessen** (vt) • **unermeßlich** (adj) • **vermessen** (adj) ['badly measured'] • **Vermessenheit** (f) • **Metze**[1] (f)	= to measure = measurable = diameter = measure, proportion = to judge = immeasurable, immense = presumptuous [lit.: 'taking before- hand,' thinking too well of one- self < L. *prae* + *sumere,* to take] = presumptuousness = peck (grain measure)	words < AS. *metan,* to measure: *1. to mete (out)* [to apportion, allot]; *2. meet* [fitting, measured, e.g., 'it is *meet* that he...' < AS. *(ge)maet,* fitting, made to fit]

GERMAN WORD	MEANING	ENGLISH COGNATE
Messer (n) [bs: implement for cutting food]	= knife, scalpel	distantly: *meat*
Messing (n) [< MHG. *messinc* (cf. AS. *maestling*) etym. uncert., but perh. < Gk. *Massagetae*, tribe of brass workers near Caspian Sea (Herodotus)]	= brass	*maslin* [dial.: brass, brass kettle < AS. *maestling*]
Mette (f) [< L. *matutinus*, of the morning (whence Ital. *mattina*, Fr. *matin*, morning)]	= early morning service of the Church	*1. matins* [an early morning service of the Church]; *2. matinee* [an early movie showing]
Metze[2] (f) [disparaging, either < *Mädchen*, maiden, or generalized < personal name *Mathilde*] • (cf. **messen** for **Metze**[1])	= harlot, strumpet, bitch	? *maiden* or ? *Mathilda*
Metzger (m) [Goth. *mats* (cf. AS. *mete*) < Gmc. **mati-*, food, esp. flesh]	= butcher	*meat* [ME. and AS. *mete* < Gmc. **mati-*, food, esp. flesh]
meucheln (vt) ['to lie in wait,' perh. cogn OFr. *muchier*, to skulk, hide] • **Meuchler** (m)	= to assassinate = assassin	*mooch* [to skulk, pilfer; to get without payment < OFr. *muchier*, to skulk, hide]
Meute (f) [< Fr. *meute*, pack of hounds; earlier: revolt (whence *mutiny*) < LL. **movita* < L. *motum*, past p. of *movere*, to move] • **Meuterei** (f) • **meutern** (vi)	= pack (of hounds); (fig.:) gang = mutiny, sedition = to mutiny	*mutiny* [< LL. **movita* < L. *motum*, past p. of *movere*, to move]
Miete (f) • **mieten** (vt) • **Mieter** (m) • **Mietshaus** (n) • **vermieten** (vt)	= pay, rent, hire = to rent, hire, lease = tenant, lessee = apartment house = to hire out (e.g., to s.o.), lease out	*meed* [recompense, pay]
mild(e) (adj) • **Milde** (f) • **mildern** (vi)	= mild, soft, gentle = mildness = to mitigate, soothe	*mild*
minder (adj) [cogn. L. *minus*, less; *minor*, younger] • **mindern** (vt & refl) and **vermindern** (vt)	= less, smaller, minor = to lessen, diminish	distantly: *1. minor; 2. minus; 3. diminish*
mischen (vt & refl) [< L. *miscere, mixtum*, to mix]	= to mix, mingle, blend	*mix* [< L. *miscere, mixtum*, to mix]

GERMAN WORD	MEANING	ENGLISH COGNATE
Mist (m) [origins assoc. with dimness and moisture; believed cogn. L. *mingere, mictum*, to urinate]	= dung, manure, filth	*1. mist; 2. micturate* [to urinate]
mit (prep & adv) [cf. AS. *mid*]	= with, together with; also, too	*mid-* in *midwife* [a person assisting (together with) a woman in childbirth < AS. *mid*, with + *wife*]
Mitte (f) • **Mittel** (n) • **mittelbar** (adj) • **unmittelbar** (adj) • **Mittler** (m) • **ermitteln** (vt) ['to get to the average, middle' < *er-* + *mittel*] • **mittels** (prep) + *gen.* • **vermitteln** (vt & vi) [bs: to act as middle man] • **unvermittelt** (adj) ['not mediated' < *un* + *vermittel-*]	= middle, center = means, average, remedy = mediate, indirect = immediate, direct = mediator = to investigate, ascertain, find out = by means of = to mediate, settle; intervene = abrupt, immediate [lit.: 'not mediated' < L. *in*, not + *medius*, middle way]	*middle*
Möbel (n) [bs: a movable thing < Fr. *meuble* < L. *mobilis*, movable]	= piece of furniture	*mobile* [< L. *mobilis*, movable]
Moder (m) • **(ver)modern** (vi) • **moderig** (adj)	= mold, putrefaction = to putrefy, rot, decay = musty, putrid	*1. mother¹* [a slimy substance formed by bacteria on the surface of fermenting liquid or vinegar]; *2. mud*
mögen (see **Macht**)		
Mohn (m) [cogn. Gk. *mekon*, poppy]	= poppy	*meconic* [of the poppy or its derivatives < Gk. *mekon*, poppy]
Mohr (m) [< Gk. *mauros*, black]	= Moor (ethnol.)	*1. Moor; 2. Mauritania*
Möhre (f) [< OHG. *moraha* (cf. Frk. *morha*), whence LL. *moricula*, 'little root,' carrot-shaped mushroom]	= carrot	*morel* [a small edible mushroom < Fr. *morille* < LL. *moricula*, 'little root,' dim. of Frk. *morha*, carrot, carrot-shaped mushroom]
mollig (adj) [< L. *mollis*, soft]	= soft, pleasant, cozy; (of persons:) chubby, plump	*1. mollify; 2. mulch* [leaves or other loose material spread on the ground around plants < ME. *molsh*, soft]
Moment (n) [< L. **mo(vi)mentum*, what moves]	= motive, factor, impulse	*movement* [< L. *movimentum, what moves]
Monat (m) [cf. AS. *monath*]	= month	*month* [< AS. *monath*]

GERMAN WORD	MEANING	ENGLISH COGNATE
Mond (m) [cf. AS. *mona*]	= moon	*moon* [< AS. *mona*]
montieren (vt) [bs: to mount part to part < Fr. *monter*, to mount] • **abmontieren** (vt) • **Monteur** (m)	= to fit, set up, assemble = to dismantle, disassemble, strip = fitter, assembler, mechanic	*mount*
Moor (n) • **moorig** (adj)	= fen, bog, swamp = marshy, boggy	*moor* [a wet wasteland]
Mord (m) • **(er)morden** (vt)	= murder = to murder	*murder*
Morgen (m) • **Morgenland** (n) [land to the east, location of morning sun] • **morgenländisch** (adj)	= morning = the East, Orient = eastern, oriental	*morning*
morsch (adj) [< L. *mortarium*, mortar] • **Mörser** (m)	= rotten, decayed, as the reduced contents in a mortar = mortar (pharm., culin.)	*mortar* [vessel in which contents are ground, reduced < L. *mortarium*, mortar]
Motte (f)	= moth	*moth*
Möwe (f) [whence Fr. *mouette*, sea gull]	= sea gull	*mew* [the common gull]
Mücke (f)	= gnat, midge	*midge*
Mühe (f) [< OHG. *muoen, muohen* < IE. **mo-*, to exert oneself, whence L. *moles*, burden, trouble > *molestare*, to trouble] • **mühen** (refl) • **mühsam** (adj) • **bemühen** (vt) ———————— • **müde** (adj) • **Müdigkeit** (f) • **ermüden** (vt & vi)	= trouble, difficulty, toil, effort = to take pains, toil = toilsome = to trouble ———————— = weary, tired, fatigued = weariness, fatigue = to tire, fatigue	distantly: *mo-* in *molest* [to burden, annoy < L. *molestare* < *moles*, burden, trouble < IE. **mo-*, exertion of oneself]
Mulde (f) [bs: a hollow recalling a milk pail < OHG. *muoltera* < L. *mulctra*, milk pail, *mulgeo, mulgere, mulsum (mulctum)*, to milk]	= trough, depression, hollow	*mul-* in *emulsion* [a substance 'milked out' < *e*, out + *mulsum* < L. *mulgeo, mulgere, mulsum (mulctum)*, to milk]
Müll (m) [bs: dry refuse; cogn. *mahlen*, to grind (ME. *mul*, dust)] • **Müllhaufen** (m) • **mulmig** (adj)	= dust, rubbish, refuse = rubbish heap = dusty, moldy	*1. mull-* in *mullock* [in Australia, refuse earth or rock left in mining < ME. *mul*, dust, particles]; *2. to mull over* [to ponder < ME. *mullen*, to pulverize < AS. *myl*, dust]

GERMAN WORD	MEANING	ENGLISH COGNATE
Mund (m) [cf. < AS. *muth*]	= mouth	*mouth* [< AS. *muth* < *munth-]
• **Mundart** (f) ['a way (*art*) people speak']	= dialect	
• **mündlich** (adj)	= oral, verbal	
• **einmünden** (vi)	= (river:) to empty (spew) into, end in	
• **Mündung** (f)	= mouth of a river, muzzle (of gun)	
• **munden** (vi) [bs: to tickle the palate (lit.: mouth)]	= to taste good, be delicious	
• **mundgerecht** (adj) ['right for the mouth']	= palatable	
Mündel (m, f, n) [bs: one protected < OHG. *munt*, protection (cf. MDu. *mond*)]	= ward, one placed under care	*mound* [bs: protection < MDu. *mond*, var. of *mont*, *munt*, protection]
• **Vormund** (m) [bs: one giving 'protection before']	= guardian	
• **Vormundschaft** (f)	= guardianship, tutelage	
munter (adj) [< OHG. *muntar* (cf. Goth. *mundon*, to strive) < IE. *mendh-, to learn, whence Gk. *manthanein*, *emathon*, to learn > Eng. *math(ematics)*]	= awake, astir, brisk. lively, alert	distantly: *math* < *mathematics* [skill requiring striving, learning < Gk. *emathon*, past t. of *manthanein*, to learn < IE. *mendh-, to learn]
• **Munterkeit** (f)	= liveliness, alertness	
• **ermuntern** (vt)	= to rouse, enliven, stir up	
• **Ermuntung** (f)	= stimulation, incentive	
Münze (f) [< OHG. *muniza* < L. epithet *Juno Moneta*, at whose temple n Rome, the *Moneta*, coins were minted; Juno was so named bec. with an earthquake she warned Romans to sacrifice < *moneo, monere, monetus*, to warn]	= mint (place of coinage); coin, medal	*1. mint* [< the *Moneta*, temple of *Juno Moneta* in Rome < L. *moneta* < *monere*, to warn]; *2. monitor* [one who warns, admonishes]
mürbe (adj) [bs: state of breaking down < OHG. *murwi* (whence Ital. *morbido*, soft) < IE. *mer-, to rub, break down (whence L. *mortalis*, subject to death; *mortarium*, vessel for grinding; *mordere, morsum*, to bite)]	= tender, mellow, well-cooked, friable, brittle	*mor-* in Latin-derived words < IE. *mer-, to rub, break down: *1. mortal*; *2. mortar* [crushed mixture of sand, lime and water]; *3. morsel* [< *mordere, morsum*, to bite]
• **zermürben** (vt)	= to wear down; break down resistance	
Muße (f) [bs: to have the occasion, possibility, or opportunity < *müssen*, a verb formerly expressing dual meaning: *obligation* (in present tense) and *opportunity* (in preterite) < OHG. *muoza* (cf. AS. *mota* < *motan*)]	= leisure	*1. must* [auxiliary verb once expressing opportunity (hence association with *leisure*) as well as requirement < ME. *moste* preterite of disused *motan*, may, to be permitted]; *2. -m-t-* in *empty* [orig.: idle, then vacant < AS. *aemettig* < *aemetta, metta*, leisure]
• **müßig** (adj)	= idle, superfluous	
• **bemüßigen** (refl)	= to find leisure for	

GERMAN WORD	MEANING	ENGLISH COGNATE
Muster (n) [< L. *monstrare*, to make known] • **mustern** (vt) • **Musterung** (f) • **Musterbild** (n) • **musterhaft** (adj)	= specimen, pattern, model, example = to inspect, review = inspection, scrutiny = model, paragon, ideal = exemplary	*1. to muster* [to gather for inspection < OFr. *moustrer* < L. *monstrare*, to make known < *monere*, to warn]; *2.* distantly: *demonstrate*
Mut (m) • **mutig** (adj) • **mutmaßen** (vt) [bs: to measure in the mind] • **mutmaßlich** (adj) • **anmuten** (vt) [bs: to appeal to the spirit] • **Anmut** (f) • **entmutigen** (vt) • **ermutigen** (vt) • **Gemüt** (n) • **gemütlich** (adj) • **hochmütig** (adj) • **vermuten** (vt) [bs: to put to mind] • **vermutlich** (adj)	= (mental) spirit, courage, heart = courageous, daring = to surmise, conjecture, presume = presumable, supposed, putative = to please = charm, grace = to discourage = to encourage, embolden = mind, feeling, disposition = genial, comfortable = highspirited = to suppose, assume = presumable, supposed	*mood*
Mutter (f) • **mütterlich** (adj)	= mother = maternal	*mother*[2]
Mütze (f) [< ML. *almutia*, cowl] • **Mützenschirm** (m)	= cap = visor	*mutch* [a close-fitting cap worn in Scotland]; *almuce* [medieval garment with a hood and fur lining]

# N		
Nabe (f) [cf. AS. *nafu*] • **Nabel** (m) • **Nabelschnur** (f), **-strang** (m)	= hub = navel (anat.) = umbilical cord	*1. nave* [hub of a wheel < AS. *nafu*]; *2. navel* [a central depression or hole < AS. *nafela*]; *3. au-* in *an auger* < faulty separation of *a nauger* [tool for piercing a hub < ME. *navegar*, lit.: 'nave-spear' < *nafu*, hub + *gar*, spear]
nachahmen (see **Ohm**)		
Nachbar (m) • **Nachbarschaft** (f)	= neighbor = neighborhood, vicinity	*neighbor* [lit.: 'nearby farmer' < AS. *neahgegebur* < *neah*, nigh, near + *gebur, boer*, farmer]
Nacht (f)	= night	*night*
Nadel (f)	= needle	*needle*

GERMAN WORD	MEANING	ENGLISH COGNATE
Nagel (m) [cf. AS. *naegel*] • **nageln** (vt)	= nail = to nail	*nail* [< AS. *naegel*]
• **Nelke** (f) ['small nail' (bec. of its nail-shape) < LG. *neilkin* < *negelkin* < *negel*, nail + -*kin*, dim. suffix] • **Gewürznelke** (f)	= clove (spice); carnation, pink = clove (spice)	+ dim. suffix -*kin* in *lambkin*, *manikin*
nagen (vt & vi)	= to gnaw	*gnaw*
nahe (prep) • **Nähe** (f) • **nahen** (vi) • **annähernd** (adj) • **nahelegen** (vt) [bs: to cause to be present in the mind (lit.: 'to place near or close by') < *nahe*, near + *legen*, to place, a loan transl. of L. *suggerere*] • **naheliegen** (vi) ['to lie close by'] • **naheliegend** (adj)	= near = nearness = to approach = approximately = to suggest [< L. *suggestus*, past p. of *suggerere*, to supply, to prompt (lit.: 'bring from below or close by') < *sub*, below + *gerere*, to carry] = to be obvious, suggest itself = obvious, evident	*nigh* + *lay*
nähen (vt & vi) [< Gmc. root **nae-ja-*, to sew] • **Näherin** (f) • **Naht** (f)	= to sew = seamstress = seam, suture	distantly: *nee-* in *needle*
Napf (m) [< Gmc. *hnappa*, drinking bowl (cf. Frk. *hnapp*)] • **Näpfchen** (n) • **Napfkuchen** (m)	= bowl, small basin = little bowl, basin = cake baked in a pan or basin	*1. hanap* [antiquar.: a medieval goblet < OFr. < Frk. *hnapp*]; *2. hanaper* [a case for storing a *hanap* < OFr. *hanapier*]; *3. hamper* [a container or basket with a cover < phonetic reduction of *hanaper*]
Narbe (f) [bs: compressed skin (cf. AS. *nearwe* < *nearwian*, to compress)] • **narbig** (adj) • **vernarben** (vi)	= scar = scarred; grained (of leather) = to scar over	*narrow* [bs: twisted and lacking breadth < AS. *nearwe* < *nearwian*, to compress]
Narr (m) [believed < LL. *nario*, mocker, 'nose wrinkler' < L. *naris*, nostril] • **Narrheit** (f) • **narren** (vt) • **närrisch** (adj) • **Narretei** (f)	= fool = folly = to make a fool of, dupe = foolish, silly, mad = tomfoolery	*nares* [anat.: the nasal passages, nostrils < L. *naris*, nostril]
Nase (f)	= nose	*nose*

GERMAN WORD	MEANING	ENGLISH COGNATE
naß (adj) • **Nässe** (f) • **(be)netzen** (vt) [< *be* + *naß*]	= wet; moist, humid = wetness, moisture = to moisten, wet, sprinkle	*1. Nass-* in *Nassau* [a territory in Germany, lit.: 'wet meadow' < *naß* + *Aue,* (poet.) pasture, meadow]; *2.* theorized but doubtful: *nas-* in *nasty,* i.e., wet and unpleasant]
Natter (f) [cf. AS. *naedre,* viper]	= viper, serpent	*an adder* [a poisonous snake < faulty separation of *a nadder* < AS. *naedre,* viper]
Nebel (m) [cogn. L. *nebula,* cloud, mist] • **nebeln** (vi) • **nebelig** (adj)	= fog, mist = to be foggy = foggy, misty, hazy	*nebulous* [< L. *nebula*]
necken (vt) [intens. of *nagen,* to gnaw (cf. *sarcasm,* treatment with biting effects < Gk. *sarkazein,* to tear flesh < *sarx, sarkos,* flesh)]	= to tease, kid	*1. to nag* [< *gnaw*]; *2. gnaw*
Neffe (m) [cogn. L. *nepos*]	= nephew	*nephew*
nehmen (vt) [cf. AS. *niman,* to take] • **annehmen** (vt) • **ausnehmen** (vt) • **entnehmen** (vt) • **teilnehmen** (vt) • **genehm** (adj) [bs: disposed to taking or accepting] • **genehmigen** (vi) [bs: to treat acceptably and so grant] • **angenehm** (adj) • **unangenehm** (adj) • **zunehmen** (vi) • **Zunahme** (f) ――――――――― • **Vernunft** (f) [bs: that taken in, understanding < *ver* + *nehmen,* to take] • **vernunftig** (adj)	= to take, seize = to accept receive, admit = to take out, except = to remove, withdraw = to take part, participate = agreeable, acceptable = approve of, grant = pleasant, agreeable = disagreeable = to grow larger, increase = increase, growth ――――――――― = reason = reasonable, wise	*1. numb* ['taken' < AS. *niman,* to take, seize]; *2. nimble* [bs: capable of taking, alert]
Neid (m) [< OHG. *nid,* malice (cf. AS. *nith*)] • **neiden** (vt) • **neidisch** (adj)	= envy, jealousy = to envy = envious, jealous	*nithing* [arch.: abject wretch, villain < AS. *nith,* enmity, malice]
Nelke (see **Nagel**)		
nennen (vt) • **nennbar** (adj) • **ernennen** (vt) • **Name** (m), **Namen** (n) • **nämlich** (adj, adv)	= to name, call, term = mentionable = to nominate, appoint = name, designation = the same; namely, to wit	*name*

GERMAN WORD	MEANING	ENGLISH COGNATE
Nest (n)	= nest	*nest*
nett (adj) [< Fr. *net, nette*, clean, spotless (whence Fr. *nettoyer*, to clean) < L. *nitidus*, shining, elegant] • **Nettheit, Nettigkeit** (f)	= nice, kind, agreeable = neatness or spruceness	*1. neat[1]* [clean, tidy; smart < Fr. *net*, clean < L. *nitidus*, shining, elegant]; *2. net[1]* [a clear or clean amount]
Netz (n) • **Netzhaut** (f)	= net, network, mesh, gauze, lattice = retina [< L. *rete*, net]	*net[2]*
neu (adj) • **erneuern** (vt)	= new = to renew, renovate, revive	*new*
Nichte (f) [< *nift*, fem. < *neffe*, nephew; cogn. L. *nepos*]	= niece	*niece*
Nichts (n)	= nothing(ness)	*not, naught*
nieder (adj) • **niedergehen** (vi) • **Niedergang** (m) • **niedrig** (adj) • **erniedrigen** (vt)	= low, base, mean, vulgar; inferior = to go down = decline = low, humble, mean = to reduce, lower, degrade, humiliate	*nether*
Niere (f)	= kidney	believed *-ney* in *kidney* [theorized orig. *kid-neyre*]
niesen (vi)	= to sneeze	*sneeze*
Niete (f) [< Du. *niet*, nothing (cf. OHG. *ni-wiht* (= G. *nichts*); AS. *nawuht*)]	= failure, flop, wash-out, blank draw (in lottery)	*naught* [< AS. *nawuht*]
nivellieren (vt) [< Fr. *niveau*, a dissimilation of LL. *livel* < L. *libella*, a level] • **Niveau** (n)	= to level, grade = level, standard; the instrument, a level	distantly: *level* [< LL. *livel* < L. *libella*, a level]
Norden (m) • **nördlich** (adj)	= north = northern	*north*
nörgeln (vi) [echoic] • **nörgelig** (adj) • **Nörgelei** (f)	= to grumble, nag or carp at = grumbling, nagging = grumbling, nagging	cf. unrelated but similarly echoic *snarl*
Not (f) • **notwendig** (adj) • **nötig** (adj) • **nötigen** (vt) • **benötigen** (vt)	= need, necessity = necessary = needy, in need = to oblige, necessitate = to need, require	*need*

GERMAN WORD	MEANING	ENGLISH COGNATE
nüchtern (adj) [< rigorous monastic offices sung in cloisters at all hours < L. *nocturnus,* night service]	= empty, fasting, sober, temperate, level-headed, plain	*nocturnal* [< L. *nocturnus,* of the night]
• **ernüchtern** (vt)	= to make sober, disenchant, disillusion	
Nüster (f)	= nostril	*nostril*
Nutzen (m) [< OHG. *nuz* (cf. AS. *nytt*) < Gmc. *neut-, nut-,* to make use of, enjoy, whence, too, OHG. *noz* (cf. AS. *neat*), cattle as possessions > *ginozo* (cf. AS. *neotan*), to enjoy, possess > *genießen,* to enjoy]	= use, utility, benefit	*1. neat*[2] [obs.: any animal of the ox family < AS. *neat,* bovine possession]; *2. neatherd* [cowherd]; *3. neat's foot oil* [pale yellow oil obtained by boiling feet and shinbones of cattle, used in dressing leather]
• **nutz** (adj) • **(be)nutzen** (vt) • **nützen** (vt & vi) • **nütz(e), nützlich** (adj)	= useful, profitable = to use, make use of = to use; be of use = useful, profitable	

# O		
Ochse (m) • **ochseln** (vi)	= ox, bullock = to work like an ox, study hard	*ox* [< AS. *oxa*]
öde (adj) [bs: alone; believed distantly cogn. Gk. *autos,* oneself] • **Öde** (f) • **veröden** (vt & vi)	= desolate, deserted; (fig.:) bleak = wasteland, solitude; (fig.:) bleakness = to make desolate, lay waste; become desolate	distantly: prefix *auto-* in *automobile, automatic,* etc. [< Gk. *autos,* oneself]
Ofen (m)	= oven	*oven*
offen (adj) • **öffnen** (vt) • **offenbar** (adj) • **offenbaren** (vt) • **öffentlich** (adj)	= open, public, vacant = to open = obvious, evident = to reveal, disclose = public	*open*

GERMAN WORD	MEANING	ENGLISH COGNATE
Ohm (m, n) [< OHG. *ame*, a liquid measure < L. *ama*, cask for liquid]	= a large liquid measure, cask	*aam, awm* [a liquid measure of about forty gallons < L. *ama*, cask for liquid]
• **nachahmen** (vt & vi) [orig.: 'to proximate in measure,' imitate in general < *nach*, after] • **Nachahmung** (f) • **nachahmenswert** (adj)	= to imitate, copy, simulate = imitation, copy(ing) = worthy of imitation, exemplary	*nigh, neigh-* in *neighbor* + *awm*
Ohr (n)	= ear	*ear*
opfern (vt) [< L. *operari*, to work, esp. to carry out worship with sacrifice]	= to sacrifice	*operate* [< L. *operari*, to work, esp. to carry out worship with sacrifice]
Ort (m) [cf. AS. *ord* (var. in ON. *oddi*, point of land)] • **orten** (vt) • **örtlich** (adj) • **erörten** (vt) [bs: to treat thoroughly (*er-*) from all positions (*ort*)]	= place, point, site, spot; (obs.) corner = to locate = local = to discuss	*odd* [orig.: point of land, then triangle, then from the third point or angle an odd number < ME. *odde* < ON. *oddi*, point of land (cogn. AS. *ord*, a point)]
Osten (m) • **östlich** (adj)	= east = eastern	*east*

P

Pacht (f) [< L. *paciscor, pacisci, pactus*, to agree] • **(ver)pachten** (vt) • **Pächter** (m)	= lease, tenure; rent = to (take on) lease, rent = lease-holder, tenant	*pact* [< L. *paciscor, pacisci, pactus*, to agree]
Panne (f) [of nautical origin; bs: sail of no use, thus a vessel at a standstill < Fr. *panne*, standstill, further etym. disputed; prob. < L. *pannus*, piece of cloth, sail]	= breakdown, standstill or failure; mishap	*1. panel* [< ML. *pannellus*, dim. < *pannus*, piece of cloth]; *2. pane* [a flat, rectangular division]
Panzer (m) [bs: warrior's protection worn over the abdomen < OFr. *pansiere* < *pance* < L. *pantex, panticis*, belly] • **panzern** (vt)	= armor; armored tank (milit.); shell (zool.) = to arm with mail, plate	*paunch* [abdomen, belly < OFr. *panche, pance* < L. *pantex, panticis*, belly]

GERMAN WORD	MEANING	ENGLISH COGNATE
Pardel (m) [< L. < Gk. *pardalis* (also *pardos*), leopard, panther]	= leopard	*pard* [arch.: leopard, panther < L. < Gk. *pardos*] and *leopard* [lion-panther]
passen (vi) [bs: to pass, meet an objective < Fr. *passer*, to pass, cross] • **passend** (adj) • **aufpassen** (vi) [bs: to pass or cross on (*auf*) to what matters]	= to suit, be suitable = fit, suitable, apt = to pay attention	*pass, passable*
Pate (m) [< L. *pater*, father] • **Patin** (f)	= godfather = godmother	*pat-* in *paternal* [< L. *pater*, father]
pauschal (see **Bausch**)		
pausen, durchpausen (vt) [< Fr. *poncer*, to pumice, to transfer images by dusting fine powder over holes punched in the paper drawing being transferred < VL. *pomex, pomicis* < *pumex*, pumice] • **Pause** (f)	= to trace (transfer, copy) = tracing, traced design, blueprint	*to pounce* [to transfer an image by dusting fine powder over holes punched in the original paper being copied < Fr. *poncer* < VL. *pomex, pomicis* < *pumex*, pumice (powder)]
Pavian (m) [< Du. *baviaan* < Fr. *babouin*, Ital. *babuino*]	= baboon	*baboon*
Pech (n) [< L. *pix, picis*, pitch]	= pitch, tar; (fig.:) bad luck [cf. Eng. *quagmire* < *mire*, deep mud]	*pitch*
Pegel (m) [cf. < AS. *paegel*] • **peilen** (vt) [naut.: to use a water gauge for bearings < LG. < MLG. *pegelen*]	= watergauge = to sound (depths), take bearings	*pail* [< AS. *paegel*, a gill, wine-measure]
Pein (f) [< L. *poena*, penalty, hardship] • **peinigen** (vt) ────── • **verpönt** (adj) [lit.: 'put under penalty,' threatened by fine, hence, prohibited < obs. *verpönen* < *ver* + L. *poena*, penalty]	= torment = to torment ────── = taboo, prohibited, despised	words < L. *poena*, penalty, hardship: *1. pain; 2. penal*
Peitsche (f) [< IE. **bhei-*, to strike] • **peitschen** (vt & vi)	= whip, lash = to whip, scourge	distantly: *bi-* in *bill* [bird's beak, point of weapon or anchor < IE. **bhei-*, to strike]
Pelz (m) [< ML. *pellicia* < L. *pellis*, a skin]	= fur	*pelt*
Pfad (m)	= path	*path*

GERMAN WORD	MEANING	ENGLISH COGNATE
Pfahl (m) [< L. *palus*, stake]	= stake, piling, pole	*1. pale* [stake < L. *palus*]; *2. palisade* [a fence of pointed stakes]
Pfand (n) • **pfändbar** (adj) • **pfänden** (vt) • **Pfändung** (f)	= pledge, deposit, security = seizable (as security) = to seize as a pledge, impound = seizure, distraint	*pawn* [anything given as security]
Pfarrer (m) [< Ital. *parroco* < L. *parochia* < Gk. *paroikia*, neighborhood, diocese]	= parson	*parish* [< L. *parochia* < Gk. *paroikia*, neighborhood, diocese]
Pfau (m) [< MHG. *pfawe* (cf. AS. *pawa*) < L. *pavo, pavonis*, peacock]	= peacock	*1. pavan(e)* [a stately courtly dance recalling strutting of a peacock]; *2. pea-* in *peacock* [< ME. *pacok*, AS. *pawa* < L. *pavo*, peacock]
Pfeife (f) [*pfiff, gepfiffen;* < L. *pipare*, to pipe] • **pfeifen** (vt & vi) • **Pfiff** (m) [bs: whistle as signal to trick] • **pfiffig** (adj)	= pipe, fife = to pipe, whistle, howl = whistle; hence a trick = cunning, artful	*1. fife; 2. pipe* [< L. *pipare*, to pipe]
Pfeil (m) [< OHG. *pfil* < L. *pilum*, short pike, javelin]	= arrow	*pile, piling* [shaft to support a bridge or dock]
Pfeiler (m) [< ML. *pilare* < L. *pila*, pillar]	= pillar, pier	*pillar*
Pferch (m) [< ML. *parricus*, hedged area] • **pferchen** (vt)	= fold, pen = to fold, pen, cram together	*park*
Pferd (m) [< Gaul. **voredos,* horse] • **Pferdelauf** (m) • **Schaukelpferd** (n)	= horse = race course = rocking-horse	*-frey* in *palfrey* [arch.: a saddle horse esp. for women < ML. *palafredus, palaveredos* < Gaul. **voredos,* horse]
Pfingsten (n) [ONeth. *pincoston;* Goth. *paintekuste* < Gk. *pentekoste*, fiftieth day after Resurrection]	= Pentecost	*Pentecost*
Pflanze (f) [< L. *planta*, a plant] • **pflanzen** (vt) • **fortpflanzen** (vt & refl)	= plant = to plant, set = to propagate, reproduce	*plant* [< L. *planta*, a plant]
Pflaume (f) [< OHG. *phruma* < L. *pruna*, pl. of *prunum*]	= plum, prune	*plum, prune*

GERMAN WORD	MEANING	ENGLISH COGNATE
pflegen (vt) [bs: striving after < OHG. *phlegan* (cf. AS. *plegian*) < Gmc. *pleg-*, undertaking, bestirring oneself]	= to care for, nourish, culture	*1. play* [bs: to bestir oneself < ME. *pleien* < AS. *plegan, plegian*, to be active]; *2. pledge* [bail, surety, solemn promise < ME. *plege* < OFr. *plege* (possib. < Gmc. *pleg-*, undertaking, bestirring oneself)];
• **Pflege** (f)	= care, cultivation	
• **pfleglich** (adj)	= careful	
• **Pfleger(in)** (m, f)	= fosterer, nurse, curator	
• **gepflegt** (adj)	= well-groomed, cultivated	
• **ungepflegt** (adj)	= uncared for, neglected	
• **verpflegen** (vt)	= to board, supply with food	
• **Pflicht** (f) [intens. of 'striving for']	= duty, obligation	*3. plight* [orig.: risk, undertaking < ME. *plihten*, AS. *plihtan*, to pledge, expose to danger, possib. cogn. *plegan, plegian*]
• **beipflichten** (vi)	= to assent to, endorse	
• **verpflichten** (vt)	= to make covenant, engage	
Pflock (m)	= plug, peg	*plug*
• **pflöcken** (vt)	= to plug, peg, picket	
Pflug (m)	= plow	*plow* (Brit. spelling: *plough*)
• **pflügen** (vt & vi)	= to plow	
Pfriem(en) (m) and **Pfrieme** (f) [cf. < MDu. *prieme*, dagger]	= awl, punch	*to preen* [to trim feathers with the beak < MDu. *prieme*, dagger]
Pfropf, Pfropfen (m) [< horticult.: 'that packed in' < L. *propago*, to implant, pack in]	= stopper, cork, plug, (med.:) clot	*propag-* in *propaganda* [what is to be implanted < L. *propago*, to implant, pack in]
• **pfropfen** (vt)	= to stopper, cork, cram	
Pfründe (f) [< MHG. *pfrüende* < OHG. *pfruonta* < ML. *provenda, praebenda*, things to be supplied]	= benefice, living, prebend	*1. prebend* [church revenue used to support a clergyman]; *2. provender* [dry food for livestock]
Pfuhl (m)	= pool, puddle	*pool*
Pfühl (m, n) [< L. *pulvinus*, cushion]	= cushion	*pillow* [< ME. *pylwe* < L. *pulvinus*, cushion]
Pfütze (f) [bs: pit filled with water < L. *puteus*, a well, whence Ital. *pozzo*, well]	= pool, puddle	*pit* [< AS. *pytt* < L. *puteus*, a well]
Pilger (m) [< OFr. < L. *peregrinus*]	= pilgrim	*pilgrim* [< OFr. < L. *peregrinus*, one who travels abroad]
• **pilgern** (vi)	= to make a pilgrimage	
Pilz (m) [< OHG. *buliz* < L. *boletus*, mushroom]	= mushroom, fungus, toadstool	*boletus* [a genus of fungi < L. *boletus*, mushroom]

GERMAN WORD	MEANING	ENGLISH COGNATE
Pinsel (m) [tapered like an animal's tail < OFr. *pincel* < L. *penicillus*, brush < L. *peniculus*, small tail < *penis*, tail] • **pinseln** (vt & vi) ['to apply a brush']	= artist's brush = to paint, daub	*1. pencil* [orig.: a brush, then a graphite marking tool < OFr. *pincel* < L. *penicillus*, brush < L. *peniculus*, small tail < *penis*, tail]; *2. penis* [taillike appendage < L. *penis*, tail]
Pirsch (f) [bs: marksmanship in shooting, orig. with bow (and wicker target?) < MHG. *birsen* < OFr. *berser*, to hunt with bow < Gaul. *bers*, wickerwork (as target?), whence Ital. *bersaglio*, target; *bersagliere*, marksman, rifleman] • **pirschen, birschen** (vi)	= (deer) stalking, still-hunting = to stalk game, still-hunt	*berceuse* [lullaby < Fr.: lullaby, cradle song < Fr. *berceau*, cradle (orig. of wickerwork) < *bers* believed < Gaul. *bers*, wickerwork]
Plage (f) [< L. *plaga* < Gk. *plege*, blow, misfortune < IE. *plak-²*, to strike] • **plagen** (vt)	= trouble, nuisance = to torment, trouble	*plague* [anything that afflicts troubles < Gk. *plege*, blow, misfortune < IE. *plak-²*, to strike]
Plane (f) [orig.: wagon covering (of felt?) < OHG. *blaha(ne)*, believed cogn. to *floc-* in L. *floccus*, flock (wool tufts, wool or cotton fibers)]	= awning, tilt, tarpaulin	distantly: *flock* [wool tufts, wool or cotton fibers applied to various uses, including felting < L. *floccus*, flock]
plärren (vi)	= to bawl	*to blare*
platzen (vi) [echoic expression of sudden or sharp change (cf. echoic Eng. *splatter, splash*)] • **aufplatzen** (vi)	= to burst, explode, crack, split = to burst open	cf. similar sound but different force in echoic Eng. *splatter, splash*
plaudern (vi) [cogn. L. *blaterare*, to babble]	= to chat, make small talk	*1. blather; 2. blatent* [disagreeably loud]
plump (adj) [echoic, expressing the awkward (cf. Eng. *plop*)]	= awkward, clumsy; outright	*to plump* [to fall suddenly; (adj:) blunt, straightforward]
Plunder (m) • **plündern** (vt)	= worthless stuff = to plunder	*plunder*
Pöbel (m) [< L. *populus*, people] • **pöbelhaft** (adj) • **anpöbeln** (vt)	= mob, rabble = low, vulgar, plebeian = to vilify, abuse	*1. people* [< L. *populus*, people]; *2. populace*
pochen (vi)	= to knock, tap, rap	*to poke*
poltern (vi) • **Polterer** (m) • **Gepolter** (n)	= to make a racket = noisy fellow, blusterer = rumbling, din	*poltergeist* [a ghost believed responsible for noisy disturbances]

GERMAN WORD	MEANING	ENGLISH COGNATE
Posaune (f) [< OFr. *buisine, buccine* < L. *bucina*, a crooked horn, trumpet] • **posaunen** (vt & vt)	= trumpet, trombone = to trumpet	*buccinator* [cheek muscle used in blowing < L. *buccinare*, to blow the *buccina, bucina*, a crooked horn, trumpet]
Posse (f) [bs: exaggerated face < earlier *bosse*, a carved fountain fixture, often in an amusing form (e.g., water-spewing face) < Fr. *bosse*, relief work] • **Possen** (m) • **possierlich** (adj)	= (theat.:) farce, burlesque; buffoonery = trick, prank = comic, funny	*1. boss*² [protruding ornament or knob]; *2. to emboss*
Pracht (f) [bs: a bursting, esp. of splendor < IE. **bhreg-*, to break, whence L. *fragor*, noise < *frango, fractum*, to break, and Eng. *break*] • **prachtvoll, prächtig** (adj)	= splendor, magnificence = splendid, dazzling, magnificent	*1. fracture, fragment; 2. break, outbreak*
prägen (vt) [bs: to mark deeply, 'put breaks in,' cogn. G. *brechen*, to break] • **einprägen** (vt) • **ausgeprägt** (adj)	= to stamp, coin, emboss = to impress, imprint = marked, pronounced	distantly: *break*
prahlen (vi) [bs: to make noise < MLG. *pral* < echoic] • **Prahler(in)** (m, f) • **Prahlerei** (f) • **prahlerisch** (adj)	= to brag, boast; show off = boaster, braggart = boasting, bragging = boastful, ostentatious	cf. echoic, but with different force, Eng. *bawl, bellow*
Prahm (m)	= barge	*pram* [a flat-bottomed boat]
prall (adj) • **prallen** (vi) ———— • **prellen** (vt)	= tight, stretched, plump = to bounce, rebound, spring back ———— = to make rebound (e.g., billiards); to bounce or toss on a blanket stretched out, hence, to cheat, swindle	*prall triller* [music: a bouncy trill]
Pranger (m) [bs: compressive device < Gmc. *prang-*, to compress, squeeze] • **anprangern** (vt)	= pillory = to pillory, denounce	*prong*
Pranke (f) [< LL. *branca*, paw, claw]	= paw of an animal	*branch* [bs: an extension of the trunk or body < LL. *branca*, paw, claw]
prasseln (vi) [ult. < *bersten*, to burst]	= to crackle, patter (of fire, rain)	*burst*

GERMAN WORD	MEANING	ENGLISH COGNATE
prassen (vi) [bs: to be noisy < MLG. & MDu. *brassen*, to carouse, believed ult. < *bassen*, to bark < echoic root] • **verprassen** (vt)	= to feast, carouse = to dissipate or go through (one's wealth, money)	direct Eng. cogn. lacking, but echoic sense evident; cf. *bash*
Probe (f) [< L. *probare*, to prove] • **probieren** (vt)	= experiment, trial = to try, put to the test	*1. probation; 2. probe* [< L. *probare*, to prove]
Protze (f) [< Venetian *birozzo* < Ital. *biroccio*, cart < L. *birotus*, having two wheels < *bi* + *rota*, wheel]	= wheeled gun carriage, limber	*barouche* [a carriage with collapsible hood, box seat for driver, but with four wheels instead of two < Ital. *biroccio*, cart < L. *birotus*, having two wheels < *bi* + *rota*, wheel]
protzen (vi) [bs: to swell (cogn. G. *Brust*, breast) < OHG. *priozan* < IE. *breus-*, to swell] • **protzig** (adj)	= to show off, parade, flaunt = ostentatious, snobbish	distantly: *breast* [bs: swollen < AS. *breost* < IE. *breus-*, to swell]
prüfen (vt) [< VL. *provare* < L. *probus*, proper]	= to examine, investigate	*proof* and *prove*
Prügel (m) [bs: a board used for beating < OHG. *brügel*, cogn. G. *Brücke*, bridge made of boards] • **prügeln** (vt) ['to use a board on s.o.'] • **prügeln** (refl) • **Prügelei** (f) • **verprügeln** (vt)	= cudgel, stick = to cudgel, flog, beat = to (have a) fight = fight, brawl, scrap = to wallop, trounce	distantly: *bridge (made of boards)*
prunken (vi) [cf. Du. *pronken*, to strut, parade] • **Prunk** (m) • **prunkend, prunkhaft** (adj) • **prunkvoll** (adj) • **Prunkstilleben** (n)	= to be resplendent, make a show, parade = splendor, pomp, magnificence = ostentatious, showy = splendid, gorgeous = a rich still life (theme in Du. 17thc. ptg.)	*1. to prank* [to dress in a showy manner, adorn in grand display; cogn. Du. *pronken*, to strut, parade]; *2. prank* [orig.: an act done to show off, make others stare in amazement, then a mischievous action]
Pult (n) [< ML. *pult, pulpitum*]	= desk	*pulpit* [< ML. *pult, pulpitum* < L. *pulpitum*, stage, scaffolding]
purzeln (see **empor**)		

GERMAN WORD	MEANING	ENGLISH COGNATE
putzen (vt) [etym. disputed; more likely bs: 'to clear up' (lop off) vines or trees < L. *puto, putare,* to prune, lop, clear up (instead of, as claimed, 'to clean the nose of discharge' < *Butzen,* clump, esp. of nasal discharge)]	= to clean, polish, adorn; plaster (a wall); prune, lop; trim or snuff (a candlewick)	disputed, but prob. words < L. *puto, putare,* to prune, lop, clear up (vines, trees): *1. amputate* [to cut or trim all around (*ambi,* around)]; *2. deputy* [one detached with special authority (*de,* from, off)]
• **Putz** (m)	= finery, adornments; plastering	
• **verputzen** (vt)	= to plaster	

# Q		
quabbeln (vi)	= to wobble, quiver, shake; be flabby	*to quiver, quaver* [to tremble, shake]
• **quabbelig** (adj)	= flabby, wobbly	
• **(Kaul)quappe** (f) [bs: a quivering ball < *Kaul* < *Kügel,* sphere + *quappe*]	= tadpole	
Qual (f) [cf. AS. *cwellan*]	= torment, torture	*1. quell* [to crush, subdue < AS. *cwellan*]; *2. kill*[2]
• **quälen** (vt)	= to torment, torture, distress	
• **Quäler** (m)	= tormentor	
Qualm (m)	= smoke, fumes, vapor	*culm* [a coal dust]
• **qualmen** (vi)	= to smoke, give off fumes	
• **qualmig** (adj)	= smoky	
queck, quick (adj)	= lively, brisk	*quick, quicken*
• **erquicken** (vt)	= to refresh, invigorate	
• **verquicken** (vt)	= to mix up	
quer (adj)	= transverse, slanting, oblique, cross	*queer*
• **Quere** (f)	= transverse direction, breadth	
quetschen (vt) [uncert., but prob. < L. *quatio, quatere, quassum,* to shake, beat, crush (whence freqtv. *quassare,* to smash > Fr. *casser,* to break)]	= to squeeze, crush, mash, (med.:) bruise, contuse	*1. to quash* [to suppress < L. *quassare,* to smash, freqtv. of *quatio, quatere, quassum,* to shake, crush]; *2. to kvetch* [to complain habitually ('to squeeze or pinch at') < Yiddish < G. *quetschen*]
• **Quetsche** (f)	= presser, (min.:) crusher	
• **Quetschwunde** (f)	= bruise, contusion	
Quirl (m) [< Gmc. *thwerila,* stir-stick < *tweran,* to turn]	= twirling-stick, whisk, whorl	*twirl*
• **quirlen** (vt)	= to twirl; whisk	

GERMAN WORD	MEANING	ENGLISH COGNATE
quitt (adj) [bs: quieted, settled < ML. *quittus* < LL. *quiettare*, to set free < L. *quietus*, calm, free < *quies*, rest]	= even (with); (of accounts:) settled; rid of	*1. quittance* [discharge from a debt]; *2. quit; 3. quiet*
• **quittieren** (vt)	= to give receipt	
• **Quittung** (f)	= receipt, discharge	
Quitte (f) [< OHG. *qitina, chutina* < L. *quidonia, cotonea* < Gk. *kydonion*, of Kydonia, city of Crete]	= quince	*quince* [< ME. *quyne, quine* < OFr. *cooin* < L. *cotonea* < Gk. *Kydonia*, city of the fruit's origin]

R

Rabatt (m)	= discount, rebate	*rebate* [< Ital. *rabattere*, to remove, take away]
Rabe (m)	= raven	*raven*
Rache (f) [< OHG. *rahha* (MDu. *wraak;* AS. *wrecan)*]	= revenge, vengeance	*wreak* [arch.: to avenge; to vent anger, inflict vengeance < AS. *wrecan*]
• **rachgierig, rachsüchtig** (adj)	= revengeful, vindictive	
• **rächen** (vt)	= to avenge	
Rad (n) [cogn. L. *rota*, wheel, *rotare*, to turn]	= wheel	*rotate, rotary* [< L. *rota*, wheel, *rotare*, to turn]
• **radeln** (vi)	= to ride (a bike)	
radieren (vt) [< L. *rado, radere, rasi, rasum*, to scrape, scratch, shave, erase]	= to rub out, erase; (art:) to etch	*1. abrade; 2. to raze; 3. razor*
• **Radierung** (f)	= etching	
raffen (vt)	= to snatch up, gather up	*raffle* [orig.: a game of chance, then a lottery < OFr. *rafle*]
• **aufraffen** (refl)	= to rouse o.s., muster energy	
ragen (vi) [< MHG. *rac*, tight, stiff; etym. uncert: perh. distantly related to OHG. *recchen*, Goth. *rakjan*, stretch]	= to rise above, tower	*1. to rake²* [naut.: to be slightly inclined above the horizontal or from the perpendicular; akin to Swed. *raka*, to project, stick out]; *2. rakish* [naut.: of trim appearance suggesting speed; thus dashing, smart]
• **hervorragen** (vi) [< *hervor*, forth + *ragen*]	= to project, be prominent, stand out	
• **hervorragend** (adj)	= superior, eminent [lit.: 'projecting out' < L. *e*, out + *minere*, to project]	
• **überragen** (vt)	= to tower over, surpass	
• **überragend** (adj)	= superior, outstanding	

GERMAN WORD	MEANING	ENGLISH COGNATE
Rahm (m)	= cream	*1. ream* [obs. & dial.: scum or froth on a liquid]; *2. ramekin* [baking dish for mixture of eggs and cream]
Rahmen (m) [origin unclear; believed cogn. to G. *Rand*, edge, brink (cf. AS. *rand*)] • **einrahmen** (vt), **umrahmen** (vt)	= frame, border = to frame, enframe	? *rand* [edge, border; strip of leather between heel and shoe < AS. *rand*]
Ramsch (m) [bs: that massed up < Fr. *ramas*, heap < *ramasser*, to gather up < L. *massa*, mass] • **verramschen** (vt)	= junk, trash; cheap goods = to sell goods dirt cheap	*re + mass* (i.e., heaping up)
Rand (m) [cf. AS. *rand;* Frk. **rando*] • **rändeln** (vt)	= edge, brim, border, margin = to edge, border, knurl	*rand* [edge, border; strip of leather between heel and shoe < AS. *rand*]
Rang (m) [< Fr. *rang* < OHG. *hring*, ring]	= order, tier	*rank, range, ring*
rank (adj) [cogn. L. *rectus*, right, straight]	= slim, slender	*1. rank* [orig.: upright, stretched, then growing vigorously, luxuriant; offensive]; *2.* distantly: *rector*
Ranke (f) [< ML. *hranca* but ult. origin uncert.; distantly ? < IE. **ger-*, curving, crooked; or ? < IE. **wer-*, to turn, bend] • **Rankenwerk** (n) • **ranken** (vi & refl) • **rankig** (adj)	= tendril, shoot = interlaced scrollwork = to climb, creep = creeping; with tendrils	? *crank* [crooked handle < IE. **ger-*, curving, crooked] Or ? distantly: *wrench* [< IE. **wer-*, to turn, bend]
Ränke (see **renken**)		
ranzig (adj) [< L. *rancidus*]	= rancid	*rancid* [< L. *rancidus*]
rasch (adj) • **Raschheit** (f) • **überraschen** (vt) ['to come upon quickly']	= quick, swift, hasty, prompt = quickness, swiftness, promptness = to surprise	*rash* [hasty, wreckless]
rasen (vi) • **rasend** (adj) • **Raserei** (f)	= to race, dash; rage, rave = frantic, frenzied = frenzy, rage, fury	*to race*
Rasse (f) [Fr. *race;* Ital. *razza*; ult. source uncert.]	= race, breed, blood	*race* [grouping of breed, species, etc.]
rasseln (vi)	= to rattle	*rattle*

GERMAN WORD	MEANING	ENGLISH COGNATE
Rast (f) • **rasten** (vi)	= rest, repose = to rest, repose	*rest*
Rat (m) [bs: that useful, esp. in reading, interpreting, advising about meanings (cf. AS. *raedan*); cogn. L. *ratio*, reckoning, thinking] • **raten**[1] (vi) • **ratsam** (adj) • **beraten** (vt & refl) • **Berater** (m) • **verraten** (vt) [bs: to give false advice < *ver*, neg.]	= advice, counsel; council (as body) = to give advice, counsel = advisable = to advise; consider = counselor = to betray	*1. to read* [orig.: to guess, advise, discern the meaning of < AS. *raedan*]; *2. riddle; 3. to rede* [dial.: to advise, counsel, to narrate, tell < AS. *raedan*]; *4.* distantly: *rat-* in *rational* [< L. *ratio*, reckoning, thinking]
• **raten**[2], **erraten** (vt)	= to guess, divine	
• **-rat** in compounds denotes 'thing(s) good or useful': • **Gerät** (n) • **Hausrat** (m) • **Unrat** (m) [orig.: 'what is not beneficial' < *un* + *Rat*, thing that benefits] • **Vorrat** (m) • **vorrätig** (adj)	 = tool, implement, gear = furniture = rubbish, filth = supply, provision, stock = in store, on hand, available	
Rätsel (n) • **rätselhaft** (adj) • **enträtseln** (vt)	= riddle, puzzle, enigma = puzzling, enigmatic = to decipher	*riddle*
Ratte (f)	= rat	*rat*
rauben (vt) • **berauben** (vt) • **Räuber** (m) • **räuberisch** (adj)	= to rob = to rob, deprive = robber = predatory	*1. rob; 2.* distantly: *to reave* and *bereaved*
Rauch (m) [< *riech-*, of smell, scent] • **rauchen** (vi) • **rauchern** (vt) • **verrauchen** (vi) • (see also **riechen**)	= smoke, vapor, fume = to fume, give off smoke = to smoke (meat), fumigate, perfume = to go up in smoke, pass	distantly: *reek*
raufen (vt) [ult. < *rauben*, to take by force] • **raufen** (vi) • **Rauferei** (f) • **Raufbold** (m) • **Raufhandel** (m)	= to pluck, pull, tear = to fight, scuffle = fight, scuffle = brawler, tough = brawl	*1. to reave; 2. bereaved; 3.* distantly: *to rob*
rauh (adj) [cf. AS. *ruh*] • **Rauheit** (f) • **rauhen** (vt)	= rough, rugged; coarse, harsh = roughness; coarseness = to roughen	*rough* [< AS. *ruh*]

GERMAN WORD	MEANING	ENGLISH COGNATE
Raum (m) [whence Fr. *arrimer*, to stow (naut.), pack (aviat.)] • **räumen** (vt) • **räumlich** (adj) • **einräumen** (vt) [bs: to give room to, let in < *ein*, in + *Raum*, space]	= space, area, room, expanse = to remove, clear away, vacate = spatial, stereoscopic = to grant, concede	*1. room; 2. rum-* in *rummage* [orig.: the cargo in a ship's *rum*, hold, then any miscellaneous articles]
raunen (vt & vi) [< OHG. *runen* (cf. AS. *runian*)]	= to whisper, murmur	*1. rune* [orig.: mystery, secret, then a mark with mysterious meaning]; *2. to raund, round* [arch.: to whisper < AS. *runian*, with parasitic *d*]
Raupe (f) [etym. uncert.; possib. bs: what moves on its stomach, as a seal; theorized < *Robbe*, seal]	= caterpillar	? distantly: *rab-* in *rabbit* (see **Robbe**)
rauschen (vi) • **Geräusch** (n) • **geräuschvoll** (adj) • **Rausch** (m)	= to rustle, cause noise (of leaves, water, silk); to rush, roar = noise, bustle = noisy = intoxication; transport, ecstasy	*rush*
Rebe (f) [cogn. L. *repo* (& *repto*), *repere*, to creep]	= vine, grape vine; tendril, shoot	distantly: *reptile* [< L. *repo* (& *repto*), *repere*, to creep]
rechnen (vt) • **berechnen** (vt)	= to calculate, reckon = to calculate, sum up	*reckon*
Recht (n) • **berichtigen** (vt)	= right, privilege, authority, law, justice = to authorize, empower	*right*
Recke (m) [knight errant, adventurer < MHG. *recke*, hero, ameliorated from OHG. *recheo*, *wrekkio*, one persecuted (cf. AS. *wrecca*, exile; Frk. **wrakjo*, soldier, also, male child, thus VL. *waracionem* > Fr. *garçon*)]	= hero, warrior	*wretch, wretched* [one despised < AS. *wrecca*, one driven out, exiled]
recken (vt & refl) [cf. AS. *raecan*; cogn. L. *rigidus*, rigid] • **verrecken** (vi) [bs: get rigid, stretch out; cf. L. *rig-* in *rigor mortis*, 'stiffness of death']	= to stretch (out) = (of animals:) to die, perish; (vulgar, of persons:) to croak, kick the bucket	*1. reach; 2.* distantly: *rigid*

GERMAN WORD	MEANING	ENGLISH COGNATE
Rede (f) [cogn. *raten*[1] (cf. AS. *raedan*), with meaning specialized to speech, cogn. L. *ratio*, reckoning, thinking]	= speech, oration, discourse	distantly: *1. to read* [orig.: to guess, advise, discern the meaning of < AS. *raedan*]; *2. riddle; 3. to rede* [dial.: to advise, counsel, to narrate, tell < AS. *raedan*]; *4.* distantly: *rat*- in *rational* [< L. *ratio*, reckoning, thinking]
• **reden** (vt & vi)	= to speak or talk (to)	
• **Redkunst** (f)	= rhetoric	
• **Redner** (m)	= orator, speaker	
• **verabreden** (vt)	= to agree on, arrange, fix	
• **Nachrede** (f) [bs: bad talk (*Rede*) about (*nach*, after) s.o.]	= defamation, slander	
• **überreden** (vt) [lit.: to 'over talk' s.o., talk into]	= to persuade, talk s.o. into	
Regal (n) [bs: straight bar < L. *regula*, rule, rod, standard]	= shelf	*1. regulate; 2. rule* [criterion; bar of metal < L. *regula*]
rege (adj)	= active, brisk, lively	? *ree* [adj. Scot.: excited, esp. with drink; fuddled]
• **reglos** (adj)	= motionless	
• **regen** (vt & refl)	= to stir, move	
• **anregen** (vt)	= to stimulate, suggest	
• **anregend** (adj)	= stimulating, suggestive	
• **erregen** (vt) [< *er*- prefix of completion + *regen*, to stir]	= to excite, cause	
• **erregbar** (adj)	= excitable	
• **Erreger** (m) ['what excites, causes illness']	= germ, virus	
Regel (f) [< L. *regula*, rule, rod, standard]	= rule, regulation, standard	*1. regulate; 2. rule* [criterion; bar of metal < L. *regula*]
• **regeln** (vt)	= to regulate, arrange, put in order	
Reh (n)	= roe (female deer)	*roe*
reiben (vt & vi)	= to rub, massage, grate	*rub*
• **Reibung** (f)	= friction	
• **Reibe** (f)	= grater	
reich (adj)	= rich, abundant	*rich*
• **Reichtum** (m)	= riches, wealth	
reichen (vt)	= to hand (to), serve, offer	*reach*
• **reichen** (vi)	= to reach, suffice	
reife (adj)	= ripe, mature	*ripe*
• **reifen** (vi)	= to ripen, mature	
• **Reife** (f)	= ripeness, maturity	
Reifen (m) [bs: a circular band < Gmc. *raipa*, band, strap]	= ring, hoop, tire (autom.)	*rope* [orig.: a strip, esp. forming a loop]
Reihe (f)	= row, file, line, series	*row* [< ME *rowe*, AS. *raew*]
• **reihen** (vt)	= to put or form in a row	

GERMAN WORD	MEANING	ENGLISH COGNATE
Reiher (m) [cf. Frk. *haigiro*]	= heron	*heron* [< OFr. *hairon* < Frk. *hai-giro*]
rein (adj) • **reinigen** (vt)	= clean, pure, clear = to cleanse, purify	*rhine* [a fine quality of Russian hemp < *rine* hemp < G. *rein Hanf*, clean hemp]
reisen (vi)	= to travel	*rise*
reißen (vt & vi) [*riß, gerissen;* < OHG. *rizan. wrizan*] • **Reißbrett** (n) • **Riß** (m) • **Aufriß** (m) • **Grundriß** (m) • **Reiz** (m) [bs: scratching, itch as stimulus, esp. in positive sense, cogn. *reißen*] • **reizen** (vt)	= to tear, pull, scratch; to split, burst = drawing board = tear, scratch = draft, plan, elevation (archtr.) = ground-plan, outline = irritation; charm, attraction = to irritate, provoke, excite	*write* [bs: scratched characters < AS. *writan* (cf. *character* < Gk. *character*, something engraved < *charassein*, to scratch, engrave)]
reiten (vt & vi) [*ritt, geritten*] • **Ritter** (m) • **ritterlich** (adj)	= to ride, mount, go on horseback = knight, cavalier = knightly, chivalrous, gallant	*ride*
Reiz (see **reißen**)		
Ren, Rentier (n)	= reindeer	*reindeer*
renken (vt) • **ausrenken** (vt) • **einrenken** (vt) • **verrenken** (vt) ——————————— • **Ränke** (f/pl.) [lit.: 'twistings,' i.e., crookedness] • **Ränkeschmied** (m) [lit.: 'smith of intrigues']	= to twist, turn = to dislocate, disjoint = to set right a dislocation = to contort, sprain ——————————— = intrigues, scheming = intriguer, schemer	*to wrench*
rennen (see **rinnen**)		
Rente (f) [< Fr. *rente*, revenue < *rendre*, to give back < ML. *rendere* for *reddere* < *re(d)*, back + *dare*, to give] • **rentieren** (refl) • **Rentner** (m)	= revenue, income, pension = to be profitable, pay = annuitant, pensioner	*1. rent; 2. to render*
retten (vt) • **Retter** (m) • **Rettung** (f)	= to rescue, salvage, save = saviour = rescue, delivery	*rid* [obs.: to save or deliver from difficulty; now: to free, disencumber < AS. *hreddan*]
reuen (impers. + **mich**) • **Reue** (f) • **bereuen** (vt)	= to regret, be sorry for = regret, repentance = to repent of, regret	*to rue* [to feel remorse, regret]

GERMAN WORD	MEANING	ENGLISH COGNATE
Revier (n) [< OFr. *rivière*, area along a river, river bank < L. *ripa*, river bank]	= district, quarter; precinct	words < L. *ripa*, river bank: *1. riviera; 2. arrive* [lit.: 'to land on a bank']; *3. rival* ['one from the opposite bank']; *4. riparian* [pertaining to life on a river or lake]
richten (vt) • **richtig** (adj) • **berichtigen** (vt) • **berichten** (vt) • **Bericht** (m) • **Nachricht** (f) • **Richtung** (f) • **anrichten** (vt) • **Gericht** (n) • **hinrichten** (vt) [< *hin*, there (i.e., final point)]	= to set right, arrange = right, correct = to correct, rectify = to report, give account = report = news, information = direction, way, course = to prepare, serve up = court of justice, judgement; dish, course (that set at table) = to put to death, execute	*right*
riechen (vt & vi) [*roch, gerochen*] • **Geruch** (m) • (see also **Rauch**)	= to smell = smell, odor; reputation	*reek*
Riefe (f) • **riefeln** (vt), **riffeln** (vt)	= groove, channel, flute = to flute, groove	*rifle* [so-called from the groove cut spirally within the barrel to cause rotary motion to the bullet]
Riegel (m) [< OHG. *rigil*] • **abriegeln** (vt)	= bar, bolt; cake, bar (e.g., of soap) = to block, bar, bolt	*railing*
Riemen[1] (m) [< OHG. *riomo*]	= strap, belt, sling	*riem*, also *reim*, *rheim* [strip or thong of leather < Afrikaans *riem*]
Riemen[2] (m) [theorized < L. *remus*, oar]	= oar	*-reme* in *trireme* [an ancient Roman ship having three banks of oars on each side < L. *tri* + *remus*, oar]
rieseln (vi) [< OHG. *risan*, to go, up or down] • **berieseln** (vt)	= to ripple, trickle, drizzle = to irrigate, spray	*rise* [to go up]
Riff (n)	= reef	*reef*
riffeln (see **Riefe**)		
Rille (f) • **rillen** (vt)	= groove, furrow, flute = to groove, chamfer	*rill* [a little brook]
Rind (n) [< OHG. *hrind* (cf. AS. *hrider*; MDu. *runt*, *ront* > Du. *rund*)]	= horned beast, such as oxen, cattle	*1. rinderpest* [a disease of cattle]; *2. runt* [ox or cow of small breed; creature of stunted growth < MDu. *runt*, *ront*]
Rinde (f)	= bark, rind	*rind*

GERMAN WORD	MEANING	ENGLISH COGNATE
ringen (vt & vi) [*rang, gerungen*] • **Ringer** (m) • **erringen** (vt) ['to successfully (*er-*) struggle after (*ring-*) s.t.,' 'wring for oneself'] • **Errungenschaft** (f)	= to wring; to wrestle, struggle (with) = wrestler = to gain, obtain, achieve = acquisition, achievement	*wring*
rinnen (vi) [*rann, geronnen*] • **Rinne** (f) • **rennen** (vi) [*rannte, gerannt*; bs: to make run] • **Rennbahn** (f)	= to run, flow, drip = groove, channel, gutter, flute (col.) = to race, run = racecourse	*run*
Rippe (f)	= rib, bar	*rib*
Risiko (n)	= risk, peril	*risk*
Riß (see **reißen**)		
Robbe (f) [from seal's likeness to a rabbit in bristles, whiskers < Du. *robbe*, rabbit] • **robben** (vi)	= seal (zool.) = to move like a seal, crawl	*rabbit* [< ME. *rabette*, young of the cony < MDu. *robbe*]
Rock (m)	= skirt, coat, jacket	*1. frock; 2. rochet* [vestment worn by a bishop]
Rocken and **Spinnrocken** (m)	= distaff	*1. rocket* [projectile with pointed shape]; *2. ratchet*
roden (vt) [seen in var. UGerm. *reuten* (cf. AS. *wrotan*)] • **ausroden** (vt) _____ • **ausrotten** (vt)	= to clear (land), root up = to clear (woods); root out _____ = to root out, eradicate, extirpate	*1. to root* [to search by rummaging < AS. *wrotan*]; *2.* suffix forms *-rode, -reut* in place names *Gernrode, Bayreuth*
Rogen (m)	= roe	*roe*
Roggen (m) [cf. AS. *ryge*] • **Roggenbrot** (n)	= rye = rye-bread	*rye* [< AS. *ryge*]
roh (adj) [cf. AS. *hreaw*] • **Roheit** (f) • **verrohen** (vt & vi)	= raw, rough; cruel, brutal = rawness, crudeness, roughness = to brutalize, grow brutal	*raw* [< AS. *hreaw*]
Rost[1] (m) • **Rostbraten** (m) • **rösten** (vt) • **Röster** (m) • **Röstbrot** (n)	= grating, grate, grill, gridiron = roast joint = to roast, grill, toast = roaster, toaster = toast	*1. roster* [orig.: gridiron, then a list, bec. of the grid of ruled lines used in listings < Du. *rooster*, gridiron]; *2. roast*

GERMAN WORD	MEANING	ENGLISH COGNATE
Rost[2] (m) • **rosten** (vi) • **Rostbildung** (f)	= rust, mildew = to rust, oxidize = rust formation	*rust*
Roß (n) [< OHG. *ros, hros* (cf. A.S. *hors*)]	= horse	*1. horse* [< A.S. *hors*]; *2. -rus* in *walrus* ['whale horse']
rot (adj) • **röten** (vt) • **Röte** (f)	= red = to color or dye red = redness, red color	*red*
Rotte (f) • **rotten** (refl)	= band, gang = to band together	*rout* [orig.: a band of followers, then a disorderly fight, defeat]
Rube (f)	= turnip, rape	*rape* [plant of the mustard family]
ruchbar (see **rufen**)		
ruchlos (adj) [lit.: 'without care,' 'lacking reck, concern' < MHG. *ruoche*, care, reck + *los*, without, less] • **verrucht** (adj) [bs: devoid of reck (care) < *ver*, neg. + *ruoche*] ———————— • **geruhen** (vi) [erroneously after *ruhen*, but really < MHG. *geruochen*, showing reck, care < *ruoch*, care]	= wicked, foul = villainous, heinous, wicked ———————— = to deign, condescend, be pleased to	*reckless* ['without reck' < *to reck*, to have care, concern, e.g., 'he *recks* not of peril,' + *-less*]
Rücken[1] (m) [cf. A.S. *hrycg*] • **rückwärts** (adv) • **berücksichtigen** (vt) [bs: to look back at]	= back, ridge = backwards = to pay attention to, take into consid- eration	*1. ridge* [< A.S. *hrycg*]; *2. rucksack* [a kind of knapsack strapped over the shoulders]
rücken[2] (vt & vi) • **rückweise** (adv) • **abrücken** (vt & vi) • **anrücken** (vi) • **entrücken** (vt) • **entrückt** (adj) [bs: carried off] • **verrücken** (vt) • **verrückt** (adj) ['displaced' < *ver*, wrong + *rücken*] • **vorrücken** (vt & vi)	= to move, shift = by jerks = to remove, move away = to approach = to remove, carry off = entranced, lost in thought = to displace, shift = mad, crazy, deranged = to move forward, advance	*to rock* [to move or shift front to back or side to side]
Ruder (n) • **Ruderer** (m)	= oar, rudder = oarsman, rower	*rudder*

GERMAN WORD	MEANING	ENGLISH COGNATE
rufen (vt & vi) [< OHG. *hruofan* (Goth. *hropjan*; AS. *hropan*)]	= to call, cry	*1. roup* [poultry disease character-ized by hoarseness and catarrhal discharge]; *2. roupy* [chiefly Scot.: hoarse]; *3. to roup* [arch.: to shout; to proclaim with loud voice; to sell by auction]
• **Ruf** (m)	= shout, call, cry; reputation, fame	
• **abrufen** (vt)	= to call away, recall	
• **Abruf** (m)	= recall	
• **berufen** (vt)	= to appoint (call s.o. to)	
• **berufen** (refl) (+ **auf**)	= to refer to (call oneself to)	
• **Beruf** (m)	= profession, calling, vocation [< L. *vocare*, to call]	
• **beruflich** (adj)	= professional, vocational	
• **Notruf** (m) [*Not*, need + *Ruf*]	= emergency call	
• **verrufen** (adj) [*ver*, neg. + *rufen*]	= ill-reputed	
also **ruch-** [cogn. *rufen*, via < MLG. *ruoft*]		
• **ruchbar** (adj)	= notorious	
• **anrüchig** (adj)	= notorious, disreputable	
• **berüchtigt** (adj)	= notorious, ill-famed	
• **Gerücht** (n) [bs: what is called < MHG. *gerüofte*, OHG. *gehruofti*]	= rumor, report	
rügen (vt) [< OHG. *ruogen*, to scold < Goth. *wrohjan* (cf. AS. *wregan*)]	= to reprimand, blame, scold, censure	*1. to wray* [arch.: to denounce < AS. *wregan*, to inform with accusa-tion]; *2. to bewray* [orig.: to accuse, then to make known]
• **Rüge** (f)	= admonition, censure	
Ruhe (f)	= rest, repose	*ro*, also *row* [obs.: repose, peace ('rest in ro'); also *to ro*, to rest]
• **ruhig** (adj)	= calm, tranquil	
• **ruhen** (vi)	= to rest, repose	
• **beruhen** (vi)	= to rest or be based on	
• **beruhigen** (vt)	= to calm, soothe	
rühren (vt) [< OHG. *ruora*, stirring, active (cf. AS. *hreran*)]	= to touch, cause to move; (fig.:) touch, affect	*1. -roar* in *uproar* [lit.: 'a stirring up,' movement, commotion]; *2. rare* [of cooked meat, bs: lightly touched to fire < AS. *hreran*, to move, shake]
• **rührend** (adj)	= touching, moving	
• **rührig** (adj)	= active, enterprising	
• **Rührung** (f)	= emotion, feeling	
• **anrühren** (vt)	= to touch, mix	
• **berühren** (vt)	= to touch, touch upon (a subject)	
• **Berührung** (f)	= contact, touch	
• **herrühren** (vi) (+ **von**) ['to touch here (from)']	= to come from, originate from	
Rummel (m) [echoic]	= bustle, racket, row	*rumble*
• **rumpeln** (vi)	= to rumble	
• **überrumpeln** (vt) [bs: to surprise by great noise]	= to take unawares, surprise	
• **Gerümpel** (n)	= rumbling, bumps, jolts; house junk	
Rumpf (m)	= body, trunk, hull (mar.), fuselage (aeron.)	*rump*

GERMAN WORD	MEANING	ENGLISH COGNATE
rümpfen (vt) ['to wrinkle the nose at']	= to turn up one's nose at, sniff at	*rumple* [to cause wrinkles]
Runge (f)	= stake, stanchion	*rung* [of a ladder, etc.]
Runzel (f) [< OHG. *runzala*]	= wrinkle, pucker	*wrinkle*
rupfen (vt) [intens. of *raufen*, to pluck, pull away < *rauben*, to rob] • **ruppig** (adj)	= to pull out, pluck = ragged, shabby, gruff	distantly: *rob*
Ruß (m) [< OHG. *ruoz*, suffixed form believed cogn. with root **hro-*, filth, foulness (cf. AS. *horig* < *horh*, filth, dark residue)] • **rußen** (vi) • **rußig** (adj)	= soot = to give off smoke = sooty	*hory, horry, howry* [obs. and dial.: foul, dirty, filthy < AS. *horig* < *horh*, filth, dark residue < **hro-*, filth, foulness]
Rüssel (m)	= snout, trunk (of elephant), proboscis	*to root* [dig with the snout, as a pig roots]
Rüstung (f) [< OHG. *hrustjan* (cf. AS. *hyrstan*) < Gmc. **hro(d)-st*] • **rüsten** (vt) • **Gerüst** (n) • **entrüsten** (vt) ['to take away one's armaments'] • **entrüsten** (refl) • **entrüstet** (adj)	= preparations; arming, armaments = to equip, fit out; mobilize (for war); to raise a scaffold = scaffold, trestle, truss = to anger, provoke s.o. = to get angry = indignant, angry	prob. distantly cogn.: *roost* [framework for fowl, timberwork < Gmc. **hro(d)-st*]
Rute (f)	= switch, rod	*1. rod; 2. rood* [cross made of two rods]
rutschen (vi) [believed echoic] • **Rutsch** (m) • **verrutschen** (vi) • **verrutscht** (adj)	= to slide, slip, skid = (land)slide = to slip = slipped, not straight	cf. similar sound but different force in echoic Eng. *crunch*
rütteln (vt & vi) [cogn. *roden*, to clear land] • **zerrütten** (vt)	= to rattle, shake = to derange, unsettle, shatter, ruin	*rattle*

GERMAN WORD	MEANING	ENGLISH COGNATE
S		
Saal (m) [< OHG. *sal* (cf. Frk. *sal*, whence Fr. *salle*; Ital. *sala, salone*)]	= hall, assembly room	*1. salon; 2. saloon* [< OHG. *sal*, domicile; cf. Goth. *saljan*, to dwell]
• **Geselle** (m) [< OHG. *gisello*, he with whom one shares a *sal*, room]	= companion, fellow, journeyman	
• **gesellen** (vt & refl)	= to associate with, join	
• **gesellig** (adj)	= gregarious, social, sociable	
• **Gesellschaft** (f)	= society, community	
• **Junggeselle** (m)	= bachelor	
Saat (f)	= seed, sowing	*1. seed; 2. to sow*
• **säen** (vi)	= to sow	
sabbern (vi) [< IE. *seib-*, to trickle, drip]	= to dribble, slaver, drool	distantly: *seep* [< IE. *seib-*, to trickle, drip]
Sache (f)	= thing, matter, affair	*sake*
• **sachlich** (adj)	= real, essential, positive	
• **Ursache** (f)	= cause	
• **verursachen** (vt)	= to cause	
sacht (adj)	= soft, gentle, slow	distantly: *soft*
sacken (vi) and **absacken** (vi)	= to give way, sag, sink	distantly: *sag* [< ME. *saggen* (cf. ON. *sakka*)]
Saft (m) [< OHG. *saf* (cf. AS. *saep*)]	= juice	*sap* [< AS. *saep*] and *sappy* [< AS. *saepig*]
• **saftig** (adj)	= juicy	
Säge (f)	= saw	*saw* [< AS. *sagu*]
• **sägen** (vt & vi)	= to saw	
sagen (vt & vi)	= to say	*1. say; 2. saga*
• **Sage** (f)	= story, myth, legend	
• **sagenhaft** (adj)	= legendary, mythical	
• **absagen** (vt & vi)	= to call off, cancel	
• **aussagen** (vt & vi)	= to state, declare	
• **versagen** (vt) [bs: to say no < *ver*, neg. + *sagen*]	= to refuse, deny	
• **versagen** (vi)	= to fail to function	
• **Versagen** (n)	= breakdown, failure	
• **zusagen** (vt & vi)	= to promise, accept	
Sahne (f) [< MDu. *säne* < OFr. *sain*, fat < L. *sagina*, fattening up, rich food]	= cream	*saginate* [rare: to fatten (animals) < L. *saginare* < *sagina*, fattening up, rich food]
• **sahnig** (adj)	= creamy	

GERMAN WORD	MEANING	ENGLISH COGNATE
Saite (f) [< OHG. *seit* < IE. **se-*, to bind, tie]	= chord, string (of violin, etc.)	distantly: *si-* in *sinew* [< IE. **se-*, to bind, tie]
Salbe (m) • **(ein)salben** (vt)	= ointment, salve = to rub with ointment	*salve*
Saldo (see **Sold**)		
sammeln (see **samt**²)		
Samt¹ (m) [< Ital. *sciamitu* < Gk. *hexamitos*, of six threads < *hex*, six + *mitos*, thread (whence *mitosis*, the process of biological cell division occuring along a thread of chromatin)]	= velvet	*samite* [a rich silk fabric of the Middle Ages with a warp of six threads, sometimes interwoven with gold thread < Gk. *hexamitos*, of six threads < *hex*, six + *mitos*, thread]
samt² (prep) • **sammeln** (vt) • **Sammler** (m) • **Sammlung** (f)	= together, along with = to collect, gather = collector = collection	*1. same; 2. sam* [obs. adv: together]
sanft (adj) [< OHG. *samfto* (cf. AS. *soefte*)] • **Sanftheit** (f) • **sanftmütig** (adj) • **besänftigen** (vt)	= soft, gentle, mild, meek, calm = softness, gentleness, smoothness = gentle, mild, meek, sweet = to appease, calm, soothe	*soft* [< AS. *soefte*]
Sarg (m) [< L. < Gk. *sarcophagus*]	= coffin	*sarcophagus*
satt (adj) [cogn. L. *satis*, enough, adequate] • **Sattheit** (f)	= satisfied, satiated, full = satiety, fullness	*1. sad* [filled with unhappy feeling < AS. *saed*, sated, full]; *2. satisfy* < L. *satis*, enough, adequate]
Sattel (m) • **satteln** (vi) • **umsatteln** (vi)	= saddle = to saddle = to resaddle; change occupation	*saddle*
sauber (adj) [< L. *sobrius*, sober, temperate; reasonable] • **saubern** (vt)	= clean, neat = to clean, cleanse	*sober*
Sau (f)	= sow	*sow*
sauer (adj) • **Sauerstoff** (m)	= sour = oxygen	*sour*
saufen (vt & vi)	= to drink (of animals); (vulg.:) to booze, tipple	*sup*¹ [to take liquid into the mouth]
saugen (vt & vi) • **Säugling** (m) • **Sog** (m)	= to suck = infant, babe = suction, undertow, wake	*suck, suckle*

GERMAN WORD	MEANING	ENGLISH COGNATE
Säule (f) [obscure; assoc. with framing, a base, sill < MHG. OHG. *sul* (cf. Goth. *sauls;* AS. *syl*); ? perh. distantly cogn. L. *solum*, bottom, ground, soil] • **Säulengang** (m) and **Säulenreihe** (f) • **Säulenhalle** (f) • **Säulenkopf** (m) • **Säulenkreis** (m) [*Säulen + Kreis*, circle]	= column, pillar = colonnade, row of columns = portico = capital of column = peristyle	*1. sill* [< AS. *syl*]; *2. ? soil* [< L. *solum*, bottom, ground, soil]; *3. ? sole* [of the foot]
Saum (m) • **säumen**[1] (vt) [not to be confused with **säumen**[2], to tarry, linger (**säumen**[2] is of difficult origin, with no known cognates in English)]	= hem, edge, seam, fringe = to hem, edge, border	*seam*
schaben (vt) • **Schaber** (m) • **schäbig** (adj) • **Schabe** (f) [bs: creature that scrapes or pares] _____ • **Schuppe** (f) • **schuppig** (adj) • **schuppen** (vt) • **abschuppen** (vi)	= to scrape, grate, scratch, rasp = scraper = shabby, seedy, mean = cockroach _____ = scale (skin), dandruff = scaly = to scale (fish) = to scale away or off	*shave*
Schablone (f) [< MDu. *schampelioen* < Fr. *échantillon*, pattern, specimen] • **schablonenhaft, schablonenmäßig** (adj)	= pattern, model, stencil, routine = mechanical, routine, by pattern	*scantling* [piece of timber cut in a small size, sample, pattern < Fr. *échantillon*, pattern, specimen]
Schacht (m) • **ausschachten** (vt)	= (mining:) shaft, well, hollow = to excavate, hollow out, sink	*shaft*
Schachtel, Schatulle (see **Schatz**)		
Schädel (m) [etym. uncert., but believed assoc. with an earthenware vessel. Perh. ult. < L. *scutella*, saucer, shallow bowl (cf. G. *Kopf*, head, cogn. L. *cupa*, cup)]	= skull, cranium	*? scuttle* [< L. *scutella*, saucer, shallow bowl]

GERMAN WORD	MEANING	ENGLISH COGNATE
schaden (vi) [cf. ME. *scathen*, to harm] • **Schade** (m), **Schaden** (m) • **schadhaft** (adj) ['having damage'] • **schädlich** (adj) • **schädigen** (vt) • **beschädigen** (vt) • **entschädigen** (vt) [*ent*, away + *schädigen*]	= to do damage, injure = damage, injury, harm = damaged, defective = harmful, injurious = to damage, harm, impair = to damage, injure = to compensate against damages, indemnify [< L. *in*, not + *damnum*, damage]	*1. scathing* [of language: sharp and damaging < ME. *scathen*, to harm]; *2. unscathed* [uninjured, unharmed]
schaffen (vt) [*schuf, geschaffen*] • **Schaffner** (m) • **abschaffen** (vt) • **anschaffen** (vt) • **erschaffen** (vt) • **Erschaffer** (m) • **beschäftigen** (vt) • **Geschäft** (n) ———————— directional prefixes convert the sense to mean *convey, carry:* • **fortschaffen** (vt) • **herschaffen** (vt)	= to work, produce, do, set up; convey, carry = steward, manager = to abolish, discontinue = to provide, furnish = to create, make = creator = to occupy, keep busy = shop, business ———————— = to carry away = to bring here	*to shape*
Schafott (n) [< OFr. *escafalt* < LL. *catafalicum*, wooden tower]	= scaffold	*scaffold* [< OFr. *escafalt* < LL. *catafalicum*, wooden tower]
schal (adj) • **Schalheit** (f)	= stale, insipid, flat, lacking essence = staleness, insipidness	*shallow* [< ME. *schalowe*]
Schale (f) • **schälen** (vt)	= scale, peel, shell, crust = to peel, skin, pare, shell	*1. scale; 2. shell; 3. shale*
Schalk (m) [< OHG. *scalc*, servant]	= rogue, scamp, rascal	*-shall* in *marshall* ['horse servant' < ME. & OFr. *mareschal* < OHG. *marah*, mare + *scalc*, servant]
Schall (m) [*schallte (scholl), geschallt;* bs: bursting sound < Gmc. *skel-*, perh. ult. echoic] • **schallen** (vi) • **erschallen** (vi) • **verschollen** (adj) • **Schelle** (f)	= sound = to sound, ring, peal = to resound, ring, echo = not heard of again, missing = little bell	distantly: *squall* [burst of rain, wind or sound < Scand. < Gmc. *skel-*, perh. ult. echoic]

GERMAN WORD	MEANING	ENGLISH COGNATE
schalten (vt & vi) [orig.: to push (a boat), then direct] • **Schalter** (m) • **Schaltheber** (m) • **Schaltjahr** (n) ['switch year'] • **Schalttafel** (f)	= to switch, operate, control, start; direct, manage = booking office, counter, switch, controller = switch, control lever = leap year = control panel, switchboard	*1. shaltree* [obs.: a pole used for propelling a boat < MLG. *schalden,* to push, OS. *scaldan,* to shove (a boat)]; *2.* distantly: *scow* [a flat-bottomed boat < Du. *schouwe, schoude*]
Scham (f) • **schämen** (refl)	= shame, modesty; pl.: privy parts, genitals (anat.) = to feel ashamed	*shame*
Schande (f) • **schänden** (vt) • **schändlich** (adj)	= disgrace, shame = to disgrace, dishonor = disgraceful, shameful	*shent* [arch.: disgraced, ruined]
schanzen (vi) • **Schanze** (f)	= to entrench, put up entrenchments = entrenchment	*1. to sconce* [to fortify]; *2. ensconsed* [protected]
Schar (see **scheren**)		
scharf (adj) [< IE. **sker-,* to cut, scrape] • **Schärfe** (f) • **entschärfen** (vi) ———— • **schürfen** (vi) [mining term: to dig or cut out] • **schürfen** (vt) [bs: to cut (the skin)]	= sharp, pungent, live (ammunit.) = sharpness, pungency = to deactivate an explosive ———— = to prospect (for) = to graze (e.g., one's skin)	words < IE. **sker-,* to cut, scrape: *1. sharp; 2. scrape*
scharren (vt & vi) • **Scharre** (f) • **ausscharren** (vt)	= to scrape or paw the ground (said esp. of horses, chickens) = scraper, rake = to dig up, rake	*-share* in *ploughshare* [implement for scraping into, digging up the ground]
Scharnier (n) [< Fr. *charnière,* hinge < Gallo-Rom. *cardonaria* < L. *cardo, cardinis,* hinge]	= hinge	*1. cardinal* [adj: on which something hinges, fundamental < L. *cardo, cardinis,* hinge]; *2. kern* [typog: projecting part of metal type < Fr. (Norman.) *carne,* projecting angle < L. *cardo, cardinis,* hinge]
Schatten (m) • **schattig** (adj) • **beschatten** (vt)	= shadow = shaded, shady = to shade, overshadow	*1. shadow; 2. shade*

GERMAN WORD	MEANING	ENGLISH COGNATE
Schatz (m) [< OHG. *scaz* (Goth. *skatts*, gold; wealth; ON. *skattr*, tribute, tax)]	= treasure, wealth	*1. scads; 2. scat, scatt* [Scot.: tribute, tax, esp. land tax < ON. *skattr*, tax]; *3.* disputed: *scatter*
• **(ein)schätzen** (vt)	= to estimate, value, appraise, assess	
• **überschätzen** (vt)	= overestimate	
• **verschätzen** (vt)	= misreckon, make a mistake	
• **brandschatzen** (vt)	= to lay (a town) under contribution; to pillage	
• **Schachtel** (f) [bs: box for treasure < MHG. *schahtel* < ML. *scatula* (whence Ital. *scatola*, box) < OHG. *scaz*]	= chest, box	
• **Schatulle** (f)	= cash box, money chest	
Schau (f)	= view; show, spectacle	*show*
• **schauen** (vt & vi)	= to see, behold; to look	
• **beschauen** (vt)	= to examine, inspect	
• **beschaulich** (adj)	= thoughtful, reflective	
Schauder (m)	= shudder	*shudder*
• **schaudern** (vi)	= to shudder, shiver	
• **schauderhaft** (adj)	= awful, dreadful	
Schauer (m)	= shower (of rain, hail), shiver, fit	*shower*
• **schauerlich, schaurig** (adj) [orig.: applied to horrible weather, then to anything horrible]	= horrible, hair-raising	
Schaufel (f)	= shovel, scoop, paddle	*shovel*
Schaukel (f) [bs: what is pushed; suffixed form based on OHG. *scoc*, a push forward]	= swing, device that swings, see-saw	*shock* [orig.: a push, then, more intensely, impact < OHG. *scoc*]
• **schaukeln** (vt & vi)	= to rock (a baby), make swing, make rock; to swing, rock (of a ship)	
• **Schaukelpferd** (n)	= rocking-horse	
• **Schaukelstuhl** (m)	= rocking-chair	
Schaum (m)	= foam, froth	*scum*
• **schäumen** (vi)	= to foam, lather	
• **überschäumen** (vi)	= to froth or bubble over, brim	
• **überschäumend** (adj)	= exuberant, bubbling over	
scheel (adj) [bs: with crooked look < OHG. *skelah* < IE. *skel-*, crooked, whence Gk. *skolios*, crooked]	= cross-eyed; (fig.:) envious, jealous	distantly: words < IE. *skel-*, crooked: *1. scoliosis* [crookedness of the spine < Gk. *skolios*, crooked, bent]; *2. scalene* [(of a triangle) having three unequal sides < Gk. *scalenos*, uneven, unequal]
• **schielen** (vi)	= to squint, be cross-eyed; squint or leer at	
Scheibe (n) [whence Fr. *cible*, target]	= disc, target; slice (of any loaf, bread, etc.); pane or slab of glass	*1. shive* [a thin cork for a wide-mouthed bottle]; *2. sheave* [pulley or wheel with a grooved rim]

GERMAN WORD	MEANING	ENGLISH COGNATE
scheiden (vt & vi) • **Scheidung** (f) • **entscheiden** (f) • **entscheidend** (adj) • **unterscheiden** (vt) • **bescheiden** (vt) [bs: keeping things apart, giving right information] • **Bescheid** (m) • **Bescheidheit** (f) • **gescheit** (adj) • **Scheitel** (m) [bs: point of divide, hence highest part, from which declivity begins]	= to separate, divorce; depart, retire = separating, parting, analysis, divorce = to decide, determine = decisive, conclusive = to distinguish, differentiate, discern = to allot, assign, direct; inform, instruct = accurate information, answer, reply = modesty, discretion = clever, discriminating = crown, top of head, parting of hair, vortex; summit, peak	*to shed* [to throw off, cast off (e.g. skin, hair), separate]
scheinen (vi) • **erscheinen** (vi) • **Schein** (m)	= to shine, gleam; seem = to appear, turn up = shine, light, gleam, certificate, note	*shine*
Scheit (m) [cf. ON. *skith;* > Ital. *schettinare,* to skate ('to go on skids')] • **Scheiterhaufen** (m) [lit.: 'skid heap'] ———————— • **scheitern** (vi)	= log, board, plank = funeral pyre ———————— = to run aground (naut.); be wrecked; to fail, miscarry	words < ON. *skith: 1. skid; 2. shide* [a piece of wood, plank]; *3. ski;* ———————— *4. to skid*
Scheitel (see **scheiden**)		
Schelm (m) • **schelmisch** (adj)	= rogue = roguish	*skellum* [a rogue]
schelten (vt & vi) • **Schelte** (f)	= to scold, rebuke = scolding	*scold*
Schemel (m) [bs: bench < OHG. *scamal* < L. *scamelllum,* dim. of *scamnum,* bench]	= stool	*shambles* [orig.: bench, for sale of fresh meat, then slaughterhouse, scene of disorder < ME. *schamel,* AS. *sceamul* < L. *scamellum,* dim. of *scamnum,* bench]
Schemen (m) [ult. < Gmc. *ski-m* < IE. *skeei-,* to gleam]	= phantom, shadow	*shim-* in *shimmer* [< IE. *skeei-,* to gleam]

GERMAN WORD	MEANING	ENGLISH COGNATE
Schenk (m) [bs: pouring a drink, extended also to giving a present]	= publican, inn-keeper	*1. to shench, shenk* [obs.: to pour out liquor, give a drink]; *2. -cheon* in *luncheon* [< Span. *lonja*, slice of ham + *-cheon* after Eng. *nuncheon*, refreshment taken in the afternoon, lit.: 'noon drink' < *noon* + *shench*, draught, cup]
• **Schenke** (f)	= tavern, pub	
• **schenken** (vt)	= to pour out, give, grant	
• **Schenkung** (f)	= donation, gift	
• **Schankmädchen** (n)	= barmaid	
• **beschenken** (vt)	= to make a present of	
• **Geschenk** (n)	= gift, present	
• **Fasching** (m) [< MHG. *vastschanc,* drinks before the *fast* of Ash Wednesday]	= Carnival, Shrovetide	
Schenkel (m)	= thigh	*shank*
scheren (vt)	= to shear, clip, prune	*1. shear; 2. share* [a cut off part]; *3. shire* [a division, district in Great Britain, e.g., *Wiltshire*]; *4. sheriff* [one with a cut out, defined, charge (cf. *deputy,* one detached, cut out, with special authority < L. *de,* away + *puto, putare,* to prune, lop, cut away)]
• **Schere** (f)	= scissors, shears	
• **bescheren** (vt)	= to give s.o. (presents), bestow upon	
• **Geschirr** (n) [orig.: that cut and fashioned, later restricted to implements, crockery and harnesses]	= crockery, vessel(s), harness, implement, apparatus	
• **Schar** (f) [bs: a division, cut off part]	= troop, band, group, flock	
• **scharen** (vt)	= to assemble, collect	
• **Scherge** (m) ['he with a defined, cut out, charge']	= beadle, hangman's assistant	
scherzen (vi) [whence Ital. *scherzare,* to play, jest]	= to make merry	*scherzo* [a playful movement in sonatas, symphonies]
• **Scherz** (m)	= joke, jest, fun	
• **scherzhaft** (adj)	= joking, funny, playful	
• **verscherzen** (vt)	= to pass time in joking; lose (a chance, etc.) through folly; to forfeit	
scheu (adj)	= shy, bashful, timid	*shy* and *to shy*
• **Scheu** (f)	= shyness, bashfulness	
• **scheuen** (vi)	= to be shy, shrink from	
• **scheuen** (vt)	= to shun, avoid, dread	
• **abscheulich** (adj)	= abominable	
• **verabscheuen** (vt)	= to abominate	
• **Scheusal** (n) [something before which one shies < *scheuen,* to shy, show fright + *-sal,* instrumental suffix]	= monster, fright	
• **schüchtern** (adj)	= timid, bashful	
• **Schüchternheit** (f)	= timidity, bashfulness	
• **einschüchtern** (vt) [bs: to put into timidity]	= to intimidate	

GERMAN WORD	MEANING	ENGLISH COGNATE
Scheuer (f) [bs: shed, place of cover < OHG. *sciura* (whence ML. *scura, scuria*) < IE. **skeu-*, to cover] • **Scheune** (f) [< OHG. *scugina* (cogn. Norw. *skygne*) < IE. **skeu-*, to cover]	= barn, shed, granary, upper part of farmhouse for storing grain = barn, shed	*1. equerry* [spelling influenced by unrelated L. *equus*, horse; orig.: a stable, then stable official, then an official attending to a prince < OFr. *escurie*, stable < ML. *scura, scuria* < OHG. *sciura*, shed]; *2.* distantly: *sky* [< IE. **skeu-*, to cover]
scheuern (vt) [believed < OFr. < LL. *excurare* < *ex*, thoroughly + *curare*, to care for] • **abscheuern** (vt) • **durchscheuern** (vt) • **wundscheuern** (vt)	= to scrub, polish; chafe, rub = to abrade, wear out = to rub through = to chafe, rub sore	*scour* [< OFr. < LL. *excurare* < *ex*, thoroughly + *curare*, to care for]
Scheune (see **Scheuer**)		
Schicht (f) • **schichten** (vt)	= layer, stratum; class, rank, shift = arrange, put in layers, classify	*shift* [arranged 'layer' of work, the hours of one's work]
schicklich (adj) [< MHG. *schicken*, to put in order] • **Schicklichkeit** (f) • **schicken** (vt) [bs: to put in order and send] • **Geschick** (n) ['what is settled and sent']	= proper, becoming, seemly = propriety, decorum = to send, dispatch = fate, destiny	*chic* [good style < Fr. < MHG. *schicken*, to put in order]
schieben (vt) [*schob, geschoben*] • **Schub** (m) • **Schubfach** (n), **Schublade** (f) • **verschieben** (vt)	= to push, slide = shove, push = drawer (what one draws or pulls) = to remove	*to shove*
schief (adj) • **Schiefe** (f) • **schiefgehen** (vi)	= oblique, slanting, inclined; (fig.:) wrong, erroneous = obliqueness, slant; (fig.:) perversity = to go wrong, go awry	uncert: believed cogn. *skew, skewed*
Schiefer (m) • **Schieferdach** (n) • **Schiefertafel** (f) • **schiefern** (vi) • **Schieferung** (f)	= slate, schist [a kind of stone amenable, like slate, to being split into layers < Gk. *schistos*, easily cleft < *schizein*, to cleave]; splinter = slate roof = slate tablet = to scale off, exfoliate = scaling off, exfoliation	*1. skiver* [the soft thin leather made from the outer layer of split sheepskin]; *2. to skive* [to slice or shave off in thin layers]
Schiene (f) [bs: thin plate] • **schienen** (vt)	= iron plate, hoop or band (esp. on a wheel); rail, slat, splint = to splint, tire, shoe	*shin* [bs: thin or narrow piece]

GERMAN WORD	MEANING	ENGLISH COGNATE
schießen (vt & vi) [*schoß, geschossen* (AS. *sceotan*)] • **Schuß** (m) • **Schößling** (m) • **Geschoß** (n) [that shot; next level, like shoots at intervals along a branch] • **abschüssig** (adj) ['shooting down']	= to shoot; dart, dash = shot; rush = sprout, (off)shoot = bullet, projectile; (archtr.:) story, floor = precipitous	*shoot, shot* [< AS. *sceotan*, to throw, cast]
Schiff (n) • **schiffbar** (adj)	= ship, vessel, boat, nave (of church) = navigable	*1. ship; 2. skiff*
Schild (m & n) • **schildern** (vt) [in chivalric times an aritist's occupation included decorating shields with colors and images]	= shield; sign = to describe, delineate, portray	*shield*
schillern (vi) • **schillernd** (adj) • **Schillerseide** (f)	= to fluctuate in color, iridesce, opalesce = iridescent, opalescent, shot (with color) = shot silk	*shel-* in *sheldrake* ['variegated drake,' any of several large kinds of wild ducks with variegated plumage < MDu. *schillen*, to make different, variegate]
Schimmel (m) [bs: of light, shiny color] • **schimmeln** (vi) • **schimmelig** (adj)	= mould, mildew; a white horse (like the color of pale mould) = to become mouldy = mouldy, musty	distantly: *shim-* in *shimmer*
Schindel (f) [believed < L. *scindula*, wood tile] • **shindeln** (vt)	= shingle = to cover or roof with shingles	*shingle* [believed < L. *scindula*, wood tile]
schinden (vt & refl) • **abschinden** (refl) ——————— • **Schund** (m) ['that torn, peeled away'] • **schundig** (adj)	= to flay, skin; to drudge = to work one's skin off, drudge ——————— = refuse, trash, rubbish = trashy	*to skin*
Schinken (m)	= ham	*shank*
Schirm (m) [< OHG. *skirmen*, to defend < *scerm*, shield, defense, whence Ital. *schermo*, screen (cinem.)] • **beschirmen** (vt) • **Fallschirm** (m) ['umbrella for use in a fall'] • **Regenschirm** (m)	= screen, block, umbrella = to guard, protect, defend = parachute = umbrella	*1. scrim* [loosely woven cotton]; *2. skirmish* [orig.: a defense against attackers, then an irregular engagement between small groups of fighters]; *3. scrimmage* [orig.: a skirmish]
schlafen (vi) [*schlief, geschlafen*] • **Schlaf** (m) • **schläfrig** (adj)	= to sleep = sleep = sleepy, drowsy	*sleep*

GERMAN WORD	MEANING	ENGLISH COGNATE
schlaff (adj) [bs: loose, flabby; cogn. G. *Schlaf*, sleep < IE. *sleb-*, to be weak, to sleep] • **Schlaffheit** (f)	= slack, loose, limp = slackness, limpness	*1. distantly:* sleep [< IE. *sleb-*, to be weak, sleep]
• **Schlamm** (m) [bs: what lies loose, flabby] • **schlammig** (adj) • **Schlampe** (f) [believed < *schlaff* + *Lappen*, rag] • **schlampen** (vi) • **schlampig** (adj)	= mud, mire, sludge, silt = muddy, slimy = slut, slattern = to be slovenly or disorderly = slovenly, sloppy, dirty	*2. slump* [fall, collapse]
• **schlemmen** (vi) [< *schlampen*] • **Schlemmer** (m)	= to revel, feast, carouse = reveler, glutton, gormandizer	
schlagen (vt & vi) • **Schlag** (m) • **beschlagen** (vt) • **Beschlag** (m) ['that beaten onto, added onto'] • **erschlagen** (vt) • **vorschlagen** (vt) • **Vorschlag** (m) • **Zuschlag** (m)	= to strike, hit, throb, slap = blow, stroke; sort, breed = to hammer, sheath; seize = metal fittings; (legal:) attachment of wages, seizure = to kill, slay = to propose, suggest = proposition, proposal = addition, surcharge	*1. to slug; 2. to slay; 3. slaughter*
• **Schlächter** (m)	= butcher	
• **Geschlecht** (n) [bs: as throbs, repeats in the type] • **geschlechtlich** (adj) • **Geschlechtsleben** (n)	= kind, genus, gender, sex, species = sexual = sexuality	
Schlamm, Schlampe (see **schlaff**)		
Schlange (see **schlingen**[1])		
schlank (see **schlingen**[1])		
schlau (adj)	= cunning, clever, sly	*sly*
Schlauch (m) [bs: a hollow housing] • **schlauchen** (vt & vi)	= tube, pipe, hose (esp. flexible); inner tube (tires); skin bag (wine) = to fill by means of a hose; to hose	*slough* [of snakes: the cast off skin] and *to slough*
schlecht (adj) [orig.: < OHG. *sleht*, simple, later carrying negative force, i.e., not great, too plain, hence bad] • **Schlechtigkeit** (f) • (for **schlechthin** see **schlicht**) • (for **Geschlecht** see **schlagen**)	= bad, wicked = badness, baseness, wickedness	in negative sense: *slight* and *to slight* [insignificant; to do or treat carelessly < ME. *sliht*, *sleht*]
Schlehe (f)	= sloe, wild plum	*sloe* [a plumlike fruit or its plant]

GERMAN WORD	MEANING	ENGLISH COGNATE
schleichen (vt & vi) [*schlich, geschlichen;* bs: to go smoothly < OHG. *slihhan* (cf. ME. *sliken,* to go smoothly) < IE. **(s)lei-,* slimy, slippery, smooth]	= to sneak, creep, steal along	*1. sleek* [smooth-going < ME. *sliken,* to go smoothly]; *2.* distantly: *sli-* in *slime* [< IE. **(s)lei-,* slimy, slippery, smooth]
• **Schleicher** (m)	= creeper, sneak	
• **Schleicherhandel** (m)	= illicit trade, smuggling	
• **Schlich** (m)	= trick, ruse	
Schleier (m)	= veil, haze, mist, film	*skleir* and *to skleir* [obs.: veil, to veil]
• **verschleiern** (vt)	= to veil	
• **schleierhaft** (adj)	= hazy, mysterious, hard to comprehend	
schleifen (vt) [*shliff, geschliffen;* bs: to cause to drag or slip over < IE. **[s]lei-,* slimy, slippery, smooth]	= to whet, grind, sharpen, polish, smooth	*1. slip; 2. slipper* [< IE. **[s]lei-,* slimy, slippery, smooth]
• **schleifen** (vt & vi)	= to drag, trail, pull down, dismantle	
• **Schleifer** (m)	= polisher, grinder	
• **Schliff** (m)	= polish, good manners	
• **ungeschliffen** (adj) [lit.: 'not ground down']	= coarse	
schleißen (vt & vi) [*schliß, geschlissen*]	= to slit, split; wear out	*slit, slot*
• **Schlitz** (m)	= slit, slash, fissure	
• **schlitzen** (vt & vi)	= to slit, slash	
schlemmen (see **schlaff**)		
schleppen (vt) [cogn. *schleifen,* to whet, grind]	= to carry with difficulty, haul, drag, lug	*1. schlepp* [an incompetent person < Yid. *shlepen,* to drag < G. *schleppen*]; *2. to shlep* [to move tediously]
• **schleppend** (adj)	= slow, sluggish, wearisome	
• **Schleppe** (f)	= train (of dress), trail	
• **Schlepper** (m)	= tugboat, tractor, hauler	
• **abschleppen** (vt)	= to tow, drag or haul off	
Schleuder (f) [bs: something hanging loose or slinglike < IE. **sleu-,* loose, slack]	= sling, catapult	distantly: *sleet* [bs: loose precipitation < IE. **sleu-,* loose, slack]
• **schleudern** (vt & vi) [bs: to put to sling, use in a sling]	= to fling, hurl; to skid (as if slung)	
schlicht (adj) [orig. MHG. *schlecht,* simple, but carrying positive force < OHG. *sleht* (whence Ital. *schietto,* frank, straightforward)]	= simple, plain, modest, smooth	*slight* [in positive sense: light, slender < ME. *sliht, sleht*]
• **schlichten** (vt) ['to make smooth']	= to adjust, settle by arbitration	
• **Schlichter** (m)	= arbitrator, mediator	
• **schlechthin** (adv)	= simply, plainly	
• **schlechtweg** (adv)	= plainly, absolutely	
• **schlechterdings** (adv)	= by all means, positively	

GERMAN WORD	MEANING	ENGLISH COGNATE
schließen (vt) [*schloß, geschlossen*]	= to close, shut, lock	*1. slot* [dial.: door bolt (cf. G. *Schlüssel*, key < *schließen*)]; *2. Anschluss* [Nazi German annexation of Austria in 1938]
• **schließlich** (adj)	= finally	
• **anschließen** (vt) ['to lock to']	= to attach, annex, join	
• **Anschluß** (m)	= annexation, joining	
• **ausschließen** (vt)	= to shut out, exclude	
• **ausschließlich** (adj)	= exclusive	
• **beschließen** (vt)	= to conclude, terminate	
• **Schloß** (n)	= lock (of door, etc.); castle, palace	
• **Schlüssel** (f)	= key	
But with reverse sense *to open up* with *auf-* and *er-:*		
• **aufschließen** (vt)	= to unlock, open	
• **erschließen** (vt)	= to disclose, make accessible	
schlimm (adj) [< MHG. *slimp*, awry, slanting, oblique < Gmc. root *slimp-*, crooked, whence Ital. *sghembo*, slanting]	= bad, evil, wicked	*slim* [earlier: useless, bad, then ameliorated to thin, slight]
schlingen[1] (vt) [*schlang, geschlungen*]	= to wind, loop, plait, creep round (bot.)	*1. to sling; a sling*[1];
• **Schlange** (f)	= snake; queue, line	
• **schlängen** (vi) ['to move like a snake']	= to twist, go winding	
• **schlängeln** (refl)	= to meander	
• **schlank** (adj)	= slender, slim	*2. slinky*
• **Schlankheit** (f)	= slenderness, slimness	
schlingen[2], **verschlingen** (vt) [var. of MHG. *(ver)slinden* < OHG. *(var)slintan*]	= to swallow greedily, gobble or gulp down	*sling*[2] [iced alcoholic drink with sugar, water and fruit juice]
• **Schlund** (m)	= throat, esophagus, gullet, gorge	
Schlitten (m)	= sled, sleigh, toboggan	*1. sled, sleigh; 2. slide*
• **schlittern** (vi)	= to slide	
• **Schlittschuh** (m) ['a sliding-shoe']	= skate	
Schlummer (m)	= slumber	*slumber*
• **schlummern** (vi)	= to slumber	
schlüpfen (vi)	= to slip, slide	*sloop* ['gliding boat,' a small vessel < Du. *sloep*]
• **schlüpfrig** (adj)	= slippery	
schmachten (vi) [bs: wasting away, small < OHG. *gismahteon* < *smahi*, small, cogn. L. *mica*, crumb, particle]	= to languish, pine	distantly: *mica* [mineral easily separated < L. *mica*, crumb, particle]
• **schmächtig** (adj)	= slight, thin	

GERMAN WORD	MEANING	ENGLISH COGNATE
schmähen (vt) [bs: treating small < OHG. *smahi*, small; cogn. L. *mica*, crumb, particle]	= to revile, decry, defame	distantly: *mica* [mineral easily separated < L. *mica*, crumb, particle]
• **Schmach** (f)	= insult, humiliation	
• **schmachvoll** (adj)	= disgraceful, humiliating	
schmal (adj)	= narrow, slim	*small*
• **schmälern** (vt)	= to narrow, curtail; belittle	
Schmalz (see **schmelzen**)		
Schmaus (see **schmutz**)		
schmecken (vt & vi)	= to taste, sample; to smack of	*smack of*
• **Geschmack** (n)	= taste, flavor	
• **schmatzen** (vi) [< older *schmackezen*]	= to eat noisily, smack the lips	
schmeicheln (vt) [bs: stroking; cogn. *schmieren*, to smear < IE. *smer-*, grease, fat]	= to flatter, adulate, caress	*smea-* in *smear* [< IE. *smer-*, grease, fat]
• **Schmeichelei** (f)	= flattery, fawning	
• **Schmeichler** (m)	= flatterer, adulator	
schmeißen (vt)	= to dash, hurl, slam	*smite*
schmelzen (vt & vi)	= to melt, fuse; to liquefy; (fig.:) dwindle	*1. to smelt; 2. smalt* [a species of glass, esp. deep blue in color];
• **Schmelz** (m)	= enamel	*3. schmaltz* [unctuous sentimentalism < Yid. < G. *Schmalz*]
• **Schmalz** (n)	= lard, grease, melted fat	
• **schmalzig** (adj)	= greasy; sentimental	
schmerzen (vt & vi)	= to pain; be painful	*to smart*
• **Schmerz** (m)	= pain, ache	
Schmied (m)	= (black)smith	*smith*
• **Schmiede** (f)	= forge, smithy	
• **schmieden** (vt)	= to forge, work, devise	
• **geschmiedig** (adj) [bs: easily wrought]	= supple, pliant [cf. *malleable*, pliant, 'that can be hammered' < L. *malleus*, hammer, mallet]	
schmiegen (refl)	= to nestle, bend, slip	*1. smuggle* [to slip contraband through];
• **schmiegsam** (adj) [bs: easily nestled]	= pliant, flexible, supple	
• **Schmiegsamkeit** (f)	= pliancy, flexibility, suppleness	
• **Schmuck** (m) [orig.: fine, ornamented clothing to slip into, then ornament itself]	= ornament, jewelry	*2. smock* [a loose garment, orig. a chemise that one 'slips into,' with a hole for the neck, as a pullover];
• **schmuck** (adj)	= neat, smart, trim	*3. smug* [orig.: trim, neat, 'nestled into,' later self-satisfied]
• **schmücken** (vt)	= to adorn, ornament	

GERMAN WORD	MEANING	ENGLISH COGNATE
schmieren (vt) [< IE. *smer-, grease, fat] • **Schmiere** (f)	= to grease, smear = grease	*smear* [< IE. *smer-, grease, fat]
Schminke (f) [bs: substance smeared on the face; cogn. *schmie-* in *schmieren*, to smear, ult. < IE. *smer-, grease, fat]	= rouge, make-up (theat.)	distantly: *smea-* in *smear* [< IE. *smer-, grease, fat]
Schmirgel (m) [< Ital. *smeriglio*, emery < LL. *smericulum, smerilium* (whence OFr. *emeril* > Fr. *émeri*) < L. *smyris* < Gk. *smyris, smiridos*, emery] • **smirgeln** (vt)	= emery (a variety of corundum used for grinding and polishing) = to rub, grind with emery, to sand	distantly: *emery* [< Fr. *émeri* < L. *smyris* (whence Ital. *smeriglio*) < Gk. *smyris, smiridos*, emery]
schmollen (vi) [bs: to make a face < 15thc. *smollen*, to laugh]	= to sulk, pout	*smile*
schmoren (vt & vi) [cf. AS. *smorian*] • **Schmorbraten** (m)	= to stew, be stewed = stewed meat	*smo-* in *smother* [< base of AS. *smorian*, to suffocate]
schmuck (see **schmiegen**)		
Schmutz (m) • **schmutzig** (adj) • **schmutzen** (vi) • **beschmutzen** (vt) ——————— • **schmuddelig** (adj) ——————— • **Schmaus** (m) [student slang, orig.: dirty food for swine, then elevated in meaning < *Schmutz*, filth] • **schmausen** (vi)	= dirt, filth, mud = dirty, filthy, muddy = to give off dirt; get dirty = to dirty, soil, smudge ——————— = smudgy, grimy, dingy ——————— = banquet, feast = to feast	*1. smut; 2. smudge*
Schnabel (m)	= bill, beak, spout	*1. snaffle* [a form of bridle-bit]; *2. neb, nib*
Schnake (f)	= crane fly	*snag*
schnappen (vt & vi) • **Schnäpper** (m)	= to catch, grab = snap, catch, latch	*to snap* [to bring the jaws together sharply; to grasp or speak abruptly]
schnarren (vi) [bs: uttering a harsh sound] • **Schnurrbart** (m) [bs: the 'beard' one snorts through]	= to rattle = mustache	*1. snarl; 2. snore* and *snort*
schnauben (vi) • **Schnupfen** (m)	= to snort = headcold	*sniff*
Schnauze (f)	= snout, muzzle, nose	*snout*

GERMAN WORD	MEANING	ENGLISH COGNATE
Schnecke (f) [< OHG. *snecko* (cf. AS. *snaegel*)]	= snail, slug; (archt:) volute, scroll, helix	*1. snail* [< AS. *snaegel*]; *2.* distantly: *sneak*
schneiden (vt) • **Schneide** (f) ['what cuts'] • **Schneider** (m) [bs: one who cuts cloth] • **beschneiden** (vt) • **Schnitt** (m) • **Zuschnitt** (m) • **Schnitz** (m)	= to cut = edge = tailor, dressmaker = to cut, clip, trim = cut, incision = cut, caliber, pattern = cut, slice, snip	*snide* [making cutting or sarcastic remarks]
schnell (adj) • **schnellen** (vt & vi) • **Schnelligkeit** (f) _____ • **Schnalle** (f) ['what pulls, holds quickly'] • **schnallen** (vt)	= quick, swift = to jerk = rapidity, quickness _____ = buckle = to buckle	*snell* [Scot.: quick, keen, vigorous]
schniegeln (refl)	= to dress, smarten, spruce up	*snug* [comfortable, neat, trim]
Schnuppe (f)	= snuff (of a candle); shooting star (bec. of association with a snuffed candle)	*to snuff* [to cut the top off a candle wick]
Schnur (f) • **schnüren** (vt)	= cord, string, lacing = to lace, tie, strap	*snare*
Scholle (f) [bs: something split off, something narrow and thin < OHG. *scolla* < IE. **skel-*, to split]	= flat fish (sole, flounder); plot of ground, clod of earth	*1. shell* [of a clam, nut etc.]; *2. shoal; 3. shallow; 4. skill* [bs: a separating ability]
schön (adj) • **Schönheit** (f) • **verschönern** (vt) • **unschön** (adj)	= beautiful, fair, fine = beauty, fineness = to embellish, beautify = unlovely, unsightly	*1. scone* ['fine (bread)' < MDa. *schoonbrot*]; *2. sheen*
schonen (vt) and **verschonen** (vt) [bs: to treat well, fairly < *schön*, beautiful, fine] • **Schonung** (f) • **schonend** (adj) • **verschont** (adj) ['spared,' past p. of *verschonen*, to spare one, exempt]	= to spare, save, take care of = mercy, indulgence, good care = careful, considerate = exempt	distantly: *scone* ['fine (bread)' < MDa. *schoonbrot*]
Schopf (m) [cf. AS. *scheoppa*] • **Schuppen** (f)	= tuft, shock (of hair); crest (ornith.) = shed, hangar, shack, barn	*shop* [booth orig. with roof of straw in bundles, tufts < AS. *scheoppa*]

GERMAN WORD	MEANING	ENGLISH COGNATE
Schöpfe (f), **Schöpfkelle** (m) • **schöpfen** (vt) • **erschöpfen** (vt) • **unerschöpflich** (adj)	= a scoop, dipper = to scoop, draw out; ladle = to exhaust [lit.: 'scoop out thoroughly' < L. *ex*, out + *haustus*, past p. of *haurio*, to draw, drain] = inexhaustible	*scoop*
Schöpfer (m) [< *schaffen*, to produce] • **Schöpferisch** (adj) • **Schöpferung** (f) • **Geschöpf** (n)	= creator = creative = creation, production = creature	*to shape*
Schorf (m) [bs: what itches, feels sharp (unrelated to *scar*, 'burn mark' < L. < Gk. *eschara*, brazier) < IE. **sker-*, to cut, scrape]	= scab	words < IE. **sker-*, to cut, scrape: *1. sharp; 2. scrape*
Schornstein (m)	= chimney	*shore*, as in *shore* up + *stone*
Schoß (m) [< OHG. *scozza* (cf. AS. *sceat*)]	= lap; womb; tail (of a coat)	*sheet* [loose flap of garment or membrane < AS. *sceat*]
schräg (adj) [bs: bent at a sharp angle < IE. **sker-*, to bend, turn away] • **Schräge** (f)	= oblique, slanting, sloping, diagonal = obliquity, slant, slope	distantly: *shr-k* in *shrink* [< *(s)kren-g* < *(s)kreg-* < IE. **sker-*, to bend, turn away]
Schranke (f) [bs: boards crossed to form a barrier or a closed space < MHG. *schranc* (cf. Frk. **skrank* > OFr. *escran*, partition, barrier to block heat, wind > Fr. *écran*), cogn. G. *schräg*, bent at sharp angle < IE. **sker-*, to bend, turn away] • **schränken** (vi) • **geschränkt** (adj) • **beschränken** (vt) • **Beschränkung** (f) • **Schrank** (m) [space closed off by crossed boards]	= barrier, gate, grating, (pl.:) limits = to put crosswise; fold the arms or cross one's legs = crosswise, angled = to confine, limit, restrict = limitation, restriction = cupboard, closet	*1. to shrenk* [obs.: to put a stumbling block, barrier, in the way of]; *2. screen* [barrier, grating < Fr. *écran*]
schrauben (vt) • **Schraube** (f) • **Hubschrauber** (m) ['lift-screw' < *Hub*, lifting < *heben*, to lift + *Schraube*]	= to screw, bolt = screw, bolt = helicopter	*screw*
Schreck (m) [bs: what makes one jump < IE. **(s)ker-*, to leap] • **schrecken** (vt) • **schrecklich** (adj) • **erschrecken** (vi)	= fright, terror = to frighten = dreadful = to be frightened	distantly: *scherzo* [a lively, 'leaping' movement in symphonic music < Ital. < Gmc. *scherz-* < IE. **(s)ker-*, to leap]

GERMAN WORD	MEANING	ENGLISH COGNATE
schreiben (vt & vi) [< L. *scribere, scriptum,* to write] • **Schrift** (f) • **Abschrift** (f) [a writing off (*ab*) another writing]	= to write = writing, script = copy	*scribe, script* [< L. *scribere, scriptum*]
schreien (vi) [< IE. **ker-²,* echoic base signifying loud noise and birds]	= to shout, scream	*scree-/screa-* in *1. screech; 2. scream* [< IE. **ker-²,* echoic base signifying loud noise and birds]
Schrein (m) [< L. *scrinium,* case, box] • **Schreiner** (m) • **schreinern** (vi)	= chest, casket = joiner, cabinetmaker = to work as a joiner	*shrine* [< ME. *schrin* < L. *scrinium,* case, box, orig. for holding manuscripts and writing materials, then for holding religious relic]
schreiten (vi)	= to step, stride	*stride*
schroff (adj) [< Gmc. *skarpo*] • **Schroffheit** (f)	= steep, precipitous; harsh = steepness, abruptness, ruggedness	*scarp* [a steep slope < Gmc. *skarpo*]
Schrot (m) • **Schrott** (m)	= crushed grain, grist; buckshot = scrap iron	*shred*
schrubben (vt)	= to scour, scrub, swab	*scrub*
schrumpfen (vi) • **schrump(e)lig** (adj)	= to shrink, shrivel = shriveled, crumpled	*shrimp*
schüchtern (adj) [cogn. G. *scheu,* shy] • **einschüchtern** (vt) ['to put timidity into s.o.']	= shy, bashful, timid = to intimidate, browbeat	distantly: *shy*
Schuh (m)	= shoe	*shoe*
Schuld (f) [< OHG. *sculd* < IE. **sqel-,* be indebted, guilty] • **schulden** (vt) • **schuldig** (adj) • **Unschuld** (f) • **verschulden** (vt) • **beschuldigen** (vt) • **entschuldigen** (vt) • **Entschuldigung** (f)	= fault, blame, guilt, debt = to owe = due, guilty, culpable = innocence = to encumber with guilt = to accuse, charge = to excuse, pardon = excuse, pardon	*should* [< AS. *sceolde,* past t. of *sceal,* I am obliged < IE. **sqel-,* be indebted, guilty]
Schule (f) • **schulen** (vt) • **schulmäßig** (adj) ['by school measure']	= school = to teach, train, instruct = orthodox, as is taught	*school*
Schulter (f)	= shoulder	*shoulder*
Schund (see **schinden**)		

GERMAN WORD	MEANING	ENGLISH COGNATE
Schuppe (see **schaben**) **Schuppen** (see **Schopf**)		
schürfen (see **scharf**)		
Schurke (m) • **schurkisch** (adj)	= scoundrel, knave = knavish	*shirk*
Schürze (f)	= apron, pinafore	*skirt, shirt*
schütten (vt & vi) [cf. AS. *scudan*] • **Schutt** (m) • **ausschütten** (vt) • **zuschütten** (vt) • **schütteln** (vt) • **erschüttern** (vt) • **Schotter** (m)	= to pour out; spill = rubble, refuse, debris = to pour out, empty = to fill up (a ditch) = to shake = to shake, affect strongly = gravel, broken stone	*shudder* [shake rapidly < ME. *shuderen*; ult. related to AS. *scudan*, to hasten]
Schutz (m) [believed < 16thc. *Schutt*, earthwall poured forth as protection; see *schütten*] • **(be)schützen** (vt) • **Schützling** (m, f)	= protection, safegarding = to protect, safeguard = protégé(e)	*1.* theorized: *shut* [to close off and so protect]; *2.* distantly: *shudder* [shake rapidly, pour forth as a protecting wall]
schwach (adj) • **Schwachheit** (f) • **Schwäche** (f) • **schwächlich** (adj) • **schwächen** (vt)	= weak, feeble = weakness, frailty = weakness, infirmity = feeble, delicate = to weaken, impair	*swack* [Scot.: supple, pliant]
Schwaden (m)	= track of cut grain; strip of vapor	*swath*
Schwalbe (f)	= swallow (ornith.)	*swallow*
Schwamm (m) [bs: what is porous] • **schwammig** (adj) • **Schwammingkeit** (f)	= sponge, fungus, dry rot = spongy, porous, bloated, fungous = sponginess	*swamp*
schwank (adj) [< *schwingen*, to swing] • **schwanken** (vi) • **Schwankung** (f)	= flexible, slender = to wave to and fro, sway = deviation	*1.* *swank(y)* [stylish]; *2.* distantly: *swing*
Schwanz (m) [< *schwingen*, to swing]	= tail	*swing*
schwappen (vi) [bs: to move quickly (esp. of liquids); prob. echoic]	= to splash, spill, flop	*to swap* [to conclude a bargain, trade < ME. *swappen*, to strike, move quickly]
Schwarm (m) • **schwärmen** (vi) • **Schwärmer** (m)	= swarm, flock, school; fancy, idol = to swarm; revel, gush (over), adore = enthusiast, visionary, fanatic	*swarm*

GERMAN WORD	MEANING	ENGLISH COGNATE
Schwarte (f) [cf. AS. *sweard*]	= rind (of bacon); old book	*sward* [grass-covered soil < AS. *sweard*]
schwarz (adj) • **Schwärze** (f) • **schwärzen** (vt)	= black, dark = blackness = to blacken	*swarthy*
schweben (vi) [bs: to move hither and thither, ult. < *schweifen*, to ramble, stray < IE. *swei-*, to bend, turn] • **vorschweben** (+ pers. pron.) [lit.: 'to hover before (s.o.)']	= to hover, float = to be a vague notion to one ('s.t. hovers before one' = to have s.t. in mind)	*1.* distantly: *sweep* [to trail (of a skirt), to extend in a curve]; *2. swoop; 3. swift*
Schweif (m) [bs: a trail, meander, turning from a straight path < IE. *swei-*, to bend, turn] • **schweifen** (vt & vi) ['to cause to stray, bend'] • **Schweifung** (f) • **abschweifen** (vi) ['to roam away'] • **ausschweifen** (vi) ['to stray outside, beyond'] • **ausschweifend** (adj) [bs: straying outside of reasonable limits]	= a tail; train (of dresses) = to make curved; to ramble, stray, roam = a curve, bending = to deviate, wander = to stray, roam; be dissolute = excessive, extravagant [< L. *extra* + *vagari*, to stray]; debauched	*1. sweep* [to trail (of a skirt), to extend in a curve]; *2. swoop; 3. swift*
schweigen (vi) [< MHG. *swigen* (cf. AS. *swigian*); cf. causative MHG. *sweigen* to bring silence] • **schweigend** (adj) • **schweigsam** (adj) • **geschweige** (adv) • **verschweigen** (vt) • **verschwiegen** (adj)	= to be silent, be quiet = silent = silent, taciturn = to say nothing of, not to mention = to keep secret, conceal = reticent, discrete, secret	*? swig* [obs.: an early game at cards in which all the players were to be silent]
Schwein (n)	= pig, hog, swine	*swine*
schwelen (vi) • **schwül** (adj) • **Schwüle** (f)	= to smolder = oppressive, muggy, sultry, damp = sultriness, stiffling heat	*1. swelter; 2. sultry*
schwelgen (vi) [< IE. *swel-*, to devour] • **Schwelger** (m) • **Schwelgerei** (f) • **schwelgerisch** (adj)	= to feast, revel in = reveler, epicure = revelry, gluttony = luxurious, reveling	*swallow* [< AS. *swelgan* < *swel-*, to devour]
schwellen (vi) [*schwoll, geschwollen*] • **schwülstig** (adj) • **Geschwulst** (f)	= to swell (out) = bombastic, turgid = swelling, tumor	*swell*

GERMAN WORD	MEANING	ENGLISH COGNATE
schwenden (see **Schwindel**)		
schwer (adj) • **beschweren** (vt) • **beschweren** (refl) • **Beschwer** (n), **-de** (f) • **beschwerlich** (adj) • **erschweren** (vt) • **schwerblütig** (adj)	= heavy, weighty, severe = to burden, lie heavy on = to complain = burden, complaint = troublesome = to make more difficult, aggravate = thickblooded; heavy, grave	*1. sweer* [obs.: grievous, oppressive, disinclined to heavy effort]; *2. zwaar* [a full-shaped variety of apple < Penn. Du. *zwaar*, heavy]
Schwert (n)	= sword	*sword*
Schwester (f)	= sister; nurse	*sister*
Schwimmen (vi) • **überschwemmen** (vi)	= to swim, float, overflow with water = to inundate, flood, deluge	
Schwindel (m) [orig.: a fall into powerlessness] • **schwindeln** (vi) • **Schwindler** (m) _____ • **schwinden** (vi), also **entschwinden, verschwinden** [bs: to dwindle, fall into total, complete powerlessness] _____ • **(ver)schwenden** (vt) • **Schwund** (m)	= dizziness, vertigo; swindle = to cheat, swindle = swindler, cheat _____ = to vanish, disappear _____ = to make disappear, squander = extinction	*swindle*
schwingen (vt & vi) [*schwang, geschwungen*] • **schwenken** (vt) • **Schwung** (m) • **schwunghaft** (adj)	= to brandish, swing; oscillate = to swing, wave; rinse = swing, verve, buoyancy = flourishing, brisk	*swing*
schwitzen (vi) • **Schweiß** (m)	= to sweat, perspire = sweat, perspiration	*sweat*
schwören (vt & vi) • **Schwuren** (m)	= to swear (an oath, etc.); vow = oath, vow	*swear*
schwül (see **schwelen**)		
See (f) • **See** (m)	= sea = lake	*sea*
Seehund (m) [< MLG. *selhund*, OHG. *selah* (cf. AS. *seolh*)]	= seal (zool.)	*seal* [< AS. *seolh*]
Seele (m) • **seelisch** (adj) • **beseelen** (vt)	= soul = psychic, mental = to animate	*soul*

GERMAN WORD	MEANING	ENGLISH COGNATE
Segel (n) [cf. AS. *segl*] • **segeln** (vt & vi) • **Segler** (m)	= sail = to sail = sailing vessel; yachtsman	*sail, sailor* [< AS. *segl*]
Segen (m) [bs: beneficent sign, esp. of the cross < L. *signum*, a sign] • **segnen** (vt)	= blessing = to bless	*1. sign; 2. signal*
sehen (vt & vi) • **ansehen** (vt) • **ansehlich** (adj) ['to be looked upon'] • **angesehen** (adj) ['looked at'] • **aussehen** (vi) • **übersehen** (vt) • **zusehends** (adv) • (see also **Sicht**)	= to see, observe; see = to view, regard = considerable = respected, esteemed = to appear, look = to run the eyes over, survey; fail to notice, miss, overlook = visibly	*see, sight*
Sehne (f) • **sehnig** (adj)	= sinew, tendon; string = sinewy, stringy	*sinew*
seicht (adj) [uncert.; theorized orig. of swampy land where water collects; cogn. *seihen, sickern*] • **Seichtheit, Seichtigkeit** (f)	= shallow, low; superficial, insipid = shallowness, insipidity	perh. distantly: *sic-* in *desiccate* [to dry up < L. *siccus*, dry ('flowed out') < IE. **seik(w)-*, to flow]
Seide (f) [< OHG. *sida* < ML. *seda serica*, bristle of *Seres* (China) < L. *seta*, bristle]	= silk	*setaceous* [having bristles, bristle-like < L. *seta*, bristle]
seihen (vt) [< OHG. *sihan* < IE. **seik(w)-*, to flow, run out, whence L. *siccus*, dry ('flowed out'), cogn. *seihen, sickern*] • **Seihe** (f) • **versiegen** (vi) [< MHG. *versigen* < *versihen*]	= to strain (out), filter = filter, strainer = to dry up; be exhausted	distantly: *sic-* in *desiccate* [to dry up < L. *siccus*, dry ('flowed out') < IE. **seik(w)-*, to flow]
Seite (f)	= side, page (of a book)	*side*
Sekt (m) [originally designating a sweet wine made from dried grapes < Ital. *secco* (Fr. *sec*) < L. *siccus*, dry]	= champagne, sparkling wine	*sic-* in *desiccate* [to dry up < L. *siccus*, dry]
selbst (pron & adv) • **selbständig** (adj) • **daselbst** (adv)	= self, in person; even = self-reliant, independent = there; in that very place	*self*

GERMAN WORD	MEANING	ENGLISH COGNATE
selig (adj) • **Seligkeit** (f)	= blessed, blissful = bliss, great joy	*silly* [orig.: happy, blessed, innocent < AS. *saelig*]
senden (vt) [*sandte, gesandt*] • **entsenden** (vt) • **Gesandter** (m) • **Gesinde** (n) [orig.: those sent, those on the campaign, followers of an army < *ge* + *Sinn*, formerly physical passage, way, going (cogn. *send*), later transf. to 'mental direction,' as in *sense*] • **Gesindel** (n)	= to send, dispatch, broadcast = to send off, dispatch = envoy, diplomat = servants = rabble, mob	*send*
Senf (m) [< L. *sinape*, mustard]	= mustard	*sinapism* [a mustard plaster]
sengen (vt & vi)	= to scorch, singe; get singed	*to singe*
Sessel (m) [< *sitzen*, to sit] • **seßhaft** (adj)	= easy chair, arm chair = settled, established, sedentary	*a settle* [a long bench with arms, back and chest beneath the seat]
setzen (vt) [causative of *sitzen*] • **Satz** (m) [set of words] • **Absatz** (m) • **Gesetz** (n) ['what is set down'] • **auseinandersetzen** (vt) • **Aussatz** (m) [< MHG. *uzsetze*, sitting out, apart (due to the contagious disease)] • **Aussätziger** (m) • **entsetzen** (vt) ['to make s.o. unsettled'] • **Entsetzen** (n) • **ersetzen** (vt) • **Ersatz** (m) • **fortsetzen** (vt) ['to set forth'] • **übersetzen** (vt) ['to set across or over (*über*)' (cf. L. *translate* < *trans*, across + *latum*, past p. of *ferre*, to carry)] • **zusetzen** (vt) ['to put s.t. to s.t.'] • **Zusatz** (m) • **zusätzlich** (adj) • (see also **sitzen**)	= to set = sentence, proposition = paragraph = law = to explain, analyze = leprosy = leper = to frighten = horror = to replace, substitute, compensate for = replacement, substitute, compensation = to continue, pursue = to translate = to add = addition, admixture = additional	*1. to set; 2. ersatz* [substitute, inferior quality]
Seuche (see **siech**)		

GERMAN WORD	MEANING	ENGLISH COGNATE
sezieren (vt) [< L. *sectum*, past p. of *secare*, to cut]	= to dissect	*section, dissect*
sich (reflexive pronoun)	= oneself, herself, himself, itself	*-zy* in *cozy* [< Nor. *kose sig* (= G. *kose sich*), make oneself comfortable, lit.: 'caress oneself']
sicher (adj) [< L. *securus*, without care or worry] • **Sicherheit** (f) • **versichern** (vt) • **Versicherung** (f)	= secure, safe, sure, certain = security, sureness, certainty = to assure, affirm = assurance, insurance	*secure*
Sicht (f) • **sichten** (vt) • **sichtlich** (adj) • **Absicht** (f) • **Rücksicht** (f) [bs: a looking back at] • **Umsicht** (f) • **Vorsicht** (f) • **sichtbar** (adj) • **beabsichtigen** (vi) • **ersichtlich** (adj) • **angesichts** (prep) + *gen.* • **hinsichtlich** (prep) + *gen.* • **durchsichtig** (adj) • **einsichtig** (adj) • **umsichtig** (adj) • **vorsichtig** (adj)	= sight, visibility, view = to sight = visibly = intention, aim, purpose = regard, consideration = circumspection, caution = caution, foresight = visible = to intend = evident = in view of = with regard to = transparent, clear, lucid = intelligent = circumspect = cautious	*sight*
sickern (vi) [iterative < *seihen* < IE. **seik(w)-*, to flow, run out, whence L. *siccus*, dry (flowed out)] • **Sickergrube** (f) [< *sicker* + *Grube*, groove] • **versickern** (vi)	= to trickle, drip, leak = drainage pit = to trickle away	*sic-* in *desiccate* [to dry up < L. *siccus*, dry (flowed out) < IE. **seik(w)-*, to flow]
Sieb (n) • **(durch)sieben** (vt)	= sieve, strainer, screen = to sieve, sift, screen	*1. sieve; 2. seep*
siech (adj) [cf. AS. *seoc*] • **siechen** (vi) ————— • **Seuche** (f) • **verseuchen** (vt) ————— • **Sucht** (f) • **süchtig** (adj)	= sick = to be ailing, be sick ————— = epidemic, contagious disease = to infect ————— = disease, mania, addiction = addictive, craving	*sick* [< AS. *seoc*]
siedeln (vi) • **Siedler** (m)	= to settle, colonize = settler	*settle, settler*

GERMAN WORD	MEANING	ENGLISH COGNATE
sieden (vt & vi)	= to boil, simmer	*seethe*
Sieg (m) • **siegen** (vi) • **Sieger** (m) • **besiegen** (vt)	= victory = to be victorious = victor, conqueror, winner = to conquer, defeat, beat	*Sieg-* in names *Siegfried, Siefert* [winning peace, carrying victory]
Siegel (n) [< L. *sigilllum*, seal, mark] • **siegeln** (vt)	= seal, signet = to seal, stamp with a seal	*seal* [< ME. *seel* < L. *sigilllum*, seal, mark]
Sims (m) [< Fr. *cimaise* and ML. **simatus*, equipped with a moulding < L. *cymatium*, moulding having an undulating section < Gk. *kymation* < *kyma*, wave, something swelling] • **Gesims** (n)	= ledge, cornice, moulding, sill (of window) = ledge, cornice, moulding, sill	*cyma* [archt.: a moulding whose profile is partly concave, partly convex] and *cymatium* [the moulding topping an entablature]
sinken (vi) [*sank, gesunken*] • **senken** (vt) • **senkrecht** (adj)	= to sink, go down, fall = to lower, let down = perpendicular, vertical	*sink*
Sinn (m) • **sinnig** (adj) • **sinnlich** (adj) • **sinnvoll** (adj) • **sinnen** (vi) [*sann, gesonnen*] • **gesinnt** (adj) • **Sinnbild** (m) • **sinnbildlich** (adj) • **gesonnen** (adj) • **besinnen** (refl)	= sense; meaning = thoughtful = sensual, material = meaningful, significant = to purpose, intend = disposed = symbol, emblem = symbolic = inclined, willing, minded = to consider; remember	*sense*
Sippe (f) • **Sippschaft** (f) • **versippt** (adj)	= tribe; kinship, relations, family = relations = closely related	*1. sib* [a blood relative, kin]; *2. sib-* in *sibling*
Sitte (f) [< OHG. *situ*, Goth. *sidus;* suffixed < IE. **s(w)e-*, of own kind, whence L. *suetus*, usual, familiar; L. *sui-*, one's own; Gk. *ethos*, custom] • **Sittenbild** (n) • **sittig** (adj) • **sittlich** (adj) • **Unsitte** (f)	= custom, habit, usage; pl.: morals, manners = genre picture = well-mannered; chaste = moral, ethical; decent = bad habit, abuse	distantly: words < IE. **s(w)e-*, of own kind: *1. consuetude* [custom, habit < L. *suetus* < *suesco*, to be accustomed]; *2. suicide; 3. ethos, ethic* [< Gk. *ethos*, believed orig. < *s(w)eth-*]
Sittich (m) [< ML. *sitacus* < Gk. *psittacos*, parrot] • **Wellensittich** (m) [named for undulating, wavelike plumage < *Welle*, wave]	= parakeet = lovebird	*psittacosus* [a disease passed from the parrot family to humans < Gk. *psittacos*, parrot]

GERMAN WORD	MEANING	ENGLISH COGNATE
sitzen (vi) [*saß, gesessen*] • **besitzen** (vt) • **Besitz** (m) ———————— • **ansässig** (adj) • **angesessen, seßhaft** and **einge-sessen** (adj) • **aufsässig** (adj) • **Insasse** (m) ['one seated in an area'] • (see also **setzen**)	= to sit = to possess = possession ———————— = resident, settled = settled, established = rebellious, refractory = inhabitant, inmate	*sit, sat, seated*
Sohle (f) [< L. *solea*, sole]	= sole (of foot); bottom, floor	*sole*
Sohn (m)	= son	*son*
Sold (m) [bs: solid money < L. *solidus*, solid, genuine, a piece of money] • **besolden** (vt) • **Soldat** (m) • **Söldner** (m) ———————— • **Saldo** (m) [bs: secure, settled < L. *solidus*, firm; sum, total] • **saldieren** (vt) ['to make solid, treat the sum']	= pay = to pay, give salary = soldier = mercenary ———————— = balance (econom.) = to balance, settle (an account)	*1. solid* [< L. *solidus*, solid, genuine; sum, total]; *2. soldier* [one serving in an army for pay < L. *solidus*, a piece of money]
Söller (m) [< OHG. *solari* < L. *solarium*, a place exposed to the sun, *sol*]	= loft, balcony, terrace of a building	*solarium* [a room or gallery exposed to the sun < L. *sol*, sun]
sonder- (prefix in compounds) [cf. AS. *sunder*] • **sonderbar** (adj) [bs: apart, separated] • **sonderlich** (adj) • **Sonderling** (m) • **sondern** (vt) • **sondern** (conj) • **besonder** (adj) • **besonders** (adv) • **absondern** (vt & refl) • **Sondergotik**	= *special, extra, apart* = odd, peculiar = special, peculiar = freak, eccentric = to separate, set asunder = but (a 'separating' conjunction) = special, separate = especially, particularly = to separate, secrete = Late Gothic (late medieval art)	*1. asunder; 2. sundry* [separated, various < AS. *sundrian*, to break apart < *sunder*, apart]
Sonne (f) • **sonnig** (adj) • **Sonntag** (m) • **Sonnabend** (m) [Sunday eve]	= sun = sunny = Sunday = Saturday	*sun*

GERMAN WORD	MEANING	ENGLISH COGNATE
Sorge (f) [cf. AS. *sorh, sorg*]	= sorrow, care, uneasiness	*sorrow* [ME. *sorowe*, AS. *sorh, sorg*]
• **sorgen** (vt)	= to be anxious, care for	
• **sorglos** (adj)	= careless	
• **sorglich** (adj)	= anxious, careful	
• **versorgen** (vt)	= to provide with, look after	
spähen (vi)	= to look out, peer	*spy*
• **Späher** (m)	= look-out, scout	
spalten (vt & refl)	= to split, flake, cleave	*1. spalding* [a split and dried fish]; *2. to spald* [to split, splay out]; *3. spaldingknife; 4. spall* [a flake < ME. *spalle*, prob. var. of *spalde*, chip < *spalden*, to split], and *to spall* [to split]; *5. spelt* [a grain that splits off easily in threshing]
• **Spalt** (m), **Spaltung** (f)	= a split, fissure, splitting, schism	
• **Spalte** (f) ['splitting of text layout on a page']	= (typog.:) column	
• **abspalten** (vt & vi)	= to split off	
• **Zwiespalt** (m) ['a splitting into two (*zwei*) sides']	= disunion, discord, dissension	
• **zwiespaltig** (m)	= discordant, disunited	
Spange (f)	= clasp, buckle, clip	*spangle* [a bright ornament]
• **Spengler** (m) [bs: one who fastens, uses clasps]	= plumber	
spannen (vt & vi)	= to stretch; be stretched tight	*span*
• **Spannung** (f)	= tension, stress	
• **spannend** (adj)	= exciting, gripping	
• **entspannend** (adj)	= relaxing	
• **Spanne** (f)	= short distance, short space of time	
• **Abspannung** (f)	= fatigue	
• **ausspannen** (vt & vi)	= to stretch out; to relax	
• **Ausspannung** (f)	= recreation	
• **umspannen** (vt) ['to stretch around']	= to encompass, comprise	
sparen (vt)	= to save, economize	*spare*
• **spärlich** (adj)	= scanty, sparse, thin	
• **sparsam** (adj)	= thrifty	
Sparren (m)	= spar, rafter, rafter-end, chevron (heraldry)	*spar* [(naut.:) a mast or boom; dial.: a pole or piece of timber]
• **Sperre** (f) [< *Sparren*, spar, rafter]	= barrier, (toll) gate, barricade	
• **sperren** (vt & vi) ['to put up spars,' 'be in spars']	= to close, cut off; jam, get stuck	
• **absperren** (vt)	= to shut, block up	
• **aufsperren** (vt)	= to open wide	
• **einsperren** (vt)	= to imprison	
• **versperren** (vt)	= to obstruct, barricade	

GERMAN WORD	MEANING	ENGLISH COGNATE
Spaß (m) [bs: 'letting go,' lit.: 'expansion,' < Ital. *spasso*, amusement, pastime (*spassare*, to amuse) < L. *expansus* < *expandere*, to expand, spread]	= fun, jest, joke	*expanse* and *expansion*
• **spaßen** (vi)	= to jest, have fun	
• **spaßig** (adj)	= funny, comical	
• **Spaßer** (m)	= joker	
spazieren (vi) [bs: to go freely in a space < Ital. *spaziare* < L. *spatiari* < *spatium*, open space, interval, walk]	= to go for a walk, stroll	*1. space; 2. expatiate* [orig.: to roam or wander freely, then to speak at length < L. *exspatiari*, to go out of one's course < *ex*, out + *spatium*, space]
• **Spaziergang** (m)	= walk, stroll	
Specht (m)	= woodpecker	*speight* [obs.: woodpecker]
Speck (m)	= bacon	*speck* [fatty meat, fat of a whale]
• **spicken** (vt)	= to lard, smoke; to cram, fill	
Speer (m)	= spear, javelin, lance	*spear*
Speicher (m) ['a place for ears of grain' < OHG. *spihhari* < L. *spicarium*, granary < *spica*, ear of grain]	= granary, storage warehouse	*spike* [ear of grain < L. *spica*]
• **speichern** (vt) [bs: to store 'spikes,' grain]	= to store up, accumulate, hoard	
speien (vt & vi)	= to spit out; vomit	*spew*
Speise (f) [< ML. *spe(n)sa*, what is given out, esp. food]	= food	*spend, expense*
• **speisen** (vt & vi)	= to feed; take meals, dine	
Spelunke (f) [bs: cavelike place for drinking < L. *spelunca*, cave < Gk. *spelynx*, *spelynka* (= *spelaion*), cave]	= drinking den, dive	*spelunker* [person whose hobby is *speleology*, the science of exploring caves < Gk. *spelynx*, *spelynka*, cave; var.: Gk. *spelaion* (= *spelynx*), cave]
Spende (f) [< ML. *spendo* < L. *expendere*, to weigh out, pay out]	= gift, alms, contribution	*spend*
• **spenden** (vt)	= to dispense, bestow	
• **spendieren** (vt)	= to make a gift of, spend lavishly	
• **Spender** (m)	= donor	
sperren (see **Sparren**)		
Spiegel (m) [< ML. *speglum* < L. *speculum*, mirror]	= mirror, looking glass	*speculum* [reflector in a telescope < L. *speculum*, mirror]
• **spiegeln** (refl)	= to be reflected	
• **Spiegelung** (f)	= reflection, mirage	

GERMAN WORD	MEANING	ENGLISH COGNATE
Spiel (n) [orig.: dance, playing movement] • **spielen** (vt & vi) • **Spieler** (m)	= play, game, sport, performance = to play, perform = player, actor, gambler	*1. glockenspiel* [a percussion instrument that produces bell tones when played by striking hammers]; *2.* family name: *Spielmann*, musician, minstrel; *3. spiel* [talk, speech]
Spind (m, n) [bs: a place for consumptions < ML. *spenda* < *expensum*, past p. of *expendere*, to spend, use up]	= cupboard, wardrobe, locker	*spend, expense*
Spinne (f) • **spinnen** (vt)	= spider = to spin	*spin, spinner* [of a web]
Spieß (m) _____ • **Spitze** (f) • **spitz, spitzich** (adj) • **überspitzt** (adj) ['over pointed' < *über*, excess]	= spear, lance, pike _____ = point, peak = pointed, sharp = exaggerated [*exaggerate*, lit.: 'to heap up' < L. *ex* + *agger*, heap]	*spit* [pointed rod; narrow point of land]
spleißen (vt & vi)	= to split, crack, splice	*splice*
Sporn (m) [< OHG. *sporo*] • **spornen** (vt) • **anspornen** (vt) • **Ansporn** (m)	= spur, goad; incentive, stimulus = to give spur to = to stimulate, incite = stimulus, incitement	*1. spur; 2. to spurn* [orig.: 'to kick with the foot,' now 'to reject with contempt']
Spott (m) [cogn. G. *speien*, to spit] • **spotten** (vi) • **Spottbild** (n) • **spöttisch** (adj) • **Gespött** (n)	= mockery = to scoff at, deride, scoff = caricature = derisive, satirical = derision	distantly: *to spit;* also *to spew*
sprechen (vt & vi) • **ansprechen** (vt) • **entsprechen** (vt) • **widersprechen** (vt) _____ • **Sprache** (f) • **Spruch** (m) • **Anspruch** (m) • **beanspruchen** (vt)	= to speak; talk = to address = to answer = to contradict _____ = speech, language = saying, decree = appeal, claim = to demand, claim	*speak* [< AS. *specan* < *sprecan*] and *speech* [< AS. *spaec* < *spraec*]
spreiten (vt) • **spreizen** (vt)	= to spread = to spread, straddle	*spread*
sprießen (vi) • **ersprießen** (vi) • **ersprießlich** (adj) • **Sproß** (m) _____ • **spritzen** (vt & vi) • **Spritze** (f)	= to sprout = to shoot forth = beneficial = sprout, shoot, germ _____ = to squirt, sprinkle, spray, sprit, = syringe; squirt, shot, injection	*1. sprout; 2. sprit*

GERMAN WORD	MEANING	ENGLISH COGNATE
springen (vi) • **entspringen** (vi) • **sprengen** (vt & vi) ['to cause to spring'] • **Sprengel** (m) [bs: a church's district (i.e., area of 'sprinkling of holy water')] • **Ursprung** (m) [*ur*, origin + *springen*] • **ursprunglich** (adj)	= to spring, jump, bounce = to escape = to sprinkle, make spring, break open, make explode; gallop = diocese, parish, administrative see = origin = original	*1. spring; 2. sprinkle*
spritzen (see **sprießen**)		
spröde (adj) [< MHG. *broede*]	= brittle, inflexible; prudish	*brit-* in *brittle* [< ME. *britel, brutel*]
sprühen (vt & vi) • **sprüdeln** (vi)	= to send forth, emit (sparks), spray; to drizzle, scintillate, sparkle = to bubble forth, effervesce	distantly: *spray*
Spule (f) • **spulen** (vt)	= spool, reel = to reel, spool	*spool*
Spur (f) [< OHG. *spor* (cf. AS. *spor*)] • **spurlos** (adv) • **spüren** (vt) • **Spürsinn** (m) • **nachspüren** (vi) • **verspüren** (vt)	= trace, track, print = without a trace = to feel, sense, perceive = scent; flair = to track, trace = to feel, sense, perceive	*a spoor* [the track of an animal, < Du. *spoor*; cf. AS. *spor*] and *to spoor* [to track by spoor]
Staat (m) • **staatlich** (adj)	= state = federal, of the state	*stead*
Stadel (m) [cf. AS. *stathol,* foundation]	= barn, shed	*1. staddle* [the supporting framework of a stack, as of hay < ME. *stathel* < AS. *stathol,* foundation]; *2. stal-* in *stalwart* [sturdy, firmly made < AS. *staelwyrthe* < *stathol-wyrthe* < *stathol,* foundation + *wyrthe,* worth]
Stadt (f) • **stadtisch** (adj)	= town, city = municipal	*stead*
Staffel (f) [bs: by set steps or posts] • **Staffelei** (f)	= relay, relay race = easel	*1. distantly: step; 2. staff*
Stahl (m) • **stählen** (vt) • **stählern** (adj)	= steel = to temper, harden = of steel	*steel*

GERMAN WORD	MEANING	ENGLISH COGNATE
Stamm (m) • **stammen** (vi) • **stämmig** (adj) [bs: stemlike, stalklike] • **angestammt** (adj) [bs: built in the stock]	= stem, trunk, stock; family, tribe = to derive or come from = stocky, thickset, squat = hereditary, innate	*stem* [a plant stalk]
stammeln (see **stemmen**)		
stampfen (vt & vi) [> Ital. *stampare*, to stamp, print]	= to mash, stamp; to paw	*1. to stamp; 2. to stomp; 3. stamp* [a sign or mark impressed]
Stand (see **stehen**)		
Stange (f) • **Gestänge** (n)	= pole, stick = structural system of poles; antlers	*stanchion* [an upright bar used as a support]
Stapel (m)	= pile, stack, stocks, emporium	*staple* [commodity, chief item of trade]
Star (m) [< L. *sturnus*, starling]	= starling	*starling*
stark (adj) • **Stärke** (f) • **stärken** (vt) • **bestärken** (vt)	= strong, robust = strength, vigor = to strengthen = to confirm	*1. stark* [rigid, standing out sharply, e.g., 'stark contrast']; *2. starch* [what stiffens or strengthens cloth]
starr (adj) [< Gmc. *ster-, st-r-*, rigid] • **Starrheit** (f) • **starren** (+ **auf**) (vi) • **erstarren** (vi) ――――――――――― • **sträuben** (vt & refl) • **sträuben** (+ **gegen**) (refl) • **struppig** (adj)	= rigid, stiff, numb, transfixed = rigidity, stiffness = to stare at = to grow stiff; be solidified ――――――――――― = to ruffle, stand on end (hair, etc.) = to oppose, kick against = rough (of hair), bristly, unkempt	*1. stare* [bs: having fixed eyes, rigidly transfixed]; *2.* distantly: *stark* [rigid, standing out sharply, e.g., 'stark contrast']
Statt (n/f) • **austatten** (vt) • **bestatten** (vt) ['to put to a resting place'] • **gestatten** (vt) ['to give place to, make room for'] • **stattfinden** (vi)	= place, stead; venue = to supply, furnish, fit out = to bury, inter = to allow, permit = to take place	*stead*
Staub (see **stieben**)		
stauen (vt) [< Du. *stouwen*, to make stay]	= to dam; stow	*to stow* [to pack, fill tightly]
staunen (vi) [bs: to make stay; intensif. < *stauen*, to dam, stow; cogn. L. *stupere*, to be amazed] • **staunenswert, erstaunlich** (adj)	= to be astonished, marvel at = astonishing, amazing	*1.* distantly: *to stow* [to pack, fill tightly]; *2.* distantly: *stu-* in *stupendous*

GERMAN WORD	MEANING	ENGLISH COGNATE
stechen (vt & vi) [*stach, gestochen*]	= to prick, sting, bite, engrave	*1. to stick; 2. stuck*
• **Stich** (m)	= engraving	
• **bestechen** (vt & vi) [< mining, orig.: to tap or broach (*stechen*) for a sample, then to test or prove by improper means]	= to bribe, corrupt; (fig.:) to fascinate	
• **bestechlich** (adj)	= corrupt, bribable	
• **Bestechung** (f)	= bribery	
• **Bestechungsgeld** (n)	= bribe	
• **Stachel** (m)	= prickle, thorn; sting	
• **stachelig** (adj)	= prickly, thorny	
• **stichhaltig** (adj) [bs: stab proof, holding against puncture < *stechen* + *halten*, hold]	= valid, sound	
• **Stichhaltigkeit** (f)	= validity, soundness	
• **Stichprobe** (f) [foundry term: a pouring of molten metal from which a test is made < *Stich*, thrust + L. *probare*, to test]	= random test, sample, spot check	
stecken (vt & vi) [cogn. G. *stechen*, to prick]	= to insert, put, stick s.t. somewhere; to get stuck, jammed, stick fast	*1. to stick; 2. stuck*
• **anstecken** (vi)	= to stick on, infect	
• **Ansteckung** (f)	= infection, contagion	
• **verstecken** (vt)	= to hide, conceal	
• **Besteck** (n) [orig.: case, then the things therein]	= set of instruments (medic.); cutlery, knife and fork	
• **ersticken** (vt & vi) ['to totally jam up, not give/get air']	= to smother, stifle; choke, suffocate	
• **stickig** (adj)	= stifling, stuffy, suffocating	
• **Stickstoff** (m) [bs: substance that stifles flame]	= nitrogen	
Steg (see **steigen**)		
stehen (vi) [*stand, gestanden*]	= to stand	*stand*
• **Stand** (m)	= position, class, rank	
• **anständig** (adj)	= decent, proper, respectable	
• **bestehen** (vi)	= to consist	
• **entstehen** (vi)	= to arise, originate	
• **gestehen** (vt & vi) ['to stand at tribunal']	= to confess, admit, avow	
• **Geständnis** (n)	= confession (esp. law), admission	
• **beanstanden** (vt) [bs: to take right ground in faulting]	= to object to, complain about	
• **verstehen** (vt)	= to understand	
• **Verstand** (m)	= intellect, understanding, judgement	
• **verständig** (adj)	= reasonable, rational, wise, prudent	
• **verständlich** (adj)	= comprehensible	
• **vorstehen** (vi)	= to project; give direction to, manage	
• **Vorsteher** (m)	= manager, director	
• **Umstand** (m)	= circumstance	
• **Zustand** (m)	= condition, state	

GERMAN WORD	MEANING	ENGLISH COGNATE
stehlen (vt & vi) [*stahl, gestolen*]	= to steal	*steal*
• **Stehler** (m)	= thief	
• **Stehlen** (n)	= stealing, theft	
• **Diebstahl** (m)	= theft, larceny	
steif (adj)	= stiff, rigid	*stiff*
• **Steifheit** (adj)	= stiffness, rigidity	
• **steifen** (vt)	= to make stiff, prop, stay	
steigen (vi) [cf. AS. *stigan*]	= to rise, ascend, mount up	*1. sty* [< AS. *stigend*, lit.: 'thing rising,' a swelling on the eyelid < present p. of *stigan*, to climb, mount]; *2. stair* [< AS. *staeger*, scaffolding, assoc. with climbing < AS. *stigan*];
• **Stiege** (f)	= stairs	
• **einsteigen** (vi)	= to get in (a car)	
• **aussteigen** (vi)	= to get off or out of (a car)	
• **Steigbügel** (see **Bügel**)		
• **steigern** (vt) ['to cause to rise']	= to raise, increase	
• **Abstieg** (m)	= descent	
• **Anstieg** (m)	= ascent	
• **steil** (adj) [bs: rising abruptly < OHG. *steigal* < *steigen*]	= steep, precipitous	*3. -stile* in *turnstile* [orig.: a steep arrangement to be climbed, later bars controling passage over or through a fence < AS. *stigel* < *stigan*, to climb];
• **Steilheit** (f)	= steepness	
• **Steilhang** (m)	= a steep slope, precipice	
• **Stegreif** (**aus dem __**) ['straight from the stirrup,' without dismounting, hence unprepared, direct < obs. OHG. *steigereif*, stirrup, lit.: 'mounting rope or loop' < *reif*, rope (cf. AS. *stigrap*)]	= extempore (speech), ad-lib, impromptu, extemporaneous	*4. stirrup* [lit.: 'mounting loop' < AS. *stigrap* < *stigan*, to climb + *rap*, rope]
• **Stegreifdichter** (m)	= extemporizer, improvisator	
• **Steg** (m) [bs: elevated path, what is raised]	= landing pier, foot-bridge, (elevated) path, catwalk, bridge (music & eyeglasses)	
steil (see steigen)		
Stein (m) and **Gestein** (n)	= stone, rock	*stone*
Stelle (f)	= place, spot	*1. stall; 2. stalemate*
• **stellen** (vt)	= to place, put, set	
• **Stellung** (f)	= position	
• **ausstellen** (vt)	= to exhibit	
• **entstellen** (vt)	= to deform, distort	
• **verstellen** (vt)	= to misplace	
• **vorstellen** (vt)	= to put forward, introduce	
• **vorstellen** (refl) ['to put before for oneself']	= to imagine	
• **Vorstellung** (f)	= presentation, notion	
• **Gestalt** (f)	= form, shape, figure	
Stelze (f)	= stilt	*stilt*

GERMAN WORD	MEANING	ENGLISH COGNATE
stemmen (vt) • **stemmen** (refl)	= to stem, dam, stand firm against = to resist, oppose	*1. to stem* [to stop or dam up];
• **stammeln** (vi) [freqtv. < *stemmen*]	= to stammer, stutter	*2. stammer* [to speak with involuntary stops or blocks]
• **stumm** (adj) [bs: vocally stemmed or dammed] • **ungestüm** (adj) [bs: unchecked, not stemmed < *un,* not + *stemmen*]	= mute, silent = impetuous, violent	
sterben (vi) [*starb, gestorben*] • **sterblich** (adj)	= to die = mortal	*starve*
Stern (m) • **Sternbild** (n) [bs: formation of stars] • **Sternkunde** (f) [*kunde < kennen*, to know] • **Gestirn** (n)	= star = constellation = astronomy = constellation	*star*
stetig (adj) • **stets** (adv) • **bestätigen** (vt) [bs: to render steady or certain] • **Gestade** (n) [bs: steady land]	= steady = steadily, continually = to confirm, verify = shore, coast	*steady*
Steuer[1] (n) • **steuern** (vt & vi)	= steering wheel, rudder = to steer, navigate	*steer*
Steuer[2] (f) [< OHG. *stiura*, support; etym. uncert.; theorized < *stouwen*, to make stay, cogn. Eng. *to stow*. But perh. OHG. *stiura* reduced < L. *ostiorum*, in *exactio ostiorum*, tax per house, lit.: 'tax (exaction) of doors' (doc. in Caes. and Cic.) < *exactio* + gen. pl. of *ostium*, door] • **besteueren** (vt) • **besteuerbar** (adj) • **Steuerbeamte** (m) • **Steuerzahler** (m) • **beisteuern** (vt & vi) [*bei-*, added to + *steuern*]	= tax, duty = to tax, levy taxes = taxable, assessable = revenue officer = tax payer = to contribute [< L. *con* + *tribus*, payment assessed]	cogn. uncert.: ? *to stow* Or ? words derived < L. *ostium,* door: *1. ostiary* [one guarding the entrance of a church; Rom. Cath. Ch.: the lowest of the minor orders < *ostiarius*, pertaining to a door]; *2. usher* ['doorman' < OFr. *ussier* < L. *ostiarius*, of a door]
Stich, stichhaltig, Stichprobe (see **stechen**)		
sticken (vt & vi) [cogn. *stecken*, to stick]	= to embroider	*stitch*

GERMAN WORD	MEANING	ENGLISH COGNATE
stickig, ersticken, Stickstoff (see **stecken**)		
stieben (vi) [*stob, gestoben;* cogn. with Gk. *typhos,* steam, smoke] • **stöbern** (vi)	= to move like dust, fly about in small particles; spray, scatter = to scatter; rummage about; to snow (in fine particles)	*stew* [< OFr. *estuver* < LL. *extufare* < *ex* + Gk. *typhos,* steam]
• **Staub** (m) [< OHG. *stoup,* cogn. Gk. *typhos,* steam, smoke] • **stauben** (vi) • **stäuben** (vt) • **bestäuben** (vt)	= dust, powder = to give off or raise dust = to dust = to cover with dust	
Stiefel (m) [orig.: a summer boot, then any boot < L. **aestivale,* of summer < *aestas,* summer, whence Ital. *stivale,* boot]	= boot (footwear)	*estival* [pertaining to summer < L. **aestivale,* of summer < *aestas,* summer]
Stift[1] (n) ['what is regulated with cause' < Gmc. **stihtan,* to found, arrange (cf. AS. *stihtian;* MDu. *stichten*)] • **stiften** (vt) • **Stifter** (m) • **anstiften** (vt)	= seminary, monastery, convent; charitable institution, foundation = to endow, found, institute = founder, sponsor, donor = to cause, instigate, plot	*stick-* in *stickler* [one who arranges uncompromisingly < *to stickle,* to raise objections, settle disputes, dispose < ME. *stightlen,* freqtv. of *stighten* < AS. *stihtian,* to dispose, regulate, arrange]
Stift[2] (m) [uncert.; theorized < L. *stipes, stipitis,* stalk, trunk; post, stake] • **Bleistift** (m) • **Kreidestift** (m)	= pin, peg, pivot, bolt, pencil = lead pencil = chalk stick	*stipe* [the stalk that supports a fern, frond or mushroom cap < L. *stipes, stipitis,* stalk, trunk; post, stake]
still (adj) • **Stille** (f) • **stillen** (vt)	= still, quiet = stillness, quiet = to soothe, appease	*still*
Stimme (f) [< OHG. *stimna;* cogn. Goth. *stibna,* AS. *stefn*] • **stimmen** (vt & vi) • **Stimmung** (f) • **stimmlich** (adj) • **Stimme** (f) [bs: voice as a vote] • **bestimmen** (vt) ['to delimit by voice'] • **beistimmen** and **übereinstimmen** (vi) • **einstimmig** (adj) • **umstimmen** (vi) [bs: to change s.o.'s vote or voice < *um-,* over again + *stimmen*]	= tune, voice, vote = to tune; be in tune, harmonize, be right, to agree = pitch, tuning; mood, frame of mind = vocal, of the voice = vote (acclamation) = to fix, determine [< L. *de* + *terminus,* limit] = to agree = unanimous = to change s.o.'s mind, bring s.o. round	*steven* [obs. except dial.: a loud voice, outcry < AS. *stefn,* cogn. Goth. *stibna,* voice]

GERMAN WORD	MEANING	ENGLISH COGNATE
stochern (vt)	= to stoke, poke	*stoke*
Stock (m) • **Stock(werk)** (m) ['framework of beams'] • **vielstöckig** (adj)	= stick, cane = story, floor (of a building) = many-storied (of buildings)	*1. a stick; 2. stock* [plant stem; main part; beam, frame of timbers; goods]
stocken (vi) • **Stockung** (f) • **stockig** (adj)	= to stop, be at standstill, stagnate = stoppage, standstill = mouldy, mildewed, fusty, decayed	*stuck*
Stollen (m)	= post, support; tunnel, gallery	*stull* [mining prop]
stolpern (vi) [cogn. *Stufe*, step, stair] • **stolperig** (adj)	= to stumble, trip = stumbling; rough	distantly: *step*
stolz (adj) [cogn. *Stelze*, stilt] • **Stolz** (m) • **stolzieren** (vi)	= proud, haughty = pride = to strut, flaunt	*1. stout* [courageous; thickset < OFr. *estout, estolt* < OHG. *stolz*]; *2. stilt*
stopfen (vt) • **einstopfen** (vt)	= to stuff, cram, plug, fill = to stuff in, fill up	*1. stop* [orig.: to fill, plug, then obstruct]; *2. stopper* [for bottles, etc.]
Stör (m)	= sturgeon	*sturgeon*
stören (vt) • **störend** (adj) • **aufstören** (vt) • **zerstören** (vt) ['to stir apart'] • **zerstörbar** (adj)	= to disturb, trouble, annoy = disturbing, troublesome = to stir up = to destroy, demolish = destructible	*stir* [bs: to agitate, shake]
störrig (adj) [intens. of *starr*, stiff, rigid] • **Störrigkeit** (f)	= stubborn, obstinate = stubbornness, obstinacy	*1. stare* [bs: having fixed eyes, rigidly transfixed]; *2. stark* [rigid, standing out sharply]
stoßen (vt & vi) [< OHG. *stuten* (cf. ME. *stutten*)] • **Stoß** (m) • **Anstoß** (m) • **anstößig** (adj) • **zustoßen** (vi) [bs: to get pushed to one] • **Zusammenstoß** (m)	= to push, shove, thrust = a push, shove, blow; pile to which things are pushed = impulse, offense = offensive = to happen, befall = collision	*stutter* [to speak with involuntary thrusts, spasms < freqtv. of ME. *stutten*]
strafen (vt) • **Strafe** (f) • **strafbar** (adj) • **sträffällig** (adj) • **sträflich** (adj) • **Geldstrafe** (f) ['money punishment']	= to punish = punishment, penalty = punishable, penal = liable to prosecution = culpable, reprehensible = a fine	*to strafe* [to attack with gunfire, esp. by using aircraft]

GERMAN WORD	MEANING	ENGLISH COGNATE
straff (adj) [believed distantly cogn. G. *starr*, rigid, fixed] • **straffen** (vt) • **Straffheit** (f)	= tight, taut; strict, rigid = to tighten, stretch, make taut = tightness, tautness; strictness	*1. strappado* [a form of torture with victim's arms pulled with a tight jerk < Ital., believed < Gmc.]; *2.* distantly: *stare* [bs: having fixed eyes, rigidly transfixed]
Strahl (m) [< OHG. *strala*, arrow; cogn. Russ. *strela*, arrow] • **strahlen** (vi) • **strahlig** (adj) • **Strahlung** (f)	= ray, beam, flash, stream, jet = to emit rays, flash = radiating, radiated = radiation, rays	*Streletz, Streltsy* [special troops of archers in 16thc. Russia < Russ. *strelitz*, archer < *strela*, arrow (G. *strahl*)]
Strähne (f)	= lock or hank of hair, strand, skein	*stran-* in *strand*[1]
Strand (m) • **stranden** (vi)	= beach, shore = to be beached, run ashore	*strand*[2], *be stranded*
Strang (m)	= cord, rope, harness trace, (railroad) track	*string*
sträuben (see **starr**)		
Strauß[1] (m) [bs: that swells out, goes stiffly < MHG. *gestriuze*] <hr>• **strotzen** (vi) [bs: to swell out, abound] • **strotzend** (adj)	= crest, tuft; bouquet (of flowers); also, stiff contention, strife, combat <hr>= to abound in, teem with, burst with = abundant, exuberant	distantly: *1. a strut* [stiff projection; obs.: strife, contention]; <hr>*2. to strut* [to swell out, go stiffly]
Strauß[2] (m) [Ital. *struzzo* < LL. *avis struthius* < Gk. *strouthion*, ostrich]	= ostrich	*ostrich* [< LL. *avis struthius* < Gk. *strouthion*, ostrich]
streben (vi) • **strebsam** (adj) • **Streben** (n) • **Streber** (m)	= to strive, aspire = ambitious, striving = effort, endeavor = ambitious person	*to strive*
strecken (vt) • **austrecken** (vt) • **Strecke** (f) <hr>• **Strick** (f) • **verstricken** (vt) [to work with line, yarn] • **verstrickt** (adj)	= to stretch, extend = to extend = extent, stretch <hr>= line, rope = to spend (time) knitting; to entangle = entangled	*stretch*
streichen (vt) [*strich, gestrichen*] • **Strich** (m) • **streicheln** (vt) [bs: to stroke repeatedly]	= to spread on, paint, rub = stroke, line, dash = to caress, stroke	*stroke, strike*

GERMAN WORD	MEANING	ENGLISH COGNATE
Streit (m) [bs: stiffening < OHG. *strit* < IE. *ster-*, to be stiff, rigid] • **streiten** (vi) [*stritt, gestritten*] • **streitig** (adj) • **umstritten** (adj)	= quarrel, conflict, dispute = to quarrel, dispute = debatable, controversial = controversial, disputed	*stride* [a long, vigorous step < AS. *stridan* < IE. *ster-*, to be stiff, rigid]
streng (adj) • **Strenge** (f)	= severe, strict, stern = severity, strictness	*strong*
streuen (vt) [< OHG. *strewen* (Goth. *straujan*), whence Ital. *sdraiarsi*, to stretch (strew) oneself out] • **Streu** (f) ['that strewn']	= to strew, scatter = litter, bed (e.g., of straw)	*strew*
Stroh (n)	= straw	*straw*
Strolch (m) [< Ital. *strolegh, strologo*, fortune teller, astrologer < L. *astrologus* < Gk. *astrologos*, astronomer] • **strolchen** (vi)	= scamp, vagabond, tramp = to rove, ramble, loaf	*1. astrologer; 2. to stroll* [to walk idly, as a wandering fortune teller]
Strom (m) • **strömen** (vi) • **Strömung** (f)	= stream, river, current = to stream, flow, rush = current, drift, trend	*stream*
strotzen (see **Strauß**[1])		
Strudel (m) • **strudeln** (vi)	= swirl, whirlpool, eddy; strudel pastry = to swirl, eddy, boil	*strudel* [a pastry rolled several times around a filling]
struppig (see **starr**)		
Stube (f)	= a room, chamber	*stove* [orig.: a heated room, then the heating device]
Stück (n)	= piece, fragment; (theat:) play	*stick*
Stufe (f) • **Stufenfolge** (f) • **stufenweise** (adj) • **abstufen** (vt) • **einstufen** (vi)	= step, degree, grade, stage = gradation [< L. *gradus*, step] = gradually ('by steps') = to gradate, modulate = to classify, rate, grade	*step*
Stuhl (m)	= chair, seat, stool; loom	*stool*
stumm (see **stemmen**)		

GERMAN WORD	MEANING	ENGLISH COGNATE
stumpf (adj) • **Stumpf** (m) • **Stummel** (m) • **verstümmeln** (vt) [bs: to render into stumps]	= blunt(ed), obtuse (of angles), dull, apathetic = stump, trunk = stump, remnant, end = to mutilate; garble	*stump* [a cut or reduced end]
Stunde (f) • **stundenlang** (adv)	= hour, a lesson, period = for hours	*stound* [arch. and dial.: a time, moment]
Sturm (m) • **stürmen** (vt & vi)	= storm, tempest, gale = to storm, assault, charge	*storm*
Sturz (m) [bs: a fall forward and downward] • **stürzen** (vt & vi) • **Absturz** (m) • **absturzen** (vi) • **bestürzen** (vt) [bs: to cause to start] • **einstürzen** (vi) • **Umsturz** (m)	= a tumble; overthrow (of govt.) = to cause to fall, overthrow; to fall, plunge forth = a fall, plunge = to fall down, crash = to startle, dismay = to cave in = overthrow, upheaval	*start* [bs: a sudden move forward]
Stute (f) [orig.: group of horses for breeding (a male, females), then the female]	= mare	*1. stud[1]* [a group of horses for breeding; their site; esp. the male horse]; *2. steed* [a riding horse]
Stütze (f) • **stützen** (vt)	= a support, prop, stay = to support, prop, stay	*stud[2]* [an upright post, crossbar, peg]
suchen (vt) • **Suche** (f) • **besuchen** (vt) • **versuchen** (vt)	= to seek, search for = search, quest = to visit = to try, attempt	*seek, sought*
Sucht (see **siech**)		
Süden (m) • **südlich** (adj)	= south = southern	*south*
suhlen (vi) [cf. Frk. *sulljan*] • **Suhle** (f)	= to wallow in mud (said of swine) = wallow	*sully* [to soil < OFr. *souiller* < Frk. *sulljan*]
Sühne (f) [cf. Frk. *sunnea,* penance for a need, whence Frk. *bisunnjan,* to atone for a fault or for what is necessary, hence Fr. *besoin,* necessity < be + *sunnea*] • **sühnen** (vt) _____ • **versöhnen** (vt) • **Versöhnung** (f) • **versöhnlich** (adj)	= expiation, atonement = to expiate, atone for _____ = to reconcile = reconciliation = conciliatory	*1. essoin* [law: an excuse for non-appearance in court < ML. *exsoniare* < *ex* + Frk. *sunnea,* expiation, penance for a need]; *2. besogne* [obs.: a raw recruit, 'one in need']; *3. bisonio* [contempt.: a needy beggar, base fellow < Ital. *bisogno,* need (cogn. Fr. *besoin,* necessity) < Frk. *sunnea,* expiation, need (whence Fr. *soin,* care)]

GERMAN WORD	MEANING	ENGLISH COGNATE
Sültze (f)	= jellied meat or fish	distantly: *silt*
Sumpf (m) • **sumpfig** (adj)	= swamp, marsh = swampy, marshy, boggy	*sump* [a pit or well in which liquid collects, a cesspool]
Sünde (f) • **Sünder** (m) • **sündig, sündhaft** (adj) • **Sündflut, Sintflut** (f) ['sin flood']	= sin = sinner = sinful = the world's flood, Deluge	*sin*
süß (adj) • **Süßigkeit** (f)	= sweet = sweetness	*sweet*

T

Tafel (f) [< L. *tabula*, board] • **tafeln** (vi) • **täfeln** (vt) • **Täfelung** (f)	= (black)board, panel, slate, plaque, plate (books), food table, banquet = to dine, feast, banquet = to floor, panel, inlay = paneling, wainscoting	*table, tablet* [< L. *tabula*, board]
Tag (m) [cf. AS. *daeg*] • **tagen** (vi) • **Tagung** (f) • **vertagen** (vt & refl)	= day = to dawn; to meet for the day = meeting, session = to adjourn, recess	*day* [< ME. *dei, dai* < AS. *daeg*]
Tal (n)	= valley	*dale*
Talar (m) [a garment whose length reaches the ankles < L. *talaris* < *talus*, ankle, heel]	= ankle length gown (eccl., jurispr., academ., historical, etc.)	words < L. *talus*, ankle, heel: *1. talaria* [winged sandals or ankle wings of Mercury]; *2. talon* [claw or spur of a bird of prey]
Talg (m) • **Talglicht** (n)	= tallow = candle	*tallow*
Tand (m) [bs: trifling < L. *tantum*, so much] • **tändeln** (vi) • **Tändelei** (f)	= bauble; trifles, knick-knacks = to dally, trifle, flirt = dallying, trifling	*1. tanto* [music: direction to perform 'so much,' 'to this degree' < Ital, *tanto* < L. *tantum*]; *2. to dandle* [to dance a child on one's knee]
Tang (m)	= seaweed	*tangle*
Tanne (f) • **Tannenbaum** (m)	= fir(tree) = fir(tree)	*Tannenbaum* [firtree, esp. of Yuletide carol]
tanzen (vi)	= to dance	*dance*

GERMAN WORD	MEANING	ENGLISH COGNATE
Tapete (f)	= wallpaper	*tapestry* [< LL. *tapitium*]
tapfer (adj)	= brave, valiant, fearless	*dapper* [orig.: heavy, powerful, now trim, spruce]
tappen (vi) [bs: to handle as with paws < MHG. *tape*, paw, metathesis of Romance **patta*, paw (whence Fr. *patte*, paw)]	= to grope, fumble, paw	*patten* [clog, wooden sandal < OFr. *patin* < *patte*, paw, foot]
• **täppisch** (adj)	= clumsy, awkward	
• **ertappen** (vt) [*er-*, thoroughly + *tapp-*]	= to catch; surprise	
tarnen (vt)	= to disguise, camouflage, mask	*1. dern* [obs. adj.: concealed, secret, dark]; *2. tarnish*
Tasche (f) [pouch orig. for money from taxes < L. *taxare*, to assess]	= pocket, pouch	*tax* [< L. *taxare*, to assess]
tasten (vt & vi) [< OFr. *taster* < LL. **tastare*, freqtv. of L. *taxare*, to feel or touch, assess, judge of; hence OFr. **tastonner* > Fr. *tâtonner*, to grope]	= to touch, feel (a thing); to grope, fumble	*1. taste* [to touch or assess with the tongue < LL. **tastare*, freqtv. of L. *taxare*, to feel or touch, assess, judge of]; *2. tax* [an assessment < L. *taxare*, to assess, judge of]
• **tastbar** (adj)	= palpable	
• **Taster** (m)	= feeler, antenna (zool.)	
• **Taste** (f) ['touch piece']	= key, press key	
• **antasten** (vt) [bs: to lay hands on]	= to touch; to handle negatively or impugn	
• **unantastbar** (adj)	= inviolable, that may not be touched	
Tat (see **tun**)		
Tau[1] (m) [bs: reduced to liquid; seen in G. *dau-* as well as *tau-*]	= dew	*1. dew* [< AS. *deaw*]; *2.* distantly: *thaw*
• **tauen**[1] (vi)	= to form dew	
Tau[2] (n) [< MLG. *touw* < *tiohan*, to pull (= OHG. *ziohan*; cogn. AS. *togian*, to pull; *teon*, to draw)]	= cable, rope (for ships)	*1. a tie* [< AS. *teag, teah*]; *2. tow* [rope < AS. *togian*, to pull, tug]
taub (adj)	= deaf, numb	*deaf*
• **Taubheit** (f)	= deafness, numbness	
Taube (f)	= dove	*dove*
tauchen (vt & vi) [< OHG. *tuhhan* (cf. AS. **ducan*)]	= to submerge; to plunge	*1. to duck* [go down, dive < AS. **ducan*]; *2. duck* [a plunging fowl]
• **Taucher** (m)	= diver	
• **auftauchen** (vi)	= to emerge, appear, turn up	

GERMAN WORD	MEANING	ENGLISH COGNATE
tauen[2], also **auftauen** (vt & vi) [cf. AS. *thawian*] • **Tauwetter** (n) _____ • **verdauen** (vt) [< *ver* + *dau-,* thaw]	= to make thaw; thaw out, get thawed = a thaw _____ = to digest	*thaw* [< AS. *thawian*]
taufen (vt) [< OHG. *touffan* (cf. Goth. *daup-jan;* AS. *dyppan, dyfan*), whence Ital. *tuffare,* to plunge, immerse] • **Taufe** (f) • **(Johannes der) Täufer** (m) • **tupfen** (vt) [orig.: dip lightly, quickly touch] • **Tüpfel** (m)	= to baptize, christen, name = baptism, christening [cf. Gk. *bap-tizo,* I immerse] = John the Baptist = to dot, dab, touch lightly = dot, spot	*1. dip* [< AS. *dyppan*]; *2. dive* [< AS. *dyfan*]; *3. dope* [< Du. *doop,* orig.: a sauce or dip, then opium, coating material]
taugen (vi) [< MHG., OHG. *tugan* (cf. Goth. *dugan;* AS. *dugan*) < IE. **dheugh-,* to be strong, valiant] • **tauglich** (adj) _____ • **tüchtig** (adj) [< MHG. *tuht* past t. < *tugan*] • **Tüchtigkeit** (f) • **seetüchtig** (adj) _____ • **Tugend** (f) [< OHG. *tugunt* < *tugan*] • **tugendhaft** (adj)	= to be good or fit, be of use = good, fit, useful, able _____ = efficient, able, fit, good = efficiency, ability = (of ships:) seaworthy _____ = virtue = virtuous	*1. dog* [valiant or useful thing < AS. *docga, dogga* < *dugan,* to be of use < IE. **dheugh-,* to be strong, valiant]; *2. doughty* [valiant, strong < AS. *dohtig* (= G. *tüchtig*) < *dohte,* past t. of *dugan*]
Taumel (m) [< OHG. *tumon,* to go in circles, to and fro, cogn. G. *Dunst* < IE. **dheu-,* to rise, move in a cloud] • **taumeln** (vi)	= giddiness, ecstasy = to reel, stagger, be giddy	distantly: *du-* in *dust* [< IE. **dheu-,* to rise, move in a cloud]
tauschen (vt) [bs: amelioration of 'a dubious deal' < MHG. *tuschen,* var. of MHG. *tiuschen,* to deceive, whence G. *täuschen,* to deceive] • **Tausch** (m) • **Tauschhandel** (m) • **vertauschen** (vt) • (see also **täuschen**)	= to exchange, barter = exchange, barter = barter = to exchange	(see entry **täuschen**)

GERMAN WORD	MEANING	ENGLISH COGNATE
täuschen (vt) [< MHG. *tiuschen*, to speak untruth; ult. origin uncert.; ? < IE. **dheu-*, to rise as a cloud, and notions of defective perception, whence G. *Dunst*, dust; OHG. *tusig* > *töricht*, foolish; and Eng. *dusk, dizzy*). Or ? < an echoic root expressing a completed act (cf. echoic sense of G. *schwappen*, to splash, move quickly, esp. of liquids, and cogn. Eng. *to swap*, to conclude a bargain, trade)]	= to deceive, delude, cheat	cognates uncert.: ? words < IE. **dheu-*, to rise as a cloud, and notions of defective perception: *1. dusk; 2. dizzy; 3. doze*
• **täuschend** (adj)	= deceptive	Or ? < an echoic root for a completed act: cf. Eng. *touch* < OFr. *tochier* < Romance *toccare* < echoic *toc*, imitating a knock, quick hit. Cf. also G. *schwappen*, to splash, move quickly, esp. of liquids, and cogn. Eng. *to swap*, to conclude a bargain, trade.
• **Täuschung** (f)	= deception, delusion	
• **enttäuschen** (vt) ['to undeceive, rid of delusion' (a loan transl. of Fr. *détromper, désabuser*, meaning same)]	= to disappoint, disillusion [*disillusion*, lit.: 'to undeceive,' 'fail to satisfy another's delusory expectations']	
• **vortäuschen** (vt)	= to feign, pretend	
• (see also **tauschen**)		
Teer (m)	= tar	*tar*
Teich (m)	= pool, pond	*ditch*
Teig (m) [cf. AS. *dag*]	= dough	*dough* [< ME. *dogh*; AS. *dag*]
• **teigig** (adj)	= doughy, pasty	
teilen (vt) [cf. AS. *daelan*]	= to divide, portion out	*1. deal*[2] [a part, share < AS. *daelan*, to divide, share]; *2. dole* [money or food given out in charity] and *to dole out* [< AS. *daelan*, to divide, share];
• **Teil** (n)	= part, piece, portion	
• **abteilen** (vt)	= to separate, partition off	
• **austeilen** (vt)	= to distribute, divide	
• **mitteilen** (vt)	= to communicate s.t.	
• **Mitteilung** (f)	= communication	
• **Gegenteil** (n) [lit.: 'opposite part']	= the contrary, reverse	
• **Nachteil** (n) ['the last (worst) part' < *nach*, after]	= disadvantage	
• **benachteiligen** (vt)	= to put at a disadvantage, to wrong	
• **Benachteiligung** (f)	= disadvantage, discrimination	
• **Vorteil** (n) ['the best part' < *vor*, first]	= advantage, profit	
• **bevorteilen** (n)	= to take advantage of, profit from	
• **übervorteilen** (vt) ['to take excess profit']	= to overcharge, cheat	
• **Urteil** (n)	= judgement, decision	*3. ordeal* [orig.: trial having physical dangers, lit.: 'what is dealt']
• **Vorurteil** (n)	= prejudice, prejudgement	

GERMAN WORD	MEANING	ENGLISH COGNATE
Teller (m) [orig.: a board on which to cut meat, then any platter < MHG. *talier* (cf. Ital. *tagliare*, to cut; Fr. *tailler*) < LL. *taliare*, to cut, split]	= plate, platter	words from LL. *taliare*, to cut, split: *1. tailor* [one who cuts cloth]; *2. tally* [orig.: a stick on which notches were cut to record numbers]; *3. retail* [what is cut again (*re-*, again) to be sold in small units]; *4. detail* [a part cut away (*de*, from)]
• **Tellerbrett** (n)	= plate rack	
• **Tellerschrank** (m)	= cupboard	
• **Tellertuch** (n)	= dishcloth	
Tenne (f)	= threshing floor, barn floor	*den* [place where grass is trodden down, lair]
Teppich (m) • **Wandteppich** (m) ['wall carpet']	= carpet, rug = tapestry	*tapestry* [< LL. *tapitium*]
teuer (adj) • **beteuern** (vt) [bs: to declare what is cherished]	= dear, expensive, cherished = to solemnly declare, swear	*dear*
Theke (f) [< Gk. *theke*, case for storage]	= display case, counter (in a shop); bar (in a tavern)	*1. -thec-* in *apothecary* [< Gk. *apo*, away + *theke*, case for storage]; *2. tick* [a cloth casing for a mattress < Gk. *theke*, case for storage]; *3. ticking* [cloth used to make a mattress casing]
tief (adj) • **Tiefe** (f) • **vertiefen** (vt)	= deep = depth = to deepen	*deep*
Tier (n) [cf. AS. *deor*] • **tierisch** (adj)	= animal = bestial, brutal	*deer* [< AS. *deor*, any wild animal]
tilgen (vt) [< L. *delere*, to efface]	= to delete, annul, efface	*del-* in *delete*
Tinte (f) [< L. *tincta*, dye]	= ink	*1. tint; 2. tincture*
Tisch (m) [flat area < L. *discus* < Gk. *diskos*] • **Tischler** (m) ['table maker,' worker of wood] • **tischlern** (vt & vi) • **Tischlerei** (f)	= table = joiner, carpenter = to do carpentry = carpentry	*1. disc; 2. desk*
Tochter (f)	= daughter	*daughter*
Tod (see **tot**)		
toll (adj) [cf. AS. *dol*] • **Tollheit** (f) • **Tollhaus** (n)	= mad, crazy = madness = madhouse, bedlam	*dull* [bs: mentally slow, not keen < AS. *dol*, foolish, stupid]

GERMAN WORD	MEANING	ENGLISH COGNATE
Tölpel (m) [bs: villager < MHG. *törpel, dörper* < MDu. *dorp* (G. *Dorf*), village]	= clumsy fellow, oaf	distantly: *thorp* [arch.: village, hamlet]
• **Tölpelei** (f)	= awkwardness	
• **tölpelhaft** (adj)	= awkward, clumsy	
Ton[1] (m) [bs: tight, thick matter < *tahen*, gen. suffix on MHG. *tahe*, < OHG. *daha*; cogn. G. *dicht*, tight]	= clay	distantly: *tigh-* in *tight*
• **tönern** (adj)	= clayey, earthen, of clay	
Ton[2] (m) [< L. < Gk. *tonos*]	= tone, timbre, accent, stress; tint, shade	*tone* [< L. < Gk. *tonos*]
• **tönen** (vi & vt)	= to sound, ring, resound; tint	
Topf (m)	= pot, vessel, crock	*top* [a pot-shaped toy that spins on a tapered base]
• **Töpfer** (m)	= potter	
• **Töpferei** (f)	= ceramic art; workshop	
Torf (m)	= peat	*turf*
töricht (adj) [< OHG. *tusig* (cf. AS. *dysig*)]	= foolish	*dizzy* [< AS. *dysig*, foolish, later unsteady, bewildered]
• **Tor**[1] (m), **Törin** (f)	= fool	
tosen (vi) [bs: great swelling of force, noise < IE. *teu-*, to swell, whence Gmc. *tus-* > *tusunt*, 'swollen hundred,' a thousand)]	= to roar, rage	distantly: *thous-* in *thousand* [< AS. *thusend* < *thus-hundi*, 'a swollen hundred' < IE. *teu-*, to swell]
• **Getöse** (n)	= din, noise	
tot (adj)	= dead, deceased	*1. dead; 2. death*
• **töten** (vt)	= to kill, murder; deaden	
• **Tötung** (m)	= killing, homicide	
• **Tod** (m)	= death	
• **tödlich** (adj)	= deadly, mortal, lethal	
traben (vi) [bs: going on foot, trampling < MHG. *draben* (cf. Frk. *trap-*) < Gmc. *trep-*, what one treads]	= to trot	distantly: *1. tramp, trample;*
• **Trab** (m)	= trot	
• **Trabant** (m) [bs: follower, one treading after < MHG. *drabant*, who follows on foot, bodyguard]	= satellite	
• **hochtrabend** (adj) [lit.: 'high-stepping,' 'high-trotting']	= high-flown, pompous	
• **Treppe** (m)	= staircase, stairs	*2. trap* [orig.: what one steps on, then anything that catches the victim unawares]
• **Attrappe** (f) [bs: what catches the eye < Fr. *attraper*, to entrap < Frk. *trap-* < Gmc. *trep-*, what one treads]	= dummy; (display) mockup	

GERMAN WORD	MEANING	ENGLISH COGNATE
Tracht (see **tragen**)		
trachten (vi) [< L. *tractare*, to conduct, transact] • **Betracht** (m), **Betrachtung** (f) • **betrachten** (vt) • **beträchtlich** (adj)	= to strive for, aspire to, endeavor after = consideration, regard = to examine, regard = considerable, important	*tractable* [< L. *tractare*, to conduct, lead, transact]
tragen (vt & vi) [cf. AS. *dragan*] • **tragbar** (adj) • **Träger** (m) • **Antrag** (m) ['that carried to'] • **einträglich** (adj) ['bringing in'] • **eintragen** (vt) [bookkeeping term: 'to carry in,' to register yield, losses or gains] • **Eintrag** (m) ['that brought in'] • **beeinträchtigen** (vt) [bookkeeping term; bs: to register misfortune (the negative force of *eintragen*, to register yield, losses or gains)] • **erträglich** (adj) ['as can be thoroughly (*er-*) borne'] • **nachträglich** (adj) ['brought afterwards'] • **Betrag** (m) [bs: that carried] • **betragen** (vt & refl) • **Vertrag** (m) ['carried by all' < *ver*, thorough] • **Tracht** (f) ['what one wears, bears'] • **Eintracht** (f) [bs: striving to carry one sentiment < *ein*, one + *tragen*] • **Zwietracht** (f) [bs: two sides carrying opposing views < *zwei*, two + *tragen*] • **Getreide** (n) ['that born, yielded (of the earth)']	= to carry, bear, wear, yield (crops) = portable; reasonable = carrier, bearer; girder = offer, proposal = profitable = to book, register yield or profits; also to bring in a negative result, misfortune, etc. = an entry, item; (fig.:) that brought in, esp. a bad befalling, injury = to impair, bring harm or injury to [cf. Eng. *casualty*, a chance event, esp. an unfortunate one < L. *casus*, chance event] = tolerable = subsequent = amount, sum = to amount to; to behave = agreement, treaty = attire, costume, fashion = harmony, concord = discord = grain, cereal produce	words < AS. *dragan*, to carry: *1. drag; 2. dray* [a low cart]; *3. draw*
Träne (f) [bs: exuded substance] • **tränen** (vi) • **Tränengas** (n)	= tear (of eye) = to run with tears = tear gas	*trane oil* [oil from whale blubber < Du. *traan*, exuded oil]
Traube (f) [uncert.; perh. 'drooping fruit' < ? IE. **dreu-*, to droop, fall] • **Weintraube** (f)	= bunch of grapes, cluster = grape, grape bunch	uncert.; ? *droop, drip* [< IE. **dreu-*, to droop, fall]

GERMAN WORD	MEANING	ENGLISH COGNATE
trauen (vt) [cogn. G. *treu* (cf. AS. *truon, tre-owian*, to have trust in)] • **trauen lassen** (refl) • **Trauung** (f), **Traurung** (m) • **traulich** (adj) • **Traulichkeit** (f) • **(an)vertrauen** (vi)	= to marry off, to unite in marriage; have trust in = to get married = marriage ceremony = intimate, famiiar = intimacy = to entrust	*1. to trow* [arch.: to have trust or confidence in]; *2. troth* [loyalty, faithfulness] and *to troth, betroth; 3. true*
Traum (m) [< IE. **dreugh-*, to deceive] • **träumen** (vi) • **träumerisch** (adj)	= dream = to dream = fanciful, visionary	*dream* [< IE. **dreugh-*, to deceive]
traurig (adj) • **trauern** (vi) • **Trauer** (f)	= mournful, grieved = to mourn, be in grief = sorrow, affliction, mourning	*dreary*
treffen (vt & vi) [< OHG. *treffan* (cf. AS. *drepan*) < Gmc. **drep-*, to hit] • **Treffer** (m) • **triftig** (adj) [bs: hitting the target] • **Triftigkeit** (f) • **trefflich** (adj) • **betreffen** (vt) • **betreffs** (prep) + *gen.*	= to hit, reach the mark, light upon, encounter, meet = a hit, good shot, prize = convincing, sound, valid = soundness, plausibility = excellent, exquisite, choice = to concern, refer to = concerning	*to drepe* [obs.: to strike, kill < AS. *drepan* < Gmc. **drep-*, to hit] and *dreper* [obs.: murderer]
treiben (vt) [< *treiben* (cf. AS. *drifan*] • **antreiben** (vt) • **Antrieb** (m) • **betreiben** (vt) • **Betrieb** (m) • **betriebsam** (adj) • **Trift** (f) [bs: a driving of livestock, or its locale < *treiben*, to drive]	= to drive, propel = to incite, drive on = impulse = to manage (e.g,. a business) = management, enterprise, factory = active, busy, industrious = pasture; drove, herd; cattle track	*1. to drive; 2. drift* [< AS. *drifan*, to drive]
treideln (vt & vi) [< LG. < Fr. *trailler* < LL. *tragulare to drag < L. *tragula*, a drag, sledge] • **Treidelpfad** (m)	= to tow = towpath	*1. to trail* [to drag along behind < Fr. *trailler* < L. *tragula*, drag, sledge]; *2. to trawl, trawler*
trennen (vt) [root *t-r-n* cogn. G. *zehren*, to consume (cf. AS. *teran*, to rend)] • **trennbar** (adj) • **abtrünnig** (adj) ['separating from others']	= to sever, separate = separable = rebellious	distantly: *to tear* [< AS. *teran*, to rend]
Treppe (see **traben**)		

GERMAN WORD	MEANING	ENGLISH COGNATE
treten (vi & vt) [*trat, getreten*]	= to tread, step; kick, trample	*tread*
• **vertreten** (vt) ['to tread for']	= to represent	
• **Vertreter** (m)	= representative, agent, proxy	
• **stellvertretend** (adj) ['treading in place of' < *Stelle*, place]	= representative, deputy, vicarious	
• **betreten** (vt)	= to step on, enter (a room, etc.)	
• **betreten** (adj) ['trodden on']	= embarrassed, at a loss	
• **Tritt** (m)	= tread, step	
• **Trotz** (m) [origin uncert.; < MHG. *traz*, believed an intensification of *Tritt*, step, as 'a step in defiance']	= defiance, obstinacy	*tread*, with added connotation of defiance
• **trotzig** (adj)	= defiant, obstinate	
• **trotzen** (vi)	= to defy, be obstinate	
• **abtrotzen** (vt)	= to wrest (a th. from s.o.) by defiance	
• **ertrotzen** (vt) [< *er*, thoroughly + *trotzen*]	= to extort, obtain by defiance	
treu (adj)	= faithful, true, loyal	*true*
• **Treue** (f) [< OHG. *triuwa* (cf. Goth. *triggwa*, treaty, whence ML. *treuga*; Ital. *tregua*; Fr. *trêve*, truce, armistice)]	= faithfulness, loyalty	
• **treulich** (adj)	= truly, trustily	
Trichter (m) [bs: wide opening through which s.t. is passed < OHG. *trahtari* < ML. *tractarius* < L. *trajectorium* < *trajectum* past p. of *trajicere* (*transjicere*), to cause to go across or through]	= funnel, crater, horn (of wind instrument)	*trajectory* [< L. *trajectorium* < *trajectum* past p. of *trajicere* (*transjicere*), to cause to go across or through]
triefen (vi)	= to drip	*drip, drop*
• **Traufe** (f)	= eaves	
• **träufeln** (vi)	= to drip	
Trift (see **treiben**]		
trinken (vt & vi) [*trank, getrunken*]	= to drink	*1. drink; 2. drunk*
• **tränken** (vt) [bs: to make drink, soak]	= to drench, soak	
• **Tränk** (m), **Getränk** (n)	= drink, beverage	
• **trunken** (adj)	= drunken, intoxicated	
• **ertrinken** (vi)	= to be drowned	
• **ertränken** (vt)	= to make drown	
trocken (adj) [cf. AS. *dryge*]	= dry	*1. dry* [< AS. *dryge*]; *2. drug* [< Fr. *drogue* < MDu. *droge*, a dry substance]; *3. drought*
• **trocknen** (vt & vi)	= to dry; dry up	
• **vertrocknen** (vi)	= to dry up	

GERMAN WORD	MEANING	ENGLISH COGNATE
Trog (m)	= trough, vat	*trough*
Trommel (n)	= drum, cylinder, barrel	*drum*
tropfen (vi) • **Tropfen** (m) • **tröpfeln** (vi)	= to drip, leak, trickle = drop = to drop, trickle	*drop*
Trosse (f) [bs: bundled lines < Fr. *trousse,* bundle < LL. *torsare* < *torsus,* var. of *tortus* < *torquere,* to twist]	= cable, hawser	*1. trousseau* [orig.: a bundle, then the collection of a bride's clothes and linens]; *2. truss* [a framework; bundle (of hay)]
Trotz (see **treten**)		
trüb (adj) [< IE. **dher-,* to make muddy; dark] • **trüben** (vt) • **Trübheit** (f) • **trübselig** (adj) • **Trübsal** (f) • **Treber** (pl.)	= turbid, muddy, gloomy = to becloud, make dark = turbidity, dreariness = sad, melancholy = distress, affliction = draff, sediment in brewing, wine- making	*1. draff* [dregs, sediment < ON. *draf,* cogn. G. *Treber,* dregs, ult. < IE. **dher-,* muddy, darkness]; *2.* distantly: *drab*
Trubel (f) [< Fr. *trouble,* disturbance]	= bustle, fuss, turbulence	*trouble*
Trug (m) [bs: that deceptive like a dream < IE. **dreugh-,* to deceive] • **Trugbild** (n) • **trügen** (vt & vi) • **Betrug** (m) • **betrügen** (vt)	= deceit, fraud = phantom, illusion = to deceive; be deceptive = deceit, fraud = to deceive, cheat	*drea-* in *dream* [< Gmc. *draugma* < IE. **dreugh-,* to deceive]
Trümmer (m/pl. of **Trumm**) [< OHG. *drum,* end piece; cogn. L. *terminus,* border, end]	= fragments, ruins, broken pieces, wreckage (naut.)	*thrum* [orig.: a word from weaving referring to ends, or termini, of the warp threads, as well as to fringing; also in naut. usage to mean bundles of rope placed to prevent chafing]
Tuch (n) [cf. Du. *doek*] • **tuchen** (adj) • **Badetuch** (n) • **Leichentuch** (n) • **Lendentuch** (n) • **Tellertuch** (n)	= cloth, fabric = of cloth = bath towel = shroud = loincloth = dishcloth	*duck* [a light cotton or linen < Du. *doek,* cloth]
tüchtig (see **taugen**)		

GERMAN WORD	MEANING	ENGLISH COGNATE
Tücke (f) [echoic; based on plural of MHG. *tuc*, sudden movement (esp. of a sinister nature), a bad blow (cf. echoic Eng. *tick*, quick sound; also cf. force in echoic but unsinister Eng. *whopping*, overwhelming)]	= malice, insidiousness, spite	cf. echoic *tick* [a quick sound], *tick-tock*
• **tückisch** (adj)	= malicious, insidious, spiteful, treacherous	
• **Heimtücke** (f)	= malice, treachery	
• **heimtückisch** (adj)	= malicious, treacherous	
Tugend (see **taugen**)		
tummeln (vi) [< IE. **dheu-*, to rise, move in a cloud]	= to romp, bestir o.s.	*1*, distantly: *du-* in *dust* [< IE. **dheu-*, to rise, move in a cloud]; *2.* theorized: *tumble*
• **Getümmel** (n)	= turmoil, tumult	
Tümpel (m)	= pool, deep part of a lake	*dimple*
tun (vt & vi) [*tat, getan*]	= to do, make, put	*1. do; 2. done;*
• **tunlich** (adj)	= practicable, feasible	
• **Untertan** (m) [bs: one 'done under' < *unter* + *tan*, past p. of *tun*, (cf. *subject* < *sub*, under + *jectum*, thrown)]	= a subject (person), one owing allegiance to another	*3. under + done;*
• **untertänig** (adj)	= submissive, humble	
• **Tat** (f) ['that done' < *tat* past p. < *tun*]	= act, deed, offense	*4. deed*
• **Täter** (m)	= perpetrator, offender	
• **tätig** (adj)	= active, busy	
• **betätigen** (refl)	= to take an active part in	
• **tätlich** (adj)	= violent	
• **Tatort** (m) [< *Tat* + *Ort*, place]	= place or scene of a crime	
• **Tatsache** (f) [< *Tat* + *Sache*, thing]	= fact	
tünchen (vt) ['to make white like a tunic' < L. *tunica*, tunic]	= to whitewash	*tunic* [a white garment worn in ancient Rome]
• **Tünche** (f)	= whitewash	
Tür (f)	= door	*door*
• **Tor**^{2} (n)	= gateway, goal (soccer)	
turnen (vi) [bs: to do turns, flips < L. *tornare*, to turn around]	= to do gymnastics	*1. turn; 2. tourney*
• **Turnen** (m)	= gymnastics	
• **Turner(in)** (m, f)	= gymnast	

GERMAN WORD	MEANING	ENGLISH COGNATE
Tusche (f) [< Fr. *toucher*, to touch, touch up with inks or colors] • **tuschen** (vi)	= watercolor, India ink = to draw with ink	*touch*
Tüte (f) ['tooter,' orig.: paper rolled like a cone or 'horn' to contain s.t. < echoic *tuten*, to toot, sound a horn]	= paper bag	*toot* [echoic]

# U		
übel (adj) • **Übel** (n) • **übelwollen** (vi) • **übelnehmen, verübeln** (vt)	= evil, bad = evil = to wish s.o. ill = to take s.t. ill or amiss	*evil*
üben (vt & vi) [*üb*- cogn. with *op*- in L. *opus*, work, *operari*, to work] • **Übung** (f) • **üblich** (adj) [bs: as is practiced] • **verüben** (vt)	= to practice, exercise = practice, exercise = customary, usual = to commit, perpetrate	*1.* op- in *operate*; *2.* opera [musical 'works' < Ital. *opera* < L. *opera*, pl. of *opus*, a work]
über (prep) • **übrig** (adj) • **übrigens** (adv) • **erübrigen** (vt) ['to keep over' < *er*-, thoroughly]	= over = left, remaining = besides = to save, spare	*over*
überwinden (see **Gewinn**)		
Ufer (n) [< MHG. *uover*, whence name *Hannover* < *am ho(he)n overe*, 'on the high bank' (cf. AS. *ofer*)]	= bank (of river); shore, edge of sea	*1.* -over in *Hannover* (German city, Eng. *Hanover*); *2.* -or (< *ofer*) in *Windsor* [< AS. *Windles ofer*]
Uhr (f) [< L. *hora*]	= clock, watch	*hour* [< L. *hora*]
umsonst (adv) [bs: 'for so,' 'for so little' < *um*, concerning + *so* < MHG. *um sus*]	= gratis, for nothing; in vain, to no purpose	*ambi*- [L. prefix: around, about] + *so*
umzingeln (vt) [< *um*, around + *zingel* < L. *cingulum*, belt, girdle, encircling zone]	= to surround, encircle, encompass, envelop	words < L. *cingulum*, belt, girdle: *1. cingulum* [belt; band of color (zool.)]; *2. cinch* [to tighten; a sure hold]; *3. shingles* [blisters around the waist < ML. *cingulus*, girdle]

GERMAN WORD	MEANING	ENGLISH COGNATE
unantastbar (see **tasten**)		
Unflat (m) ['that not flushed away' < MHG. *unvlat* < *un* + obs. *vlaejen*, to rinse, flush < *flae-*, cogn. Gmc. **flowan*, flow, and **floduz*, flood < IE. **pleu-*, to flow] • **unflätig** (adj)	= filth, dirt = filthy, dirty	*un* + words < Gmc. **flowan*, flow, and **floduz*, flood: *1. flow; 2. flood; 3. float; 4.* distantly: *pluvious* [rainy < L. *pluvere*, to rain < IE. **pleu-*, to flow]
ungeheuer (see **Heirat**)		
ungestüm (see **stemmen**)		
Ungetüm (n) [bs: abnormal thing, that outside of order < **un-ga-domia*, what is not rightly decreed < *un*, without, not + *ge* + *tum* < Goth. *doms*, judgement (cf. AS. *dom*, what is decreed) < IE. **dhe-*, to place, set down]	= monster	*un* + *1. doom* [orig.: judgement, then tragic fate < AS. *dom*, what is decreed < IE. **dhe-*, to place, set down]; *2. deem* [to judge, believe]; *3.* suffix *-dom* [state, condition, power < *doom*, what is laid down, e.g., *kingdom*]
Unke (f) [< merging of OHG. *unc* snake (cogn. L. *anguis*, snake), and *eutze*, toad] • **unken** (vi)	= toad; (fig.:) grumbler = to croak; grumble	*anguine* [of or like a snake < L. *anguis*, snake < IE. **angwhi* or **eghi-*, snake]
unlängst (adv) ['not long ago,' *un*, neg. + *längst*, long ago]	= lately, recently	*un* + *long*
Untertan (see **tun**)		
üppig (adj) [believed to mean excess, *üp-* < *über*, over] • **Üppigkeit** (f)	= luxuriant, opulent, lush, sumptuous = luxury, opulence	distantly: *1. ov-* in *over*; *2. up* [in sense of increase, e.g., *dress up*]
Urkunde (f) [< *erkennen*, to recognize] • **beurkunden** (vt)	= document, deed, legal instrument = to attest, certify, authenticate	*know*

# V		
Vater (m) • **väterlich** (adj)	= father = paternal	*father*
verblüffen (vt) [perh. echoic]	= to perplex, dumbfound	*to bluff* [to mislead]

GERMAN WORD	MEANING	ENGLISH COGNATE
verdammen (vt) [< *ver* + L. *damnum*, damage, harm]	= to condemn, damn	*damn* [< L. *damnum*, damage, harm]
• **verdammt** (adj)	= damned	
• **Verdammnis** (f)	= damnation	
verdrießen (vt) [*verdroß, verdrossen;* < *ver* + OHG. stem *drioz-* believed cogn. to L. *trudo, trudere, trusum,* to push, press]	= to vex, annoy	distantly: *-trude* as in *intrude, intrusion* [< L. *trudo, trudere, trusum,* to push, press]
• **verdrossen** (adj)	= annoyed	
• **verdrießlich** (adj)	= annoying, unpleasant	
• **Verdruß** (m)	= vexation, displeasure	
• **überdruß** (m) [bs: pushed to full capacity]	= satiety, weariness	
• **überdrüssig** (adj)	= weary or tired of	
verfemen (vt) ['to banish' < *ver* + MHG. *vieme,* judgement; cf. *Vehmgericht,* secret tribunal of old Westphalia]	= to outlaw; ostracize (socially)	*Vehmic* [historical term pertaining to the *Vehmgericht,* a secret tribunal which enacted banishment on individuals in old Westphalia]
vergessen (vt) [*vergass, vergessen*]	= to forget	*forget*
• **vergeßlich** (adj)	= forgetful	
vergeuden (vt) [bs: opening wide < *ver* + MHG. *giuden,* to waste < *giu-,* cogn. G. *gähnen,* to yawn, gape]	= to dissipate, squander	distantly: *to yawn*
verletzen (see **letzt**)		
verlieren (vt & vi) [*verlor, verloren*]	= to lose	*1. vorlorn; 2. lose*
• **Verlust** (m)	= loss	
Vermögen (see **Macht**)		
Vernunft (see **nehmen**)		
verpönt (see **Pein**)		
versehren (vt) [*ver* + *sehr*, painful]	= to injure, disable	*sore*
• **versehrt** (adj)	= disabled, impaired	
• **Versehrte(r)** (m)	= disabled person	
versöhnen (see **Sühne**)		
verteidigen (vt) [orig.: < jurispr.: 'to defend the day's case,' then to defend anything < *ver,* causative + *Tag,* day + *Ding,* thing, legal case]	= to defend	*for + day + thing*
• **Verteidiger** (m)	= defender; counsel for defense	

GERMAN WORD	MEANING	ENGLISH COGNATE
Verzicht (see **zeihen**)		
Vettel (f) [< L. *vetula*, old woman < *vetus*, old]	= hag, harridan	*vet-* in *veteran* [< L. *vetus*, old]
Vetter (m) [bs: father's brother's son, cogn. *Vater*, father]	= cousin	*1. father; 2. paternal* [< L. *pater*, father]
Vieh (n) [< Gmc. **fehu-* (cf. AS. *feoh*)] • **viehisch** (adj) • **Viehhof** (m)	= livestock, cattle, beast = bestial, brutal = stockyard	*1. fee* [< ME. *feo* < AS. *feoh*, cattle, esp. as payment]; *2. fe-* in *fellow* [one who set down payment in a cooperative venture < AS. *feolaga* < *feoh* + *laga*, to lay, place]
viel (adj) [< OHG. *filu;* root *v-l* = *p-l* in Gk. *poly-*, many, much] • **vielfach** (adj & adv) • **vielleicht** (adv) ['very light'] • **vielseitig** (adj) ['many-sided']	= many, much; very = multiple; frequently = perhaps, maybe = versatile	distantly: *poly-* in *polyphonic, polygamy* [< Gk. *poly-*, many]
Vlies (n)	= fleece	*fleece*
Vogel (m) [< OHG. *fogal* (cf. AS. *fugel*)] • **Vogelbauer** (n)	= bird = bird-cage	*fowl* [< ME. *fowel* < AS. *fugol, fugel*, bird]
Vogt (m) [legal official < MHG. *voget, fogat* < L. *advocatus*, one called to give counsel < *ad*, to + *vocare*, to call]	= overseer, bailiff, steward	*advocate* [< L. *advocatus*, counselor, one called to give counsel < *ad*, to + *vocare*, to call]
Volk (n) • **volkstümlich** (adj) ['what is held by the people or folk'] • **Volkstümlichkeit** (f) • **bevolkern** (vt)	= people, nation = popular [< L. *populus*, people] = popularity = to populate	*folk*
voll, völlig (adj) • **vollenden** (vt) • **vollkommen** (adj) • **vollständig** (adj) • **vollständigen** (vt)	= full, entire, complete = to finish, bring to an end = consummate, complete, full = complete = to complete	*full*

GERMAN WORD	MEANING	ENGLISH COGNATE
# W		
Waage (f) [< OHG. *waga* < IE. **wegh-*, to set in motion, move back and forth]	= balance, scales	*1.* weigh [< ME. *weien, wegen*]; *2.* distantly: *wag* [< AS. *wagian*, to oscillate]
• **waagerecht** (adj) ['balanced right,' straight across]	= horizontal	
• **wägen** (vt) [bs: to move, esp. back and forth < *waga*, scales]	= to weigh	
• **erwägen** (vt) ['to weigh out fully,' 'weigh for one-self' < *er*, thoroughly + *wägen*]	= to consider, deliberate [< L. *deliberare*, to weigh well < *de* intens. prefix + *libra*, balance, scale]	
• **Erwägung** (f)	= consideration, deliberation	
• (see also **wagen**, **wiegen**)		
wach (adj)	= awake	*1.* watch; *2.* wake; *3.* bivouac
• **wachen** (vi)	= to keep watch	
• **bewachen** (vt)	= to watch, guard	
• **wecken** (vt)	= to wake s.o.	
• **Wecker** (m)	= alarm clock	
Wachs (n)	= wax	*wax* and *to wax*[1] [to apply a protective coating]
• **wachsen**[1] (vt)	= to apply wax to	
wachsen[2] (vi) [*wuchs, gewaschen* (cf. AS. *weaxan*, to grow)]	= to grow, increase, expand	*1. to wax*[2] [to increase, grow, said esp. of the moon < ME. *waxen*, AS. *weaxan*, to grow]; *2. waist* [part of the body that increases, expands]
• **erwachsen** (vi)	= to arise, develop	
• **erwachsen** (adj)	= adult, grown-up	
• **verwachsen** (adj)	= deformed, humpbacked	
• **Wachstum** (n), **Zuwachs** (m)	= increase	
• **Wuchs** (m)	= growth, stature, figure	
• **Wucher** (m)	= usury	
• **Wucherer** (m)	= usurer	
• **Wuchergewinn** (m)	= excess profit	
• **Nachwuchs** (m)	= rising generation	
Waffe (f) [< OHG. *waffan* (cf. AS. *waepen*; MDu. *wapen*)]	= weapon	*weapon* [< AS. *waepen*]
• **(be)waffnen** (vt)	= to arm, fit with weapons	
• **entwaffnen** (vt)	= to disarm	
• **Waffestillstand** (m)	= armistice, truce	
• **Wappen** (n) [< MDu. *wapen*, arm(s), weapon (cogn. G. *Waffe*)]	= coat of arms	

GERMAN WORD	MEANING	ENGLISH COGNATE
wagen[1] (vt & refl) [bs: to put in the balance < OHG. *waga* < IE. **wegh-,* to set in motion, move back and forth]	= to venture, risk, dare	*1. weigh* [< ME. *weien, wegen*]; *2.* distantly: *wag* [< AS. *wagian,* to oscillate]
• **Wagnis** (n)	= venture, risk, hazard	
• **Wagehals** (m) ['one risking one's neck' < *wagen + Hals,* neck]	= dare devil	
• **wagehalsig** (adj)	= daring, foolhardy	
• **Wagehalsigkeit** (n)	= venture, risk	
• **Wagemut** (m)	= daring	
• (see also **Waage, wiegen**)		
Wagen[2] (m)	= carriage, coach, car, truck	*wagon*
• **Wagenspur** (f) [lit.: 'wagon track']	= rut	
wägen (see **Waage**)		
Wahl (f)	= choice, selection, election	*1. wale* [Scot. & dial.: a choosing; that chosen as best] and *to wale* [to choose]; *2. wally* [Scot.: fine, first-rate, choice]
• **wählen** (vt)	= to choose, select, elect	
• **wählbar** (vt & vi)	= eligible	
• **Wähler** (m)	= elector, voter	
• **wählerisch** (adj) [bs: choosy, fussy in choices]	= particular about, fastidious, choosy	
• **Wählzettel** (m)	= ballot, voting paper	
• **Auswahl** (f)	= choice, selection	
• **auswählen** (vt)	= to choose out, select	
Wahn (m)	= false or erroneous opinion; delusion, folly	*to ween* [to think, suppose, imagine]
• **wähnen** (vt)	= to fancy, imagine, believe	
• **Wahnsinn** (m)	= insanity, madness	
• **wahnsinnig, -witzig** (adj)	= insane, mad	
wahr (adj) [< IE. **wero-,* true; whence L. *verus,* true]	= true, genuine	distantly: *ver-* in *veracity* [< L. *verus,* true < IE. **wero-,* true]
• **wahrhaft** (adj)	= truthful, veracious	
• **Wahrheit** (f)	= truth	
• **wahrscheinlich** (adj) ['appearing true']	= probable, likely	
• **bewähren** (vt)	= to verify, prove	
• **bewähren** (refl)	= to prove a success, stand the test	
• **bewährt** (adj)	= proven, tried	
• **albern** (adj) ['all true' < OHG. *alawari,* honest < *al,* all + *war,* true]	= silly, foolish (orig.: honest, kindly)	*all + ver-*
• **Albernheit** (f)	= silliness, foolishness	

GERMAN WORD	MEANING	ENGLISH COGNATE
wahren (vt) [bs: keeping watch (cf. Frk. *waron;* whence Fr. *gar-, garage*) < Gmc. *war-* < IE. **wer-,* to watch out, perceive]	= to safeguard, maintain	words < Gmc. *war-* < IE. **wer-,* to watch out, perceive: *1. wary;* *2. aware; 3. beware; 4. warren* [a preserve, then the den of a rabbit]; *5. garage* [via OFr. *garer,* to protect < Frk. *waron*];
• **Wahrung** (f)	= safeguarding	
• **wahrnehmen** (vt)	= to perceive, take notice	
• **bewahren** (vt)	= to keep, preserve	
• **gewahr** (adj)	= under notice, aware of	
• **gewahren** (vt)	= to discern, notice	
• **verwahren** (adj)	= uncared for, neglected	
─────────	─────────	─────────
• **Gewähr** (f) [disputed; bs: to furnish surety, cover < *giweren,* prob. < IE. **wer-*]	= guarantee, security	*6. war-* in *warrant; 7. guar-* in *guarantee* [< OFr. *garantie* ult. < Frk. *waron*];
• **gewähren** (vt)	= to grant, allow, furnish	
• **Gewährsmann** (m)	= informant, source	
• **gewährte** (adj)	= allowed, afforded	
• **Währung** (f) [etym. disputed; prob. bs: what is assured, secure < MHG. *werunge*]	= monetary standard, currency	
─────────	─────────	─────────
• **Ware** (f) [bs: thing kept under watch, perh. via AS. *waru*]	= ware, article of commerce, product	*8. wares*
währen (vi) [< IE. **wes-,* to stay, dwell]	= to last, continue	*were* [subjunctive of verb *to be* < AS. *waere* < IE. **wes-,* to stay, dwell]
• **während** (prep; cj)	= during; while	
Waise (f) [origin unclear; root *wai-* believed to signify 'one separated' < IE. **weidh,* to separate, divide, whence *Witwe,* widow]	= orphan	words < IE. **weidh-,* to separate, divide: *1. widow; 2. -vide* in *divide*
Wal (m)	= whale	*whale*
Wald (m)	= forest, woodland	*weald* [forest, wooded country]
walken (vt)	= to full cloth; to mill (cloth, leather)	*walk* [earlier: to roll or compress s.t., tread, then to traverse on foot]
Wall (m) [< L. *vallum,* rampart]	= rampart, embankment, dam	*wall*
wallen[1] (also **aufwallen**) (vi) [< *Welle,* wave, billow]	= to wave, undulate, bubble	*1. a well; 2. to well up*
• **Wallung** (f)	= ebulition, excitement, agitation	
• **wällen** (vi)	= to boil, simmer	
─────────	─────────	
• **Wulst** (m)	= swelling, pad, roll	
• **wulsten** (vt & vi)	= to make into a pad or roll; to puff, swell	
• **wulstig** (adj)	= roll-shaped, puffed, swelled	

GERMAN WORD	MEANING	ENGLISH COGNATE
wallen[2] (vi) [uncert.; believed bs: to go to and fro; *wall-*, prob. < *wadl-* < OHG. *wadalon*, whence *Wedel*, tail, frond, what is wagged] • **Wallfahrer** (m) • **Wallfahrt** (f)	= to go on a pilgrimage = pilgrim = pilgrimage	? *1*. distantly: *wheedle;* [orig.: to wag, fan, then to flatter, coax, cogn. OHG. *wadalon*]; *2. to wedel* [to ski downhill by moving rear of skis side to side, making quick, short turns]
Walroß (n) [< *Wal*, whale + *Roß*, horse]	= walrus	*walrus*
walten (vt & vi) • **Gewalt** (f) • **gewaltig** (adj) • **gewaltsam** (adj) • **Gewaltsamkeit** (f) • **vergewaltigen** (vt) • **verwalten** (vt) • **Verwalter** (m)	= to govern; wield power = power, force, violence = powerful, mighty = violent, forcible = violence, vorce = to violate, rape = to administer, manage = manager, director	*wield*
Walze (f) • **walzen, wälzen** (vt) • **abwälzen** (vt) • **Walzer** (m) • **Wälzer** (m) ['something rolled' < loan transl. of L. *volumen*, scrolled papyrus < *volvere*, to turn, roll]	= roller, cylinder = to roll round = to roll or shift away = waltz (dance) = hefty book or volume [< L. *volumen*, scrolled papyrus, what is rolled round < *volvere*, to turn, roll]	*waltz* [a rolling, turning dance; also a cylinder, roller]
Wamme (f)	= belly part (furmaking); paunch	*womb*
Wams (n) [< ML. *wambasium* < MGk. *bambax*, cotton]	= jacket; doublet	*wampus, wamus, wammus* [a medieval quilted jacket worn under armor]
Wand (see **winden**)		
wandeln (refl) • **Wandel** (m) • **wandelbar** (adj) • **Wandlung** (f)	= to change = change = changeable, variable = change, transformation	*wandle* [changeable; Scot.: supple, agile]
Wange (see **winken**)		
wanken (see **winken**)		
Wanne (f) [< L. *vannus*, a winnowing fan, a pan or tub used to toss, ventilate and collect winnowed grain] • **Badewanne** (f)	= tub, vat, trough, winnowing fan = bathtub	*fan* [orig.: utensil or pan used in winnowing to toss and blow off chaff and so collect the grain, then any device for creating a current of air < L. *vannus*, winnowing pan]
Wanze (f) [bs: a bug living in cracks in a wall (*Wand*), shortened < OHG. *wantlus*, wall louse < *want*, wall + *lus*, louse]	= bedbug	distantly: *to wind* [G. *Wand*, woven wickerwork partition, wall] + *louse*

GERMAN WORD	MEANING	ENGLISH COGNATE
Ware (see **wahren**)		
warm (adj) • **Wärme** (f)	= warm, hot = warmth, heat	*warm*
warnen and **verwarnen** (vt) • **(Ver)Warnung** (f)	= to warn, caution, admonish = warning, admonition	*warn* and *warning*
warten (vi) [< Gmc. *wardon*] • **erwärten** (vt) • **Wärter** (m) • **Warte** (f)	= to wait, stay, be in store for s.o. = to wait for, expect = attendant, keeper, male nurse = watch tower, look-out	*1. ward* and *steward; 2. guard* [< Fr. *garder,* to keep, watch over < Frk. **wardon*]
Warze (f)	= wart	*wart*
waschen (vt, vi, refl) • **Wäsche** (f)	= to wash = laundry, washing; lingerie	*wash*
Wasser (n) • **wässern** (vt) • **wässerig** (adj) • **Wasserstoff** (m)	= water = to water, irrigate, soak, steep = watery = hydrogen	*water*
waten (vi)	= to wade	*wade*
Watte (f) • **wattieren** (vt)	= cotton pad = to wad, pad	*wad*
weben (vt & vi) • **Weberei** (f) • **Gewebe** (n) • **Honigwabe** (f) [bees' 'web' for storing honey]	= to weave = weaving mill, woven material = textile, tissue, texture, web, weft = honeycomb	*weave*
Wechsel (m) • **wechseln** (vt & vi) • **Wechsler** (m) • **wechselseitig** (adj)	= (ex)change, rotation = to change, exchange = money-changer = mutual, reciprocal	distantly: *week* [period which changes every seven days]
wecken (see **wach**)		
Wedel (m) [bs: 'wagger' < OHG. *wadalon,* to go to and fro] • **wedeln** (vi) • **anwedeln** (vt)	= tail, sprinkling brush, frond; fan = to wag (the tail); to fawn, crawl, cringe = to fawn over or wag the tail at	*1. to wheedle* [orig.: to wag, fan, then to flatter, coax]; *2. to wedel* [to ski downhill by moving rear of skis side to side, making quick, short turns]

GERMAN WORD	MEANING	ENGLISH COGNATE
Weg (m) [what goes, 'moves' from place to place (cf. AS. *wagian*, to oscillate) < IE. **wegh*, to go, transport]	= way, road, path, route	*1. way; 2. away;*
• **bewegen** (vt & refl)	= to cause to move, stir, excite, agitate	*3. wag* [< AS. *wagian*, to oscillate];
• **bewegbar** (adj)	= movable, mobile	
• **beweglich** (adj)	= active, stirring, nimble	
• **Beweggrund** (m) ['a ground for moving']	= motive, reason	
• **abwegig** (adj) ['away from the way']	= devious, misleading	
• **verwegen** (adj) [bs: intense movement, intensification of *weg-*]	= daring, audacious, bold	
• **Verwegenheit** (f)	= audacity, boldness	
• **unentwegt** (adv) [bs: on-going, 'not put out of the way' < *un*, not + *ent*, apart + *Weg*]	= untiringly, continuously	
• **wegfallen** (vi)	= to be omitted	
• **wegnehmen** (vt)	= to take up (time or space)	
• **wegen** (prep) + *gen.* ['from this way']	= because of	
• **aufwiegeln** (vt) [*auf* + *wiegeln*, freqtv. of *weg-*]	= to stir up, instigate	*4. wiggle;*
• **wackeln** (vi)	= to wobble, be loose	*5. waggle*
• **wackelig** (adj)	= shaky, tottery, loose	
weh (adj) [< OHG. *we* (cf. AS. *wa*; Goth. *wai*, whence Ital. *guaio*, trouble)]	= sore, painful, aching	*woe* [< AS. *wa*]
• **Weh** (n)	= pain, grief, woe	
• **Wehen** (n/pl.)	= travail, labor pains	
• **wehklagen** (vi)	= to lament	
• **Heimweh** (n)	= homesickness, nostalgia	
wehen (vi) [< IE. **we-*, to blow]	= to blow, drift, flutter	*wi-* in *wind* [< IE. **we-*, to blow]
• **Wehe** (f)	= drift (of snow, sand)	
Wehr (f)	= resistance, defense, weapon	*weir* [a dam or fence]
• **wehren** (vt & vi)	= to oppose, prevent	
• **wehren** (refl)	= to defend o.s., offer resistance	
• **abwehren** (vt)	= to ward off, repulse	
• **Abwehr** (f)	= warding off, defense	
• **verwehren** (vt)	= to debar, keep one from	
• **Gewehr** (n) ['what defends']	= gun, rifle	
Weib (n)	= female, woman	*wife*
• **weiblich** (adj)	= female, feminine gender, womanly	

GERMAN WORD	MEANING	ENGLISH COGNATE
weich (adj) • **weichen** (vi) • **abweichen** (vi) ['to yield away'] • **ausweichen** (vt) • **entweichen** (vi) ['to withdraw fully from']	= tender, soft = to give way, yield = to deviate, diverge = to avoid, evade = to escape, run away	*weak* [yielding, soft]
Weichbild (n) [< OHG. *wih*, place (cf. AS. *wic*); cogn. L. *vicus*, row of dwellings, quarter of a city, whence Eng. *vicinity*]	= precincts, city boundaries; outskirts	*1. wick* [arch.: village, hamlet < AS. *wic*]; *2.* suffixes *-wick* in *bailiwick* [a district under control of a bailif; special field of interest] and *-wich* in place names *Greenwich, Norwich*
Weide[1] (f) [cf. AS. *withthe*]	= willow	*withey, withe* [a willow, willow twig < AS. *withthe*]
Weide[2] (f) [of hunting, of pastures < OHG. *weida*, feed (cf. Frk. **waidanjan*, to search after food, pasture)] • **weiden, ausweiden**[1] (vt & vi) • **Weidmann** (m) • **weidlich** (adj & adv) [orig.: 'suitable to the hunt'] **Weid-** *applied to belly, viscera:* • **ausweiden**[2] (vt & vi) • **Eingeweide** (n/pl) [hunting term: that fed to the dogs] • **Augenweide** (f) [bs: feed for the eyes]	= pasture, meadow = to turn out to grass, feed = huntsman, sportsman = (adj:) valiant, brave; (adv:) to one's heart's content, thoroughly = to eviscerate, disembowel = viscera, entrails, intestines = welcome sight	*gain* [< OFr. *gaaignier* < Frk. **waidanjan*, to search after food, pasture]
weigern (refl) [bs: to resist < OHG. *weigar*, rash < *wigan*, to fight, combat (cf. Goth. *weihan*, to fight) < IE. **weik-*[1], to fight, whence L. *vinco, vincere, victus*, to vanquish, defeat, refute] • **verweigern** (vt) • **Geweih** (n) [< MHG. *gewige*; etym. disputed; prob. bs: 'fighters,' that used for fighting < *wigan*, to fight, combat]	= to decline, refuse, be unwilling = to refuse, deny, disobey = antlers	*vic-* and *wig-* in words < IE. **weik-*[1], to fight: *1.* distantly: *vic-invictor* [< L. *vinco, vincere, victus*, to vanquish, defeat, refute; *2. wight*[2] [arch. and dial.: courageous, skilled in arms, warlike < ON. < Gmc. *wig-*, battle, fight]; *3.* suffix *-wig* in names: *Ludwig* < *hluda*, famous + *wig*, fighter]
Weihe (f) [< OHG. *wihen* < IE. **weik-*[2], assoc. with magic and religious notions] • **weihen** (vt) • **weihevoll** (adj) • **Weihestätt** (f) • **Weihnachten** (n) • **Weihrauch** (m) [< *Weih-* + *Rauch*, smoke] • **entweihen** (vt)	= consecration, inauguration, dedication, solemn mood = to consecrate, ordain = solemn = shrine = Christmas = incense = to desecrate, profane	*wi-, vi-* in words < IE. **weik-*[2], assoc. with magic and religious notions: *1. wile*, guile [< Anglo-Norm. *vihl*, strategem]; *2. witch* [< AS. *wicca*]; *3. victim* [< L. *victima*, sacrifice]

GERMAN WORD	MEANING	ENGLISH COGNATE
Weiher (m) [< MHG. *wiwaere* < L. *vivarium*, fish pond, game preserve < *vivere*, to live]	= fish pond	*vivarium* [enclosed place for raising plants or animals in a simulated environment < L. *vivarium*, fish pond, game preserve < *vivere*, to live]
Weiler (m) [< ML. *villare*, farm < L. *villa*, farm, country home]	= hamlet	*villa*
weinen (vi) • **beweinen** (vi) • **beweinenswert** (adj)	= to weep = to weep for = deplorable	*whine*
weise[1] (adj) [< *wissen*, to know] • **Weisheit** (f) • **weissagen** (vt & vi) [< *wissen* + erron. based on *sagen*, to say]	= wise, prudent, cunning = wisdom, learning, science = to prophecy, foretell	*wise, wisdom*
Weise[2] (f) [bs: making known < *wissen*, to know] • **weisen** (vt & vi) • **Weisung** (f) • **abweisen** (vt) ['to point off'] • **anweisen** (vt) • **beweisen** (vt) • **Beweis** (m) • **erweisen** (vt) • **hinweisen** (vt) • **Hinweis** (m) • **nachweisen** (vt) • **Nachweis** (m) • **verweisen** (vt)	= way, manner, custom = to demonstrate, point out = direction, instruction = to refuse, repel = to direct, instruct = to demonstrate, prove = evidence, proof = to prove = to point at, refer to = reference = to show, demonstrate = evidence, proof = to refer to	*wise* in: **1.** *clockwise* and **2.** *'in no wise'*
weiß (adj) • **weißen** (vt) • **Weiße** (f)	= white = to whiten, whitewash, blanch, refine = whiteness, whitewash	*white*
weit (adj) • **Weite** (f) • **erweitern** (vt)	= wide = width = to widen, enlarge	*wide*
Weizen (m)	= wheat	*wheat*
welk (adj) • **(ver)welken** (vi)	= faded, withered; flabby = to fade, wither	*wilt* [var. of obs. *to welk*, to wither < ME. *welken*, to fade]
Welle (f) • **wellenförmig** (adj) • **wellig** (adj) • **Wellensittich** (see **Sittich**)	= wave, motion of water; shaft (min.) = undulating = wavy, undulating	*well* [flow of water from the earth; any shaft, opening] and *to well up*

GERMAN WORD	MEANING	ENGLISH COGNATE
Welpe (m)	= puppy	*whelp* [a young dog, lion, wolf, bear, etc.; child]
Welt (f) [< OHG. *weralt*, epoch, man's life < *wer*, man + *alt*, old] • **verweltlichen** (vt)	= world = to secularize	*world* [< AS. *weorold* < *wer*, man + *eald*, old]
wenden (see **winden**)		
werben (vt) [< Gmc. **hwarb-*, to turn oneself, be active < IE. **kwerp-*, to rotate] • **Gewerbe** (n) [activity esp. for earning a living] • **gewerblich** (adj) • **bewerben** (refl) • **Bewerber** (m) • **erwerben** (vt) • **Erwerb** (m) • **Wirbel** (m) • **Wirbelsäule** (f) ['turning column,' bec. the joints turn] • **Werft** (f)	= to enroll or enlist; to woo, court = trade, business, industry = commercial, industrial = to apply for, seek, solicit or bid for = applicant, bidder = to acquire, gain = acquisition, purchase = whirl, eddy, flurry = spinal (or vertebral) column, with joints that turn [cf. *vertebra* < L. *vertere*, to turn] = wharf, dockyard	*1. wharf* [place where people turn, move about, are active < AS. *hwearf* < IE. **kwerp-*, to rotate]; *2. whirl* [< ON. *hvirfla* < IE. **kwerp-*, to rotate]; *3. warble*
werden (vi) [cf. AS. *weerthan*]	= to become	*weird* [of ghosts and spirits: what is to come < ME. *wirde*, AS. *wyrd*, fate < *weerthan*, to become]
werfen (vt) [*warf, geworfen* (cf. AS. *weorpan*) = L. *jacio, jacere, jactum* (in compounds -*jecio*, -*jecere*, -*jectum*)] • **einwerfen** (vi) • **entwerfen** (vt) • **Entwurf** (m) • **umwerfen** (vt) • **unterwerfen** (vt) • **verwerfen** (vt) ────── • **Wurf** (m) • **Würfel** (m) • **würfelig** (adj)	= to throw = to object, interject = to design, plan, outline = project, plan [cf. *project*, lit.: 's.t. thrown forth' < L. *pro* + *jactum*] = to overturn, upset = to subdue, subject = to reject, refuse = a throw, cast = cube, die (gaming) = cubical, checkered	*1. to warp* [orig.: to throw, then to throw from a straight course, hence distort, twist < AS. *weorpan*]; *2. warp* [in weaving: the longitudinal, vertical threads of a textile (perh. < historical practices in preparations for weaving that might involve the throwing, extending, of the threads that would become the warp)]
Werft (see **werben**)		
Wert (m) • **wert** (adj) • **werten** (vt) • **verwerten** (vt) ['to get the value out of'] ────── • **Würde** (f) • **würdig** (adj)	= value = worthy, of worth = to value, appraise = to utilize, make use of = dignity, title, office = dignified, worthy	*worth*

GERMAN WORD	MEANING	ENGLISH COGNATE
Wesen (n) [bs: what is made to be < *gewesen*, past p. of *sein*, and cogn. Eng. *was*]	= being, essence, nature	distantly: *was* [past t. of *to be*]
• **wesentlich** (adj)	= essential	
• **abwesend** (adj) ['being away']	= absent	
• **Abwesendheit** (f)	= absence	
• **anwesen** (adj) ['being near']	= present	
• **Anwesenheit** (f)	= presence	
• **verwesen** (vi) [*ver-,* of exhaustive force]	= to rot, decay	
Westen (m)	= west	*west*
• **westlich** (adj)	= western	
Wette (f) [cf. AS. *weddian*, to pledge; Frk. **waddi,* surety, pledge (whence LL. *wadium* > OFr. *guage* > Fr. *engager,* to engage)]	= wager, bet	*1. to wed* [< AS. *weddian*, to pledge, Frk. **waddi,* a surety, pledge]; *2. -gage* in *engage* [to bind by pledge < OFr. *guage* < LL. *wadium* < Frk. **waddi*] and *mortgage* [pledge or debt due upon death (*mort*)]; *3. wager* [orig.: a pledge, then a bet < LL. *wadiare* < Frk. **waddi,* surety]; *4. wage(s)* [orig.: pledge, then recompense < ONFr. var. of *gage*]
• **wetten** (vt & vi)	= to wager, bet	
• **Wettbewerb, Wettkampf** (m)	= competition, contest	
• **wetteifern** (vi)	= to rival, emulate	
• **Wetteifer** (m)	= rivalry, emulation	
Wetter (n)	= weather	*weather*
• **wittern** (vt) [bs: to detect a scent carried by the wind < *Wetter*, weather]	= to scent, smell; (fig.:) to suspect	
• **Witterung** (f)	= weather; scent (zool., hunting)	
• **verwittern** (vt & vi) ['to go bad from weather' < *ver*, intens. prefix + *wittern*]	= to weather, disintegrate, decay, effloresce	
wetzen (vt)	= to sharpen, grind, rub	*whet*
Wichse (f) [< *Wachse*, wax]	= polish, blacking	*wax*
• **wichsen** (vt)	= to polish, shine, apply blacking	
Wicht (m)	= creature	*wight*[1] [creature, living being]
wickeln (vt)	= to roll, wrap	*wick* [bs: something spun or rolled]
• **einwickeln** (vt)	= to wrap up, envelop	
• **entwickeln** (vt & refl)	= to unfold, develop	
• **verwickeln** (vt & refl) [< *ver*, advers. prefix + *wickeln*]	= to entangle, complicate	
• **Wickel** (m)	= roller; compress	
• **Wickelkind** (n)	= child in swaddling clothes	
Widder (m)	= ram	*wether* [a male sheep], *bellwether* [a lead sheep fastened with a bell]

GERMAN WORD	MEANING	ENGLISH COGNATE
wider (prep) • **Widerkraft** (f) • **widerlegen** (vt) • **widerlich** (adj) • **Widerpart** (m) and **Widersacher** (m) • **widersprechen** (vi) • **widerstehen** (vi) • **widerwillig** (adj) • **erwidern** (vt & vi) [bs: a countering; addressing the opposite side] • **widrig** (prep)	= against, contrary = power of resistance = to refute, disprove = repugnant, disgusting = opponent, adversary = to contradict = to withstand, resist = reluctant, unwilling = to reciprocate, return; to answer, reply, retort = adverse	*with* [orig.: 'against' (preserved in *withstand*, 'to oppose, stand against'), then assuming meaning of ME. *mit, mid,* the original word for 'with, associated to,' still found in *mid-* in *midwife,* a person assisting (together with) a woman in childbirth]
widmen (vt) [orig.: act of bearing a dowry, then dedicating anything < OHG. *widamo,* dowry, itself cogn. G. *Wittum,* dower, ult. < IE. **wadh-²,* to go, whence L. *vadere,* to go]	= to dedicate, devote to	distantly: *-vade* in *invade, pervade,* and *vade-mecum* [a guiding book of reference, lit.: 'go with me' < imperat. of L. *vadere,* to go + *mecum,* with me, ult. < IE. **wadh-²,* to go]
wiegen¹ (vt & vi) [*wog, gewogen;* bs: to move, esp. back and forth < OHG. *waga,* scales] • **auswiegen** (vt) • **ausgewogen** (adj) • **überwiegen** (vt & vi) • **vorwiegend** (adj) • **Gewicht** (n) • **wichtig** (adj) ['weighty'] ——————— • **wiegen²** (vt) [bs: to move, esp. back and forth < OHG. *waga,* scales] • **Wiege** (f) ['what rocks back and forth'] • **Wiegenlied** (n) • (see also **Waage, wagen**)	= to weigh = to balance out = balanced = to outweigh, preponderate [< L. *prae,* ahead + *pondus,* weight] = preponderant, predominant = weight = important ——————— = to rock, lull = cradle = lullaby, cradlesong	*1. weigh* [< ME. *weien, wegen*]; *2.* distantly: *wag* [< AS. *wagian,* to oscillate]
Wiese (f) [< OHG. *wisa* (cf. Frk. *waso,* whence Fr. *gazon,* lawn, grass)]	= meadow	*ooze* [soft mud, esp. at the bottom of a lake; area of muddy ground, bog < ME. *woze* < AS. *wase,* grassy land]
wild (adj) • **Wild** (n) • **wildern** (vi) [bs: to steal game] • **Wilderer, Wilddieb** (m) [lit.: 'game thief']	= wild, savage = wild animal, game = to poach = poacher	*wild*

GERMAN WORD	MEANING	ENGLISH COGNATE
Wille (m) • **willentlich** (adj) • **willig** (adj) • **willigen, einwilligen** (vi) • **bewilligen** (vt) [bs: to be willing to grant < *be +* *willigen*]	= will, volition = deliberately = willing = to give consent = to grant, allow	*will*
wimmern (vi)	= to whine, wimper	*whimper*
Wimpel (m)	= pennant, streamer, pennon	*wimple* [cloth headwrap of nuns]
Wimper (m) ['wind(ing)-brow' around the eye < *winden,* to wind + *Braue,* brow]	= eyelash	*to wind + brow*
winden (vt) [*winden, wand, gewunden*] • **wenden** (vt) • **wendig** (adj) • **auswendig** (adj) [bs: turning out easily] ——————— • **Wand** (f) [bs: something twisted or woven, wickerwork] • **gewandt** (adj) [bs: able to twist oneself; cf. *versa-* *tile,* able to turn from side to side < L. *vertere,* to turn] • **Gewand** (n) ['wrapping,' 'twisting' of cloth] • **anwenden** (vt) ['turn s.t. to a use'] • **aufwenden** (vt) ['to turn (expense) up'] • **aufwendig** (adj) • **Aufwand** (m) • **einwenden** (vt) ['to twist in at,' thus, to turn against (cf. *to object,* lit.: 'to throw against' < L. *ob,* against + *jectus,* past p. of *jacere,* to throw)] • **Einwand** (m), **Einwendung** (f) • **verwenden** (vt) • **Vorwand** (m) ['something woven to conceal the front of' (cf. 'false front') < *vor +* *Wand* (loan transl. of L. *praetextum,* pretext < *prae,* before + *textum,* weaving)] ——————— • **Windel** (f)	= to wind, twist = to wind around or over = flexible, agile = outward(ly); by memory, by heart ——————— = wall, partition = agile, nimble, adroit = garment, robe, gown = to employ, apply = to expend, spend = expensive, costly = expenditure, pomp = to object = objection = to utilize, expend = pretext, pretense ——————— = baby's napkin, diaper	*1. to wind; 2. to wend*

GERMAN WORD	MEANING	ENGLISH COGNATE
winken (vi) [bs: to bend (as signal) < IE. *weng-*, to bend, go at an angle]	= to make a sign, beckon	words < IE. *weng-*, to bend, go at an angle: *1. wink; 2. wince;*
• **Wink** (m)	= sign, wave, wink	
• **Winkel** (m)	= angle, corner, nook	
• **winkelig** (adj)	= angular, crooked	
• **Winkelzug** (m) [bs: bent or crooked tug]	= trick, subterfuge, shift	
• **wanken** (vi) [< OHG. *wancal*, unsteady (cf. AS. *wancol*)]	= to stagger, totter	*3. wench* [orig.: one who goes in angles, is inconstant as an infant's steps, then transf. to a dishonorable woman < AS. *wancol*, unsteady];
• **Wange** (f) [etym. uncert.; prob. bs: the face's part 'turned' to the side (whence Ital. *guancia*, cheek), believed cogn. *winken*]	= cheek; side part; hence, too, flanges	*4. wonky* [Brit.: shaky, tottery]
wippen (vi) [bs: to swing, move up and down, pull suddenly]	= to seesaw, rock, tilt up, overturn	*to whip* [to swing a beater; to sew round in a loose stitch]
• **Wippe** (f)	= a seesaw, rocker	
• **Wipfel** (m) ['swayer']	= (tree-)top	
Wirbel (m) [< IE. *kwerp-*, to rotate]	= whirl, eddy, flurry	*warble* [< IE. *kwerp-*, to rotate]
• **Wirbelsäule** (f) ['a turning column,' bec. the joints turn]	= spinal (or vertebral) column, with joints that whirl, turn [cf. *vertebra* < L. *vertere*, to turn]	
wirken (vt & vi)	= to have an effect; work, produce; to knit, weave	*work*
• **Wirkung** (f)	= effect	
• **wirklich** (adj)	= really	
• **Wirklichkeit** (f)	= reality, actuality	
• **Werk** (n)	= work, production	
wirr (adj) [< OHG. *werra*, confusion; whence Romance words for 'war': Ital. *guerra*; Sp. *guerra*; Fr. *guerre*]	= confused, incoherent	*1. war* [orig.: confusion, later strife, a battle]; *2. guerrilla* [an irregular fighter < Sp. *guerra*, war < OHG. *werra*]
• **(ver)wirren** (vt)	= to confuse, entangle	
• **verworren** (adj)	= confused, muddled	
• **entwirren** (vt)	= to disentangle, extricate	
• **Gewirr** (n)	= confusion, tangle, snarl	
Wirt(in) (m, f) [bs: keeper, person in charge; etym. disputed]	= landlord, innkeeper, host	perh. distantly: *warden* [keeper]
• **wirten** (vi)	= to keep house	
• **wirtlich** (adj)	= economical, hospitable	
• **Wirtschaft** (f)	= housekeeping, economy, industry	
• **bewirten** (vt)	= to entertain	
• **bewirtschaften** (vt)	= to manage (a farm, etc.)	

GERMAN WORD	MEANING	ENGLISH COGNATE
Wisch (m) • **wischen** (vt) • **Wischer** (m) • **aufwischen** (vt) • **entwischen** (vi) • **erwischen** (vt) [bs: to wipe or sweep up for o.s.]	= wisp of straw = to wipe, mop = wiper = to mop, wipe up = to slip away, elude = to catch, get hold of	*1. whisk; 2. whisker*
Wisent (m)	= bison	*bison*
wispern (vt & vi)	= to whisper	*whisper*
wissen (vt) • **Wissenschaft** (f) • **Gewissen** (n) • **gewissenhaft** (adj)	= to know = knowledge, science = conscience = conscientious	*to wit*
wittern (see **Wetter**)		
Witwe (f)	= widow	*widow*
Witz (m) • **witzig** (adj)	= wit, joke, brains = witty, ingenious	*wit, witty*
Woche (f)	= week	*week*
Woge (f) [< OHG. *wag*; ON. *vagr* (whence Fr. *vague*, wave) < *bewegen*, move] • **wogen** (vi)	= wave, billow = to surge, billow, wave, heave	*vogue* [a wave of fashion < Fr. < Ital. *vogare*, to ride the waves < MHG. *wogen*]
wohl (adj) • **wohlhabend** (adj) • **Wohl** (n) • **Wohltäter** (m) • **wohltätig** (adj) • **Wohlstand** (m)	= well = well-off, affluent = welfare, health, well-being = benefactor = charitable = prosperity	*weal*
wohnen (vi) [cf. AS. *wunian*] • **Wohnung** (f) • **bewohnen** (vt) • **Bewohner, Einwohner** (m) ――――――――――― • **gewohnt** (adj) • **Gewohnheit** (f) • **gewöhnen** (vt) • **gewöhnlich** (adj) • **außergewöhnlich** (adj) • **entwöhnen** (vt) [bs: accustom away from, *ent*, away + *wohnen*] • **verwöhnen** (vt) [*ver*, neg. + *wohnen*]	= to dwell, live = dwelling, habitation = to inhabit, occupy = inhabitant, occupant ――――――――――― = customary, habitual = custom, habit = to accustom, habituate = common, ordinary, vulgar = extraordinary = to wean, accustom from suckling to eating food = to spoil, pamper	*1. be won to* [to be accustomed to < AS. *wunian*, to dwell]; *2. wonted* [accustomed, habitual, usual]; *3. to wean* [to accustom offspring to food, stop from suckling]

GERMAN WORD	MEANING	ENGLISH COGNATE
wölben (vt.) [cf. AS. *hwelfan*] • **Gewölbe** (n) • **Tonnengewölbe** (n) [< *Tonne*, barrel + *Gewölbe*] ──────── • **Walm** (m) • **walmen** (vt)	= to vault, arch, curve = vault = barrel vault ──────── = slope or hip of a roof = to slope a roof	*to whelm, overwhelm* [bs: engulf, cover over < AS. *hwelfan*]
Wolke (f) • **Wolkenkratzer** (m) ['cloud-scraper'] • **wolkig** (adj) • **bewölken** (vt)	= cloud = skyscraper = cloudy = to cloud, darken	*welken* [arch. poetic: the sky; loosely, the atmosphere]
Wolle (f) • **Baumwolle** (f)	= wool = cotton	*wool*
Wonne (f) [cf. AS. *wynn*] • **wonnig** (adj)	= delight, bliss = delightful, blissful	*win-* in *winsome* [attractive, charming < AS. *wynn*, delight, joy]
Wort (n) • **wörtlich** (adj) • **antworten** (vi) ['to give words back'] • **befürworten** (vt) ['to speak a word for']	= word = literal, verbal = to answer = to advocate	*word*
Wrack (n)	= (naut.:) wreck, wreckage, hulk	*wreck*
wühlen (vi) • **Wühler** (m) • **aufwühlen** (vt) • **zerwühlen** (vt)	= to dig, agitate; (of pigs:) to root = agitator = to turn s.t. up, stir = to root up, dishevel, rumple	*wallow*
wund (adj) • **Wunde** (f) • **verwunden** (vt)	= sore = wound, hurt = to wound, hurt	*wound*
Wunder (n) • **wundern** (vt) ['to cause wonder to'] • **bewundern** (vt)	= miracle, marvel = to surprise, astonish, cause to wonder = to admire, marvel at	*wonder*
Wunsch (m) • **wünschen** (vt) • **verwünschen** (vi) ['to wish ill' < *ver*, advers. prefix] • **Verwünschung** (f) • **verwünscht** (adj) • **verwünschen** (adj) [bewitched (with positive force)]	= desire, wish = to wish, want = to curse, execrate; to bewitch, cast a spell on = curse, malediction = cursed = enchanted, bewitched	*wish*

GERMAN WORD	MEANING	ENGLISH COGNATE
würgen (vt & vi) [cf. AS. *wyrgan*] • **erwürgen** (vt & vi)	= to choke, strangle = to strangle, throttle	*worry* [orig.: to twist, bite at, then to annoy, distress < AS. *wyrgan*, to strangle]
Wurm (m)	= worm	*worm*
Würze (f) [< MHG. *wurz*, root] • **würzen** (vt) • **würzig** (adj)	= spice, seasoning = to spice, season = spicy, seasoned	*wort* [a plant or herb, now usually in compounds: *spiderwort, bellwort*]
Wurzel (f) [< MHG. *wurz*] • **wurzeln** (vt)	= root = to take root	*wort* [a plant or herb, now usually in compounds: *spiderwort, bellwort*]
Wüste (f) • **wüst** (adj) • **verwüsten** (vt)	= waste, wilderness, desert = deserted = to lay waste, devastate	*waste, wasteland*
Wut (f) [< OHG. *wuot* (cf. AS. *wod*) < IE. **wet-*, to inspire, blow] • **wüten** (vi) • **wütend, wütig** (adj)	= fury, rage, wrath = to rage, storm = furious, raving, fierce	*1. Woden* [Teutonic god]; *2. wood*[2] [arch. or dial. adj: out of one's mind, insane; enraged < AS. *wod*]; *3. vatic* [of a prophet] and *to vaticinate* [to foretell < L. *vates*, prophet < IE. **wet-*, to inspire, blow]

Z

Zacke(n) (f) • **zackig** (adj)	= point, prong = indented, jagged	*1. tack; 2. tag; 3. zigzag*
Zagel (m) [chiefly dial. (cf. AS. *taegel*)]	= tail	*tail* [< AS. *taegel*]
zäh (adj) [cf. AS. *toh*] • **Zähigkeit** (f)	= tough, tenacious = toughness, tenacity	*tough* [< AS. *toh*]
zahlen (vt & vi) [cf. AS. *tellan*, to calculate] • **Zahl** (f) • **zahlreich** (adj) • **bezahlen** (vt) • **erzahlen** (vt) • **zählen** (vt & vi)	= to count out in payment, to pay = number, figure = numerous = to pay, pay for = to narrate, tell = to count, number, reckon	*1. tell-* in *teller* [one who counts, e.g., a bank employee who receives and pays out money, or one who counts votes < AS. *tellan*, to calculate]; *2. to tell* [to relate in order, to recount]; *3. tale*
zahm (adj) • **zähmen** (vt)	= tame = to tame, domesticate	*tame*

GERMAN WORD	MEANING	ENGLISH COGNATE
Zahn (m) [< OHG. *zan, zand* (cf. Goth. *tunthus*, AS. *toth*) < Gmc. **tanth*] • **zähnen** (vt) • **Zahnrad** (n) ['toothed wheel'] • **Löwenzahn** (m) [bs: lion's teeth, bec. of dentated edges of the leaves of this plant]	= tooth = to notch, indent = cog wheel, gear = dandelion [< Fr. *dent de lion*, tooth of a lion]	*1. tooth* [< AS. *toth* < Gmc. **tanth*]; *2.* distantly cognate: *dental* [< L. *dens, dentis*, tooth); *3. tine* [prong of a fork AS. *tind*, cogn. Gmc. **tanth*]
Zähre (f)	= tear (eye)	*tear* (eye)
Zange (f)	= tongs, pliers, pincers	*tongs*
Zank (m) [bs: tearing into as with the teeth (*Zahn*, tooth) < OHG. *zanihhon*, based on OHG. *zan, zand*, tooth < Gmc. **tanth*] • **zanken** (vi & refl) • **Zankapfel** (m)	= quarrel = to quarrel, bicker = apple of discord (myth.)	distantly: *tooth* [ult. < Gmc. **tanth*]
Zapfen (m) • **zapfen** (vt)	= plug = to tap, pierce for draining	*1. tampon, tampion* [plug]; *2. tap* [to release liquid]
Zarge (f)	= border, edge, rim, hoop	*target* [dim. of *targe*, orig. a round shield]
Zauber (m) [< OHG. *zoubar* (cogn. AS. *teafor*)] • **zaubern** (vt & vi) • **Zauberei** (f) • **Zauberer** (m)	= charm, magic, spell = to conjure; practice = sorcery magic, sorcery, witchcraft = sorcerer	*tiver* [red color used in making runes < AS. *teafor*]
Zaum (m) • **zäumen** (vt)	= bridle, reins = to bridle	*team* [eg., of horses, oxen]
Zaun (m) • **einzäunen** (vt)	= fence, hedge = to fence in	*town* [orig.: fence of a yard, then collectively a fenced settlement]
zausen (vt)	= to pull about, tease (wool)	*toss, tussle, tousle* [to fight, scuffle]
Zecke (f)	= tick (insect)	*tick*
Zeder (f)	= cedar	*cedar*
zedieren (vt) [< Fr. *céder*, to cede]	= to cede, transfer, assign	*to cede*
Zehe (f) [cf. AS. *tahe* (*z-h, t-h* cogn. to *d-g* in L. *digitus*, digit, finger)]	= toe	*1. toe* [< ME. *to* < AS. *tahe*]; *2.* distantly: *digit* [< L. *digitus*, finger]

GERMAN WORD	MEANING	ENGLISH COGNATE
zehren (vi) [cf. Goth. *gatairan;* AS. *teran*]	= to live off of, draw on, consume; (fig.:) prey upon, undermine	*to tear* [to rend, pull off]
• **zehrend** (adj)	= consumptive, wasting (medic.)	
• **zerren** (vt)	= to pull, drag, tear	
• **Zerrbild** (n)	= caricature	
• **Zorn** (m) [intens. of *zerren*]	= anger	
• **zornig** (adj)	= angry	
• **zürnen** (vi)	= to get angry	
Zeichen (n) [cf. AS. *tacn;* Frk. *tekan* (whence Fr. *tacher,* to stain, leave a mark)]	= sign, token, mark, symbol	*token* [bs: a sign, indicator < AS. *tacn*]
• **zeichnen** (vt & vi)	= to draw, design, draft, subscribe	
• **Zeichnung** (f)	= drawing, design, subscription	
• **bezeichnen** (vt)	= to mark, describe, call	
• **bezeichnend** (adj)	= characteristic	
• **verzeichnen** (vt)	= to record	
zeigen (vt) [< OHG. *zeigon* (cf. AS. *taecan*)]	= to show, point out, indicate	*teach* [< AS. *taecan*]
• **zeigen** (refl)	= to appear, show up	
• **anzeigen** (vt)	= to point to, notify, denounce	
• **aufzeigen** (vt)	= to set forth, disclose	
zeihen (vt) [cogn. Goth. *gateihan,* to make known to (cf. AS. *teona,* accusation, hurt) < IE. **deik-,* to pronounce solemnly, whence Gk. *dik-,* justice]	= to accuse [lit.: 'to bring charge to' < L. *ad* + *causa,* charge]	*1. dic-* in *syndicate* [< ML. *syndicatus,* association of managers < Gk. *syndikos,* one helping in a court of justice < *syn,* with + *dik-,* justice]; *2.* distantly: *tee-* in *teen* [arch.: assusation, then the injury, harm suffered, affliction < AS. *teona*], and *to teen* [obs. or dial.: to vex, distress]
• **verzeihen** (vt) [*ver,* nullifying + *zeihen*]	= to forgive, pardon, excuse ['to free from a charge' < L. *ex* + *causa*]	
• **verzeihlich** (adj)	= pardonable	
• **bezichtigen** (vt)	= to accuse	
• **Verzicht** (m) [bs: negative declaration]	= renunciation	
• **verzichten** (vi)	= to renounce, do without	
Zeisig (m) [cf. MDu. *siseken*]	= finch, siskin	*siskin* [any of several kinds of finches of Europe, Asia and N. America < MDu. *siseken*]
Zeit (f)	= time	*1. tide* [orig.: a period of time, as in *Eastertide,* then the ebb and flow of water at its fixed times]; *2. tidings*
• **zeitig** (adj)	= timely; mature	
• **zeitigen** (vi)	= to ripen, mature	
• **Zeitung** (f) [bs: time's events]	= newspaper	
• **zeitgenössisch** (adj) ['companion in time']	= contemporary [< L. *con,* with + *tempus,* time]	
Zelt (n) [cf. AS. *teld*]	= tent	*tilt* [a cloth canopy over a boat or stall < AS. *teld,* tent]
• **zelten** (vi)	= to camp, set up tent	
• **Zeltdecke** (f)	= awning	

GERMAN WORD	MEANING	ENGLISH COGNATE
Zettel[1] (m) [< MHG. *zedele* < L. *schedula,* dim. of *scheda,* a split piece (of papyrus) on which an inventory was written]	= slip of paper, scrap, ticket, tag, sticker	*schedule* [< L. *schedula,* dim. of *scheda,* a split piece (of papyrus) on which an inventory was written]
Zettel[2] (m) [bs: strings spread across < obs. MHG. *zetten,* to scatter, spread] • **anzetteln** (vt) ['to set warp for weaving intrigues'] • **verzetteln** (vt) ['to spread thoroughly ' < *ver,* thoroughly + *zettel,* spread]	= warp (weav.) = to plot, scheme, contrive = to scatter, disperse, waste, squander	*to ted* [to disperse, spread about (esp. the fresh mowed grass for drying)]
Zeug (n) [bs: stuff, implements, production (cf. Du. *tuig*) < MHG. *ziuc,* OHG. *(gi)ziug,* ult. < *ziehen, zog,* to pull, draw; extended sense: to produce things] • **Zeughaus** (n) • **Zeugschmied** (n) • **zeugen**[1] (vt) • **Zeuger** (m) • **Zeugung** (f) • **Zeugungkraft** (f) • **Erzeuger** (m) • **Erzeugung** (f) • **Spielzeug** (n)	= artificial product, material, cloth, stuff, tools, implements = arsenal, armory, tool house = tool-smith = to engender, produce, beget = procreator = procreation, generation = generative power = producer, begetter = production, making = plaything(s), toy(s)	*1. toy* [< Du. *tuig,* tool, implement]; *2. to taw* [to prepare or dress (e.g., dress raw material, esp. skins to be converted into leather) < AS. *tawian* (cf. OS. *togean,* OHG. *zouwen*)]
Zeuge (m) [bs: witness or testimony drawn before the tribunal < MHG. *ziuc,* OHG. *(gi)ziugon,* cogn. *ziehen, zog,* to pull, draw] • **Zeugnis** (n) • **zeugen**[2] (vi) • **bezeugen** (vt) • **überzeugen** (vt) [bs: to win over (*über*) by giving evidence (*zeug-*)]	= witness = testimony, evidence, certificate = to be witness, give evidence = to testify to, certify, attest = to convince, persuade	*1. to tug* [< ME. *tuggen, toggen* < ON. *toga* (cf. AS. *togian,* intens. of *teon,* to draw, pull)]; *2. to tow* [< AS. *togian,* intens. of *teon,* to draw, pull]
Ziege (f) [< OHG. *ziga,* prob. a term originally for the female dog as in ON. *tik,* bitch] • **Ziegenbock** (m) • **Ziegenfell** (n) • **Ziegenleder** (n)	= she-goat, nanny goat = he-goat, billy-goat = goat skin = kid leather	*tike* [a term of endearment, esp. for a lively child]
Ziegel (m) [(cf. AS. *tigele*) < L. *tegula,* tile] • **Ziegelstein** (m) ['tile-stone']	= roof tile = brick	*1. tegular* [of or like tiles < L. *tegula,* tile, slab of baked clay]; *2. tile* [contracted < *tigel* < AS. *tigele* < L. *tegula*]

GERMAN WORD	MEANING	ENGLISH COGNATE
ziehen (vt) [*zog, gezogen;* < OHG. *ziohan* (cf. AS. *teon*)]	= to pull, draw, march	*1. to tug* [< ME. *tuggen, toggen* < ON. *toga* (cf. AS. *togian,* intens. of *teon,* to draw, pull)]; *2. to tow* [< AS. *togian,* intens. of *teon,* to draw, pull]
• **Zug** (m) ['pull,' 'what is pulled']	= train, pulling, march, trait	
• **zügig** (adj) ['as pulls along']	= speedy, free, easy	
• **beziehen** (vt)	= to put cover on, pull on; draw (salary, supplies)	
• **beziehen** (vt) (+ **auf**) ['to pull to']	= to relate s.t. to	
• **Beziehung** (f)	= relation, connection	
• **bezüglich** (adj)	= relating, relative	
• **Bezug** (m)	= relation, reference; covering, case; supply, purchase	
• **(in Bezug auf +**)	= (in relation or reference to)	
• **Zugkraft** (f)	= traction; (fig.:) draw, attraction, appeal	
• **Auszug** (m)	= departure; removal; excerpt, extract	
• **Verzug** (m) [bs: hindered march < *ver,* neg.]	= delay, default	
• **unverzüglich** (adj) [bs: without delay]	= immediate, instantaneous	
• **Vorzug** (m)	= preference, priority	
• **Zügel** (m) [bs: for pulling < *zog,* pret. of *ziehen,* to pull]	= rein, bridle	
• **zügeln** (vt)	= to rein; to bridle, check	
• (see also **Zeug, Zeuge, zögern, zucken, Zucht**)		
Ziel (n) [bs: to which one strives (cf. AS. *tilian,* to bestow labor, strive for)]	= aim, goal, target	*1. to till* [orig.: to bestow attention and labor, esp. upon the land, then to prepare land for cultivation < AS. *tilian,* to bestow labor, strive for]; *2. till* [fixed point, 'with the limit or goal of' ('till then')]
• **zielen** (vi)	= to take aim at, strive for	
• **erzielen** (vt) ['to successfully (*er-*) strive for']	= to obtain, achieve	
ziemen (vi)	= to be suitable, becoming	*1. seemly* [fitting conventional standards]; *2. to seem* [< AS. *seman,* to bring to agreement]
• **ziemlich** (adj)	= seemly, suitable	
• **Zunft** (f) [bs: agreement on what is proper, seemly < OHG. *zumft* < *ziemen,* to seem, seem right + suffix *-ti*]	= guild, corporation	
• **zünftig** (adj)	= belonging to a guild; (fig.:) skilled, expert, competent	
Zier (f) [disputed; prob. < OHG. *ziari*]	= ornament, embellishment	*1. attire* [personal adornment, equipment, covering < OFr. *atirier* < *a tire,* in order, arranged < OHG. *ziari*]; *2. tire* [automot.: a covering of metal plates or rubber on a wheel]; *3. distantly: tier* [< OFr. *tiere,* arrangement, order]
• **Zierat, Zierde** (f) [suffix *-de = -th,* as in *length*]	= ornament, decoration	
• **zieren** (vt)	= to decorate, adorn	
• **zierlich** (adj)	= delicate, graceful	
• **verzieren** (vt)	= to adorn, decorate, embellish	
• **ungeziert** (adj)	= unaffected	

GERMAN WORD	MEANING	ENGLISH COGNATE
Zimmer (n) ['timber-framed room' < OHG. *zimbar*, wooden beam (cf. AS. *timber*)] • **zimmern** (vt & vi) • **Zimmermann** (m)	= room, apartment = to carpenter, construct = carpenter	*timber* [< AS. *timber*]
Zimt (m) [< OHG. *cinment* < L. *cinnamum*]	= cinnamon	*cinnamon*
Zinn (n)	= tin	*tin*
Zins (m) [< L. *census*, past p. of *censere*, to assess, tax]	= interest (finance)	*census* [an official count, esp. of population < L. *census*, past p. of *censere*, to assess, tax]
Zipfel (m) [< ME. *tippe*] • **zipfelig** (adj)	= end, tip, point = pointed, with pointed end(s)	*tip* [< ME. *tippe*]
Zirkel (m) [< L. *circulus* < *circus*, circle, orbit] • **zirkeln** (vi)	= (pair of) compasses or dividers; circle, group, company = to draw with compasses	*1. circle; 2. circus*
zittern (vi) • **zitterig** (adj) • **erzittern** (vi)	= to tremble, shake, waver, quiver = trembling, shaking = to tremble violently, shudder	*teeter*
Zitze (f)	= teat, nipple	*tit, teat*
zögern (vi) [bs: to pull here and there, hence cause delay < *ziehen, zug, gezogen*, to pull] • **verzögern** (vt)	= to linger, tarry, hesitate = to delay, retard, slow	*1. tug; 2. tow*
Zoll (m) [< ML. *toloneum* < Gr. *teloneion* < *telos*, end, hence, an added tax, 'final thing' (cf. *fine* < L. *finis*, end)] • **Zöllner** (m)	= toll, customs = customs collector	*toll* [< AS. *toll* < ML. *toloneum* < Gr. *teloneion*, place for assessing a duty < *telos*, end, hence, too, tax, 'final thing']
Zopf (m) [cf. Frk. *top*] • **zopfig** (adj) [bs: given a flourish or 'tress']	= plait of hair, tress; (fig.) pedantry, formality, antiquated custom = pedantic, antiquated	*1. tuft; 2. top; 3. toupee* [a small wig < Fr. *toupet* < Frk. *top*, tress]
Zorn (see **zehren**)		
Zotte (f) • **zottig** (adj) ——————— • **Zote** (f) [bs: 'shaggy talk,' wit like dirty, unkempt hair < *zotte*, tuft] • **zoten** (vi) • **zotenhaft, zotig** (adj)	= tuft (of hair) = shaggy, matted, tufted ——————— = dirty talk or joke, obscenity = to talk smut = obscene, dirty, lewd, indecent	*tod* [< ME *todde*, a former English weight for wool; a bushy clump of ivy]

GERMAN WORD	MEANING	ENGLISH COGNATE
Zuber (m) [bs: vessel with two handles < OHG. *zubar, zwibar* < *zwi-*, two + *beran*, bear, carry]	= tub	*two + to bear*
Zucht (f) [bs: pulling the traits desired < OHG. *zuht* (cf. AS. *tyht*), ult. < *ziehen*, to pull (cf. ME. *togen*)] • **Zuchthaus** (n) • **züchten** (vt) • **Züchtung** (f) • **züchtig** (adj)	= discipline, breeding, cultivation = house of correction = to breed, rear, cultivate = breeding, cultivation = disciplined, chaste, modest	*1. to tight* [obs.: to train, discipline < AS. *tyhtan*]; *2.* distantly: *taut* [pulled tight < ME. *tocht* < *togen*, to pull]
zucken (vi) [bs: to pull quickly, ult. < *ziehen*, to pull (cf. AS. *teon*)] • **verzucken** (vt) • **verzücken** (vt) • **verzückt** (adj) • **Verzückung** (f)	= to twitch, move convulsively = to contract, pull = to enrapture, ravish = rapt, ecstatic = rapture, ecstasy	intens. of *tug* [< ME. *tuggen,* *toggen* < ON. *toga* (cf. ME. *togen*, AS. *teon*, to draw, pull)]
Zügel (see **ziehen**)		
Zunder (m) [cf. AS. *tynder*] • **zünden** (vt & vi) • **zündend** (adj) • **Zündung** (f) • **Zündschnur** (f) • **entzünden** (vt & refl) • **entzündbar** (adj) • **Entzündung** (f)	= tinder, easily flammable material = to kindle; arouse enthusiasm; ignite, catch fire = stirring, catching = ignition = fuse = to inflame; become inflamed = inflammable = inflammation	*tinder* [< AS. *tynder*]
Zunft (see **ziemen**)		
Zunge (f)	= tongue	*tongue*
Zweck (m) [orig.: wooden peg ('twig') fixed in center of a target, then the target it- self < *Zweig*, branch, twig] • **zweckmäßig** (adj) ['fitting a purpose' < *maß*, measure] • **zwecks** (prep) + *gen.* • **bezwecken** (vt)	= aim, end, purpose = expedient, suitable = for the purpose of = to aim at, have in view	*twig*
zweifeln (vi) [bs: to waver on two sides of a di- vide < *zwei* + *fel* < *falten*, to fold] • **zweifelhaft** (adj) • **bezweifeln** (vt) • **verzweifeln** (vi) ['to be overrun by doubts']	= to be in doubt = doubtful = to doubt, question = to despair	*two-fold*

GERMAN WORD	MEANING	ENGLISH COGNATE
Zweig (m) [bs: a branch forking into two < *zwei*, two]	= branch	*1. twig;* 2. distantly: *two*
Zwerchfell (n) [< *Zwerch*, transverse + *Fell*, skin] • **überzwerch** (adj)	= (anat.:) diaphragm, midrift = diagonal, slanting, crosswise	*1. to thwart* [to extend across, ob-struct] and *2. athwart* + *fell-* in *fellmonger* [dealer in sheepskins]
Zwerg (m) [cf. AS. *dweorg*]	= dwarf	*dwarf* [< AS. *dweorg*]
zwicken (vt) [cf. AS. *twiccian*] • **Zwickel** (m) [bs: a shape pinched in at one end, pointed]	= to pinch, nip = wedge; spandrel of an arch (archt.); gusset (dressm.)	*1. to twitch* [to pull with a jerk, orig. to catch hold of, pinch in on < AS. *twiccian*]; *2. to tweak* [to pinch in, pull with a jerk]
Zwiebel (f) [< OHG. *zwibolla* < L. *cepulla*, dim. of *cepus*, onion, whence Ital. *cipolla*, onion] • **Zwiebeldach** (n) and **Zwiebel-kuppel** (f)	= onion, bulb (of flower) = onion dome	*cipolin* [an Italian marble with al-ternating streaks of color recalling the layering of the onion < Ital. *cipollino*, little onion < L. *cepulla*, dim. of *cepus*, onion]
Zwiespalt (see **spalten**)		
Zwietracht (see **tragen**)		
Zwilch (**Zwillich**) (see **Litze**)		
Zwilling(e) (m) [< OHG. *zwiniling* < *zwinal*, dou-bled < *zwei*, two]	= twin(s)	*twin* [< *twi-*, two]
zwingen (vt) [*zwang, gezwungen* (cf. AS. *twen-gan*)] • **zwingend** (adj) • **Zwinger** (m) [bs: confining area] • **Zwang** (m) • **zwängen** (vt)	= to force, compel = forcible, compelling = dungeon, keep; enclosed area, court = compulsion, coercion = to force	*1. twinge* [< AS. *twengan*, to squeeze]; *2. thong* [< AS. *thwang*, twisted string that constrains]
zwinke(r)n (vi)	= to blink (the eyes), twinkle, wink	*twinkle*
Zwirn (m)	= thread, cotton	*twine*
Zwist (m) [bs: of two opposing views < *zwei*, two] • **zwistig** (adj)	= dissension, dispute = discordant	*two*
Zwitter (m) ['of two natures' < *zwei*, two]	= hermaphrodite, hybrid, mongrel, bastard	*two*

Appendix

Terms on Art and Architecture

Aufschrift	legend	**Fußboden**	pavement
Backstein	brick	**Gebälk**	framework, beams
Baukunst	architecture	**Gebäude**	edifice
Bildgestaltung	composition	**Gefäß**	vase
Bildhauer	sculptor	**Gehrung**	bevel, mitre
Bildhauerkunst	sculpture	**Geländer**	balustrade, banister
Bildnis	portrait	**geriffelte Säule**	fluted column
Bildsäule	statue	**Geschoßtreppe**	staircase
Blendarkade	blind arcade	**Gesims**	cornice, ledge
Bogen	arch	**gestelzter Bogen**	stilted arch
Bogenlauf	archivolt	**Gewölbe**	vault
Brustung	parapet, balustrade	**gewundene Säule**	spiral column
Bühne	stage, platform	**Giebel**	pediment, gable
Bühnenbild	stage scene painting	**Glockenturm**	belfry, campanile
Dach	roof	**Grabmal**	tomb
Dachfenster	dormer window	**Grabnische**	loculus, burial niche
Dachterrasse	raised loggia	**Grundriß**	plan, layout
Decke	ceiling	**Guß, Abguß**	casting, foundry work
Denkmal	monument	**Halbkreisbogen**	round arch
Docke	baluster	**Halbkuppel**	semidome
Dockengeländer	balustrade	**Halbgeschoß**	mezzanine
Dom	duomo, cathedral	**Hängezwickel**	pendentive
dreiblättrig	trilobate	**Helldunkel**	chiaroscuro
Dreifuß	tripod	**Herd**	fireplace, hearth
Ebenmaß	proportion	**Hof**	court, couryard
Eckwandpfeiler	anta	**Holzschnitt**	woodcut
eingebettete Säule	engaged column	**Hufeneisenbogen**	horseshoe arch
Eisenbeton	reinforced concrete	**Kanzel**	pulpit
Empore	gallery, tribune	**Kanzelhaube**	pulpit sounding board
Entlastungsbogen	discharging arch	**Kanzelhimmel**	pulpit sounding board
Entwurf	sketch, project	**Keilschrift**	cuneiform
Erdgeschoß	ground story	**Kelch**	chalice, goblet
Erdhügel	tumulus	**Kettenbogen**	catenary arch
erhabene Arbeit	relief work (cameos)	**Kielbogen**	ogee arch ("keel" arch)
Erker	oriel, bay window	**Kleeblatt**	trefoil ("cloverleaf")
Farbentonwert	value (color)	**Kleeblattbogen**	lobed arch
Farbschicht	impasto	**Kunst**	art
Farbstoff	pigment	**Kunsthalle**	museum
Farbton	tint	**Kuppel**	dome, cupola
Fassade	facade	**Lettner**	rood screen
Felsmalerie	rock painting	**Lichtwert**	value
Fensterkreuz	mullion	**Lisene**	pilaster
Firnis	varnish	**Mauer**	wall
Fruchtschnur	festoon	**Muster**	model, sample
Füllhorn	cornucopia	**Pfeiler**	pillar

Pinsel	paintbrush	**Tonnengewölbe**	barrel vault
Querbogen	transverse arch	**Treppe**	staircase
Querschiff, -haus	transept	**Tünche**	whitewash
Radierung	engraving, etching	**Turm**	tower
Rahmen	cornice, frame	**Umgang**	ambulatory, gallery
Rankenwerk	rinceau, vinescroll	**Umriß**	contour
Rundbogen	round arch	**Vierung**	crossing
Rundfenster	oculus, round window	**Vorhalle**	narthex, atrium
Säulengang	colonnade	**Wandsäule**	engaged column
Säulenhalle	portico	**Wappen**	coat of arms
Schatten	shadow	**Wendeltreppe**	spiral staircase
Schiff, Mittelschiff	nave	**Werkstatt**	workshop, atelier
Schnitt	section	**Zahnfries**	dentil range
Seitenschiff	side aisle	**Zeichnung**	drawing
Spitzbogen	pointed arch	**Zeltdach**	tent roof
Strebebogen	flying buttress	**Ziegel**	brick, tile
Strebepfeiler	buttress	**Zwerggalerie**	dwarf gallery
Stuck	stucco	**(Hänge)Zwickel**	spandrel, pendentive
Täuschung	tromp-l'oeil	**Zwinger**	keep, court

References

Chambers, W.Walker and John R. Wilkie. *A Short History of the German Language*. London: Metheun and Co. Ltd., 1970.

D'Hauterive, R. Grandsaignes. *Dictionnaire d'ancien français, moyen age et renaissance*. Paris: Librairie Larousse, 1947.

De Vries, Jan. *Nederlands Etymologisch Woordenboek*. Leiden: E.J. Brill, 1987.

Duden. Etymologie. Herkunfstswörterbuch der deutschen Sprache. edited by Günther Drosdowski and Paul Grebe, vol. 7, Mannheim: Dudenverlag, 1963.

Grimm, Jakob and Wilhelm Grimm. *Deutsches Wörterbuch*. 16 vols. in 45. Leipzig: S. Hirzel, 1854-1960.

Hagboldt, Peter. *Building the German Vocabulary*. Chicago: The University of Chicago Press, 1928.

Hirt, Hermann. *Etymologie der neuhohdeutschen Sprache. Darstellung des deutschen Wortschatzes in seiner geschichtlichen Entwicklung*. 2nd ed. Munich: C.H. Beck'sche Verlagsbuchhandlung, 1921.

Keller, Howard K. *A German Word Family Dictionary Together with English Equivalents*. Berkeley: University of California Press, 1978.

Klein, Ernest. *A Comprehensive Etymological Dictionary of the English Language*. Amsterdam: Elsevier Publications, 1971.

Kluge, Friedrich. *Etymologisches Wörterbuch der deutsche Sprache*. 22nd ed. edited by Elmar Seebold, Berlin: Walter de Gruyter, 1989.

Little, William with H. W. Fowler and J. Coulson, *The Oxford Universal Dictionary on Historical Principles*. revised and edited by C.T. Onions., 3rd ed. rev. with addenda. Oxford: Clarendon Press, 1955.

Langenscheidt New College German Dictionary. German-English, English-German. New York: Langenscheidt, 1987.

Law. M.H. *How to Read German. A Short Cut for Non-Linguists*. New York: W.W. Norton and Company Inc., 1964.

Malkiel, Yakov. *Etymological Dictionaries. A Tentative Typology*. Chicago: the University of Chicago Press, 1976.

Masciotta, Michelangelo. *Dizionario di termini artistici*. Florence: Felice le Monnier, 1969.

Meyer-Lübke, W. *Romanisches etymologisches Wörterbuch*. 2nd ed. Heidelberg: Carl Winter's Universitätsbuchhandlung, 1924.

Onions, C.T. *The Oxford Dictionary of English Etymology*. Oxford: Clarendon Press, 1966.

Oxford University. *Oxford Etymological Dictionary*. 12 vols. Oxford: Clarendon Press, 1933; rev. ed. 1971; 2nd. ed. 20 vols., 1989.

Partridge, Eric. *Origins. A Short Etymological Dictionary of Modern English.* New York: The Macmillan Company, 1958.

Pokorny, Julius. *Indogermanisches etymologisches Wörterbuch.* 2 vols. Bern and Munich: A. Francke, 1948; also 1959 and 1969.

Prehn, August. *A Practical Guide to the Scientific Study of the German Vocabulary.* New York: Oxford University Press, 1912.

Priebsch, R. and W.E. Collinson. *The German Language.* 3rd ed. London: Faber and Faber, 1934.

Purin, C.M. *A Standard German Vocabulary of 2932 Words and 1500 Idioms Illustrated in Typical Phrases and Sentences.* Boston: D.C. Heath and Co., 1937.

Réau, Louis. *Dictionnaire illustré d'art et d'archéologie.* Paris: Librairie Larousse, 1930.

Schmidt, Karl A. *Easy Ways to Enlarge Your German Vocabulary.* New York: Dover Publications, Inc., 1974.

Schwarz, Ernst. *Kurze deutsche Wortgeschichte.* Darmstadt, 1967.

Shipley, Joseph T. *Dictionary of Word Origins.* New York: The Philosophical Library, 1945.

Skeats, Walter A. *An Etymological Dictionary of the English Language.* Oxford: Clarendon Press, 1882. New and rev. ed., 1909, reprint 1956.

Sweet, Henry. *The Student's Dictionary of Anglo-Saxon.* New York: Oxford University Press, 1911.

The American Heritage Dictionary of the English Language. 3rd ed. Boston: Houghton Mifflin Company, 1992.

Wasserzieher, Ernst. *Woher? Ableitendes Wörterbuch der deutschen Sprache.* Bonn: Ferd. Dümmler, 1974.

Waterman, John T. *A History of the German Language. With Special Reference to the Cultural and Social Forces that Shaped the Standard Literary Language.* Seattle: University of Washington Press, 1966; rev. ed. 1976.

Watkins, Calvert. *The American Heritage Dictionary of Indo-European Roots.* Boston: Houghton Mifflin Company, 1985.

Webster's New World Dictionary of the American Language. Cleveland and New York: The World Publishing Co., 1962.

Webster's Ninth New Collegiate Dictionary. Springfield, Mass.: Merriam-Webster Inc., 1990.

Notes

Notes